Understanding Primary Education as a Whole

Understanding Primary Education as a Whole

Socio-cultural perspectives for leaders

Tony Birch

 Open University Press

Open University Press
McGraw Hill
8th Floor, 338 Euston Road
London
England
NW1 3BH

email: enquiries@openup.co.uk
world wide web: www.openup.co.uk

First edition published 2022

Executive Editor: Eleanor Christie
Editorial Assistant: Zoe Osman
Head of Portfolio Marketing: Bryony Waters

A catalogue record of this book is available from the British Library

ISBN-13: 9780335250691
ISBN-10: 0335250696
eISBN: 9780335250707

Library of Congress Cataloging-in-Publication Data
CIP data applied for

Typeset by Transforma Pvt. Ltd., Chennai, India

Praise page

"*This book is ideal for those leading and studying primary education. At a time when politicians seek to influence and even control schooling, those at the sharp end need to balance these pressures with an appreciation of the powerful social and cultural influences which have shaped and will continue to shape education our primary schools. School leaders and those studying primary education will find this book highly informative and thought provoking. Tony Birch has drawn on his considerable experience and deep personal understanding of recent developments and research.*"

Dr. Alan Cross, former Senior Fellow, Manchester Institute of Education, University of Manchester, UK

"*This book is essential reading for anyone who cares about education and primary education in particular. It is written by someone who understands the depth, interrelationships and complexity of the system, yet it is presented in an accessible way. There is a great deal of insight as well as challenges to our current thinking about primary education. I was personally pleased to see a strong focus on developing quality systems.*"

Les Walton CBE

"*Every generation of educational leaders, practitioners and thinkers need a literature on which to draw and from which to learn. Never before has there been so much expectation and therefore pressure on the education system. All of those leading primary education at whatever level can learn from Tony Birch's analysis of history and competing influences on primary education. This book is systematic, comprehensive and thoughtful.*"

Dr. Alison Borthwick, UK and International Freelance Education and Mathematics Consultant

"*I have been fortunate enough to be an early reader of Tony's latest publication. The style of writing and the structure of the chapters take you on a reflective pathway which guided my own reflection of my own time in education. By acknowledging the socio-cultural dynamics that surround and are interwoven with the education system you realise that there is one thing for certain – change. The decision to be made by the reader is to facilitate it or react to it. Whichever they do, my hope is that when leaders of education read the chapters in this book and make decisions influenced by Tony's research, they keep the learning of the children and young people at the heart of their outcomes."*

Rob Dean, Headteacher

"Tony Birch has a clear analytical eye coupled with rigorous academic research. He draws on years of his own practice across some of the most challenging education leadership roles. He reminds us of the complexity and challenge of primary education, the battles that have been fought around it and the changes in systems and practice that have occurred as a consequence. Most of all he brings an experience and analysis few can match. He reminds us that teaching is in an intellectually driven activity. That we should be proud of the education we provide and optimistic about the future."

Michael Tonge MA, Chief Executive Prestolee Multi Academy Trust, UK

"Understanding Primary Education as a Whole is a significant contribution to the literature on primary schooling. What is so impressive about the book, and Tony Birch is to be congratulated on this, is the way in which historical perspective has been combined with contemporary reality and the ease with which it links theory to practice, as well as practice to theory. Tony's book challenges on many levels – the reflective practitioner and leader, policy makers and administrators, as well as concerned and interested parents and citizens –all will learn from and find something of value in its pages. As well as being wise, this book is also engaging, accessible and essentially practical. Read it!"

Professor Emeritus David Hopkins, www.profdavidhopkins.com

Contents

Acknowledgements

This book has been created from my experiences and personal study of primary education. The process has been reflective and I have often been reminded, while writing, of numerous colleagues and their wisdom, insight and practice. It has certainly been a privilege to have worked with so many talented leaders, teachers, researchers, inspectors, teacher educators, advisers, governors, politicians, more recently chief executives and, of course, children. I am indebted to them for what I have learned. I admire primary educators for their many qualities: foremost a driving moral purpose but also their creativity, resilience, integrity, humour, determination and not inconsiderable amount of skill – I hope I have recognised this in the text. There are simply too many individuals to name: my heart-felt thanks to you all.

I have been profoundly lucky in my experiences too. I was a primary teacher and school leader before working in a local authority context where I was involved in teacher education, curriculum development and school improvement. I learned more from completing a master's degree and subsequently researching a PhD. Holding responsibilities for SEND and inclusion, for admissions and school place planning gave me further perspectives. Now I combine consultancy with governance in two Multi-Academy Trusts. It is through doing these things with so many great people over more than 30 years that the perspectives in this book have emerged. The book combines reflective notes made from reading, writing, discussions, meetings, conferences, observations and materials used in presentations and reports over many years, revised, rearranged and supplemented to form the chapters here.

Specifically in relation to this book, I would like to express my appreciation to Dr Alan Cross who has been my valued guide and friend and has rigorously provided feedback and encouragement on various drafts as they have developed. Thanks to Les Walton CBE for his observations, insight and enthusiasm for the project; to Professor David Hopkins and Rob Dean (head teacher and former colleague) for their perceptive comments. Professionally three others deserve my thanks: Moira Bentley and Bridget Somekh, both of whom, nearly 20 years apart, had a huge impact on my academic career; and Robin Alexander, who has – though he may not know it – been the single most significant influence on my thinking about primary education.

Last but not least my thanks to Jane and Emma who have been amazing in their love and support throughout: without them this book would never have been written.

About the book

In so many respects, primary education is something to be treasured but, of course, it is not without its challenges and has the capacity to develop further: it has a responsibility to do this. This book is optimistic: challenging yet written from the deep belief that within the system of primary education is the energy for even greater success that just needs to be unlocked.

The book is in four parts. Part 1, titled *Socio-cultural Dynamics*, comprises three chapters. Chapter 1, 'Primary education in perspective', explores why pedagogy and creating 'meaning' matters so much. Chapter 2, 'The journey of primary education', tracks its history, exploring the debates and activity that foreground how it has come to be as it is now. Chapter 3 is about the 'Global driving forces' that influence debates about primary education today.

Part 2, titled *Connecting Primary Education: Through the Looking Glass*, delves deeper into contemporary primary education. Chapter 4, 'Learning in a changing world', explores current understandings of learning, contextualised in our understandings of childhood. Chapter 5 looks at the 'Socio-cultural dynamics of pedagogy' and its components and combinations. Chapter 6 looks to the school context, focusing in particular on 'The power of leadership', while Chapter 7 – 'Together: a collaborative approach' – looks at the 'system' of primary education .

Part 3, *Towards Holistic Primary Education*, draws on *Reinventing Organizations* by Laloux (2016). It has two chapters: with a worldwide pandemic as its backdrop, Chapter 8 is titled, simply, 'Wholeness'; Chapter 9 is about 'Evolutionary purpose' and explores the idea of 'pioneering' a new version of primary education through a series of developmental trails.

Part 4 draws the book to its conclusion. Chapter 10 has the title 'Primary education: pedagogy as a whole', and explores the balance between stability and possibility. It is about maintaining a grounded primary education while recognising the transformative potential of learning in the twenty-first century. It suggests the importance of rooting developments in powerful, carefully articulated aims and values matched with a vibrant and responsive pedagogy of primary education.

Part 1

Socio-cultural Dynamics

This section is in three chapters. It begins by introducing the complexities of primary education through the lens of socio-cultural dynamics before exploring its historical origins and why it looks as it does today. It concludes by exploring the global driving forces and the contemporary issues that it faces.

It explores: *aims and purpose • structure and scale • micro-dynamics • pedagogy • the accumulations of history • spiral dynamics • 'stability, standards and subjects' • the political and global context • the energy in primary education • powerful productive forces*

English primary schools are, typically, bright, dynamic and vibrant places: they must be for they consistently engage the interests, curiosity and motivation of lively and energetic children between the ages of 4 and 11, a period when their development is, simply, remarkable. Extending children's capacities, accelerating their understanding, engaging them with a fast-changing world and building their confidence are among the driving forces of the complex and elaborate system we know as primary education, and as the Cambridge Primary Review concluded, there is room for optimism: 'primary schools appear to be under intense pressure but in good heart' and 'are highly valued by children and parents' (Alexander, 2010b, p. 488).

What makes them great? Is it the climate expressed in the warmth emanating from the relationships between adults and children? Or is it the breadth and range of the curriculum that excites children's interest? Is it the precision of the teaching that stretches and challenges children's learning? It is all of these and others, it is in the combination of many elements that great primary education finds its alchemy and an energy that has a profound impact on children.

In a system serving more than 4.5 million children through 16,000+ schools, it should be no surprise to find conflict, dilemmas, tensions and debates alongside the alchemy. The approach here is to explore the social and cultural dynamics through which primary education has evolved: how purposes, values and beliefs are formed and reformed and enacted in the leadership and pedagogy of classrooms, schools, communities and wider systems. It cannot hold all of the answers: the intention is to encourage thought and reflection and the improvement of practice and only then can it claim to have had an impact.

The chapter which follows is an exploration of primary education from a range of perspectives. It leads to a second which delves deeper into its history and considers why it takes its current form. The third chapter explores some of the powerful dynamics in play today.

Note that throughout this account I refer to primary 'schools' as an overarching descriptor. Where appropriate, usually when referring to policy matters, I differentiate, using specific terminology, between schools and Academies.

1 Primary education in perspective

This chapter is about the system of primary education, focusing on its aims, purpose, components and interrelationships. It emphasises pedagogy as the vital ingredient.

It explores: *structure, system, scale and components • aims, purpose and form • processes of change • micro-dynamics • pedagogy at the heart • the meaning of primary education*

Children were born to learn: they are competent and capable learners who, through their brain's plasticity – coupled with the power of pedagogy – can create and develop new neural pathways. Each child is an individual and has features that make them precisely who they are. As neuroscientist Joseph Le Doux explains:

> Genes dictated that your brain was a human one and that your synaptic connections, though more similar to those of members of your family than to those of members of other families, were nevertheless distinct. (LeDoux, 2003, p. 307)

LeDoux explains that it is through experience of the world that your synaptic connections adjust, further distinguishing you from everyone else.

Those who are regularly engaged with children recognise the varied and varying characteristics – curiosity, feistiness, energy, puzzlement, humour and creativity are commonly observed, sometimes alongside anger, diffidence or anxiety. The environment mediates children's development: the extent to which they have been able to partake in exercise and their diet, together with the social and intellectual stimulus with which they have engaged and even whether they have succumbed to illness or injury. As children move from their early dependency through increasing levels of autonomy, their experiences – including those at school – play a critical role and, as they accumulate, their identity is forged. The ability subsequently to flourish depends upon this as children learn to respond to praise, to adversity, to reward, to success and setbacks. Through their home, their peers, their extended family, within their community and their exposure to wider culture and society (Desforges and Abouchaar, 2003; Berliner, 2011), through their experience of complex and pervasive media, information and communications technologies, children's development will be mediated by the extent to which they have been nurtured and loved; read to and encouraged on a journey of education; influenced by the beliefs and values of faith and culture; by their friends and wider social network; their experiences of the world (including travel, sport, music and the arts) and the extent to which they have enjoyed the benefits of economic security. A child's growth and development is highly complex. Their wider world provides their experience and primary education must connect respectfully with this; as well as matters cognitive and intellectual, those responsible for primary education must respond to important issues of culture, belonging and identity (Eaude, 2019). Some children seem to live idyllic lives, whereas the lives of others, sadly, seem blighted: there is an argument that education matters most to those who are disadvantaged, not necessarily materially, but those whose lives may be troubled, beset by obstacles, uninspired or demeaned – in these circumstances, primary education can have a special wealth. Primary education at its rich and dynamic best can enliven, transform and change children's lives.

Primary education adds huge value and the cycle is continuous; the debates and decisions educators make reverberate over many years and we should recognise that the children we expose to it will make the future. If this is the case, those responsible for primary education must leave a powerful legacy and the roots, which it provides for children, will have a vital role in our future sustainability and prosperity. When we think of primary education, it should be in terms of doing something better, generation-by-generation. This is the ethos of this book, recognising the achievements of past and present and building forwards from them.

Primary education in perspective (structure, system, scale, components)

The significance of primary education, purely in terms of the scale of the endeavour, makes it worthy of consideration and a few headline figures give us a sense of the undertaking. In January 2017, for example, 4.69 million children aged 5–11 were educated in primary schools, a growth of more than half a million in the 10 years since 2007 (DfE, 2017a), at a cost of approximately £4,700 per pupil (Belfield et al., 2018). They were taught by more than 200,000 teachers and a vast cohort of classroom assistants in 16,786 primary schools (DfE, 2017b). Then there is everything else that is involved, including the interactions in each individual lesson, wide-ranging curriculum plans, meetings between teachers and parents, school buildings, programmes of teacher education, governing boards and trusts, financial allocations, publishers of educational resources, tests and inspections – the list is endless.

Most of England's children, sometime between their fourth and fifth birthday, enter our national system of primary education often having experienced some form of pre-school education. Primary education in England takes place in a variety of types of schools (community, voluntary, foundation, as well as Academies and Free Schools) covering different age ranges (infant, first, junior, middle, primary), although most children because of the structure of the school year start school aged 4 (see Riggall and Sharp, 2010). Since 1988, the 5–11 age range has been sub-divided into three stages: the Foundation Stage, followed by Key Stages 1 (ages 5–7 years) and 2 (ages 7–11 years), with a prescribed national curriculum. The large majority of children aged 5–11 years spend approximately 25 hours per week in their primary school, for 39 weeks of the year. It is likely they spend about half of this time learning English and Mathematics (Alexander, 2010b), often in age-delineated groups and classes of close to 30 children. Usually, but not always, children attend one of the primary schools in their immediate local community. This system of primary education is so deeply embedded in our society that it is not easy to consider if it is in the most appropriate form for now and the future.

The system of primary education sits in a complex cultural context. On the surface, at least, England is an affluent, democratic country with ample resources and a history of 'welfarism', where universal primary education is a long-established and prominent feature: yet this system was created in a different time when inequality was no less prevalent but contrasts with a society and culture that is vastly different today. England is now a country of around 56 million people with around 240 languages being spoken; it is no longer – if it ever was – a homogeneous nation and questions of the degrees to which uniformity, individuality and diversity counterbalance in primary education are not answered easily. Today's topography forms a complex, uneven web amid rapid social and technological advances. How primary education responds to and exemplifies our cultural diversity, how it addresses questions of equity (e.g. Ainscow et al., 2012) and how it meets the needs of each individual child are important questions. Children from diverse cultural and religious backgrounds populate our schools bringing a rich experience not always fully aligned with the values of their school. Ours is a society riven with inequality, one where affluence and poverty live side by side (e.g. Bukodi and Goldthorpe, 2018; Social Mobility Commission, 2020) leaving a trail of underachievement that should be a priority (e.g. Smithers, 2013; Jerrim et al., 2017).

Primary schools remain, unquestionably, the prime means through which most of our children begin their formal educational journey. They are also, in many cases, among the last bastions of community (Groves and West-Burnham 2020), as the disappearance of many local services and Covid-19 have demonstrated. Of course, an education is much more than schools; as the saying goes, 'it takes a village to raise a child' (see Lemke, 2002). Learning can occur anywhere, with anyone, increasingly so with the plethora of digital resources, so many schools turn in partnership towards their communities. There is a distinctive argument that primary schools, rather than being islands or oases isolated from their environment, are firmly located in society's wider socio-cultural dynamics: Castells (1997) recognised that loss of 'identity' is one of the greatest challenges of globalisation.

While some might debate the importance of schooling relative to other aspects of a child's early development, primary education is properly regarded as vital to children's start in life – it paves the way, in part, for who and what they will become (Alexander, 2010b). Jerome Bruner's proposal that 'each generation must describe afresh the nature, direction, and aims of education' (1971, p. 22) has never been more apposite: attention to the future of primary education is to everyone's benefit.

The aims, purpose and form of primary education: more questions than answers

In England today, our organised, universal and compulsory system can be taken for granted. Schools are a powerful societal construct: as our most commonly shared experience they are embedded in the fabric of society. Sometimes we can become so engaged in the details of practice that the key question, 'What is the purpose of primary education?', is overlooked, possibly alongside other strategic concerns, such as: Why is the system of primary education structured as it is? How does it relate to our wider social and cultural relations? And, can education, as Michael Apple (2013) asked, change society?

Primary education connects with children and their communities. The quality and type of education we provide for them helps to shape them as people: their development, academic success, personal and social growth and, ultimately, their contribution by way of return to society. If we accept this proposition, then primary education is much more than buildings, infrastructure and resources (or for that matter preparing children for their secondary education). Fundamentally, it is the ideas, values and practices that are constantly influencing not just children's learning and development but the cultural identity of our nation through a web of connections, relationships and dialogue.

In part, much depends on that first key question: 'What is the purpose of primary education?' (e.g. Hannon and Peterson, 2021). Is it to equip children for a rapidly changing world? Is it for social justice and to support the disadvantaged and marginalised, for example? Is it the cohesion of our increasingly diverse society? And if so, should it be community or professionally led? Is it to ensure our nation's economic competitiveness? Is it to provide societal stability, to maintain the existing hierarchies, or is it the route to individual empowerment? Some argue that it enables the nation to succeed and enhances our ability to participate and compete in the global economy. For primary education specifically, some place a premium on children learning the basic skills of literacy and numeracy, largely in preparation to do well in the next stage of education. Few doubt its importance but it needs constant consideration to reflect current times.

Questions of purpose generate further questions, particularly about the forms primary education will need to take for the future. Do we need an education system that is radical in its response to new challenges, or one that offers stability in turbulent times and a link with the past? Or, as a compromise, something that is slowly evolving, gradually responding to those new demands? More practically, is the wide use of single-age classes with generalist class teachers fit for purpose? Should English and Mathematics alone be at the core of a twenty-first-century education? And what sort of teaching would we then need? The type that transmits knowledge to children through direct instruction? An education that builds on children's curiosity, interests and motivations, helping them to become inventive problem-solvers? How, then, in an unpredictable world, do we actively decide how to educate our children? If education has a vital role and transformative possibilities, then these questions carry great importance.

Increasingly, the world our children inhabit is fragile: there are significant and seismic economic, environmental, social and technological changes taking place. Our experience of Covid-19 had a dramatic effect: demonstrably this was felt in the unprecedented widespread physical closure of our primary schools to many children but also in the remarkable adaptive responses of education professionals and parents to keep children safe, to create home learning in various formats and to do whatever was needed in children's best interests. Whatever our thoughts on the pandemic and its consequences – which will take many years to fully process – we are reminded that primary education needs to be anticipative of a world that is changing:

- *economically* – in the aftermath of the crash of 2010, fiscal emergencies of 2020 and a growing, potentially unsustainable, global consumerism;
- *environmentally* – in conditions which mean serious climate change might cause new patterns of migration and social tension in the foreseeable future;
- *socially* – as changes to family lives lead to loss of identity and anxieties affect more people; and
- *technologically* – as complex global systems radically restructure communication, reconstitute and enable immediate access to knowledge and social-media alter realities.

The context for our thinking about primary education reflects in uncertainty, ambiguity and complexity. While we are increasingly able to more fully understand our place on the planet and in our wider universe, including the effects of globalisation and our impact on fragile ecosystems, there are effects that we have not, and possibly cannot, control as technological advances race ahead, restructuring our relationship with knowledge and our concept of self. As Covid-19 revealed, apocalyptically, our vast planet constantly creates new learning: each generation is presented with new challenges but, importantly, also the opportunity to do something better.

Focusing for a moment the environment, which may be our next global disaster, reveals much: we know that there are world-wide temperature rises though even with today's multi-scenario modelling software scientists cannot be certain of their trajectory. There are issues related to greenhouse gases, the melting glaciers and ice caps, the continuing loss of vast areas of rainforest, our polluted oceans and radioactive waste which may affect our children and our children's children far more than they do us. There are significant challenges ahead, including producing enough food for a growing population, and how to address significant continued migration as a result of geopolitical forces. The future for us and Earth's other species is not a certain one. These and other developments create societal questions such as how we manage to consume less, overcome the tendency to be acquisitive, face up to threats to environmental stability and yet still flourish as a species (Fielding and Moss, 2011).

Our optimism should lie in humans having developed remarkable capacities for learning. From human activity have come wisdom, beauty, science, engineering and architecture. As a result of learning, powerful breakthroughs have been made; for example, medical innovations have helped overcome destructive diseases, scientists are developing new food production processes for the planet's growing population, and technologies evolve at breakneck speed. It is vital that primary educators understand that humanity has the capacity to respond to life differently and to make powerful transformations. Indeed, it has been suggested that human learning is slowly replacing the process of natural selection in human evolution; a potentially powerful means by which the species can overcome the further challenges it faces (see Aldrich, 2013). Moreover, if we accept that children's emotional and cognitive growth is determined in part by what they experience in school, that their brains are influenced according to the emphases of our pedagogy, then educational possibilities and choices become all the more important. Learning will, eventually, be a key means by which we transcend the challenges we face.

What does all this mean for primary education? It recognises that there is not one single educational challenge and there are a multiplicity of potential purposes to be brought together cohesively. The United Nations Convention on the Rights of the Child (UNICEF, 1990), for example, highlights a number of implications for education systems that include access to schooling, the right to freedom of expression, the development of the child's personality, talents and abilities and, through Article 23, supporting children with special educational needs. The Cambridge Primary Review (Alexander, 2010b), meanwhile, recognised the increasingly expansive nature of primary education by setting out twelve challenging aims under three headings:

- For *the individual*: well-being; engagement; empowerment; autonomy.
- For *self, others and the wider world*: encouraging respect and reciprocity; promoting independence and sustainability; empowering local, national and global citizenship; celebrating culture and community.
- For *learning, knowing and doing*: exploring, knowing, understanding and making sense; fostering skill; exciting the imagination; enacting dialogue.

As humankind transcends itself, primary education will be part of its bedrock. How best we educate our future generations in such a dynamically changing world presents a fundamental challenge that needs a coherent, carefully articulated response to which defining our purpose is front and central.

Reflection point

What are the most important aims and purposes of primary education from your perspective? What makes them more important than others that are presented? Does today's curriculum reflect these aims and purposes?

Processes of change: understanding complexity from a socio-cultural perspective

There is a tendency when thinking about education to do so in terms of individual schools and, more recently, Academies (often now in Trusts), yet primary education is a publicly funded whole. Archer, in her classic account of the evolution of the English and French education systems, defined it thus:

> .... a nation-wide and differentiated collection of institutions devoted to formal education, whose overall control and supervision is at least partly governmental, and whose component parts and processes are related to one another. (Archer, 1984, p. 19)

Primary education is just that – a complex interrelating system, forged over long periods of time and increasingly extensive and complex: it is interconnecting rather than a series of separate components. Simply the choice of the word 'system' is significant – it implies organisation, dynamics and interrelationships that stimulate thought, debate and activity – so that human endeavour is always embedded and understood in its socio-cultural context with all of its incipient variety. Primary education has socio-cultural dynamics: complex processes of change through which it evolves across the 16,000+ schools and where purposes, identities, values and beliefs are formed and reformed, enacted in the leadership and pedagogy of classrooms, schools, communities and the wider landscape every day. Policy constructs, financial infrastructure, buildings, teacher training programmes, curriculum frameworks, staffing organisations, classroom resources and, of course, the complex practices of teaching all interplay. The interest is how they interplay – how they connect. As Wertsch argues:

> The task ... is to explicate the relationships between human action, on the one hand, and the cultural, institutional, and historical contexts in which this action occurs on the other. (Wertsch, 1998, p. 24)

It is in this relationship between people and structure that systems exist and that the potential for change can be found.

First, there is the idea that education systems create value – that is, they have 'worth'. In the way that the system of primary education caters for the education of those 4.69 million children in England, decisions have been made reflecting what is perceived to be important: the value may be qualitatively dissimilar for children, parents, professionals, politicians and other stakeholders, whose interests and motivations differ. In the workings of a system dialogue is necessary about its aims and purpose and how value should be achieved, measured and judged, and realised in debates about funding allocations, curriculum choices and 'effectiveness'. The process is on-going; changes are agreed, further arguments stimulated and they continue, in shifting forms, over long periods. The changing structure of schools illustrates that systems can and should be managed so that, first and foremost, *the purposes, aims, values and pedagogies of primary education should be clear and familiar to everyone* who participates and interacts directly or indirectly with it and should be the basis for judging its success.

Second, if the purposes of primary education are to be well understood, there needs to be constructive dialogue across the system and between its various layers. *Dialogue is key to participants in the system creating their meaning and motivation* – with, for example, more than 200,000 teachers this is challenging but if not, the meanings in systems can be contradictory and some practices dysfunctional or self-interested, even when they might appear coherent and the components seem aligned. Dialogue is the means by which the system evolves as practices, from time to time, are challenged, disrupted and replaced.

The third idea is that systems can be influenced and shaped. They can be inert and unchanging, even regressive – but they need not be so, as they can be energised to be active and dynamic. Despite the complexity, there is a need to recognise that the system can be affected by a range of forces: some of these are localised, for example, in school leadership and generated from local communities but others, policy decisions and social forces, can operate at a macro-contextual level. The achievements of the system therefore depend upon the effectiveness by which the system, at a range of levels, is led, managed and organised – in the way it is connected together. Understanding the potential levers to manage and change a system is vital, Fullan (2011, 2021) argues: *the system can be shaped and developed using the right levers* – it gives a point of optimism. When given appropriate leadership, then, systems do develop and can be improved.

The fourth idea is that education systems are interdependent. Components interrelate, one with another, and exploring the interdependencies of the system is vital in satisfying the holistic sense that (1) primary education does not exist in a vacuum, and (2) the components of primary education connect and combine with one another. The economist Edward Deming's (1994) view challenged thinking about systems: left alone, he believed, individual components within a system become selfish and competitive. He argued that a strong system is subservient to its aim – and in a coherent one, the components are working cohesively towards its achievement (Deming, 1994). Otherwise, as some argue, the system can become 'self-interested' as people or organisations aim to extend and prolong their place within it beyond their worth or even when they no longer have a clear, beneficial purpose. The challenge might be thought of, as Deming describes it, as achieving '*a network of interdependent components that work together to try to accomplish the aim of the system*' (Deming, 1994, p. 50, my emphasis).

It is in their combination that systems have distinctive identities, they vary when compared one with another (see Archer, 1984; Alexander, 2000) and the diverse, culturally specific elements create unique forms (e.g. Crehan, 2016). Yet, socio-cultural dynamics are inherently positive and optimistic: human beings can create meaning and positively affect their environment through their activity (Engeström, 1999a). It is not surprising therefore that politicians, given the extensive financial investment in education systems (only health trumps education in terms of expenditure), choose to intervene, often controversially, to bring about improvements. Local Management of Schools, a National Curriculum, national Literacy and Numeracy Strategies, and a New Schools System are just some recent centrally and politically led initiatives that have also served to identify a further question: what balance should be sought, in primary education, between national, local and school/community level initiatives and responsibilities?

Given this complexity, leading and managing in education systems is necessary if they are to adapt, evolve and change yet retain their relevance and value. Exploring the system involves studying interrelationships between components in pursuance of the overall purpose (and in a system as complex as primary education, this can be elusive and contradictory); it means unlocking energy, cultivating meaning and inspiring motivation. Fullan explains:

> The ultimate goal of change is when people see themselves as stakeholders with a stake in the success of the system as a whole, with the pursuit of meaning as the elusive key. (Fullan, 2001, p. 272)

The micro-dynamics in understanding change: object, motive, voice, histories and contradiction

Why are there differences between and within education systems of the kind Alexander's (2000) classic study of the culture and pedagogy of primary education in five countries illustrated? Studying classrooms in England, France, India, Russia and the United States of America it recorded the variety of primary education which was culturally imbued, richly varied and fascinating in every sense. For Alexander, culture was deeply embedded in the pedagogy of schools. It can be seen, too, in Crehan's (2016) autobiographical and journalistic exploration of Finland, Singapore, China, Japan and Canada. Both accounts observe dialogue in systems, analyse developments and give comparative 'perspective' so that the emerging patterns can be considered: for activity theorists this complexity resides in micro-dynamics – of 'object', 'motive', 'the cultural context', 'voices', 'histories' and the 'contradictions' in systems (see Engeström, 1999a).

Objects are seen by Kaptelinin (2005) to be the complex 'reasons' which drive and motivate the activity of those within a system: they offer 'meaning'. They are more than the stated purpose, aims and intention and nuanced in their construction because they are mediated through dialogue and activity. Objects represent 'what, why and how' (Hasan and Kazlauskas, 2014) and in a system they diverge: from the Year 6 child approaching end-of-year tests, to the newly appointed Secretary of State explaining their new policy, to the head teacher approaching their school development plan – an amalgam of values, beliefs, attitudes and approaches interplay. The same object could exist as a transformational vision, or conservative and self-satisfied, even wistful atavism depending on interpretation, subsequently generating inspiration or despondency depending on the individual or group. In any case, according to Sannino and Engeström, 'the object gives activity its identity and direction' (2018, p. 45).

The quality, direction and composition of an object matters greatly: Ofsted, for example, described how the power of the leadership narrative acted as an energiser and connector for professionals, children and communities in challenging contexts (Ofsted, 2009). Objects often produce tensions: becoming an Academy was, for some – in particular the entrepreneurial – a huge opportunity, while for others, a threat to position and status. They are complex and are often ambiguous and evolving: when Ofsted introduced their most recent framework it reoriented, creating new directions and practices, particularly in terms of the curriculum (Ofsted, 2019) and generated motive, particularly for the head teachers who are judged by them. Energising an 'object' creates meaning in a system and affects motivation (from classrooms to the corridors of political power): they cannot easily be mandated and are always mediated by the socio-cultural dynamics of the system.

What motivates people is never a simple construct but rather the complex interrelations of a series of features and processes; nevertheless, the more intense the motive, the greater the energy expended to reach the goal. *Motives* are deeply psychological: the teacher constantly driven by the test performance of their children may, eventually, find their energies dwindling, while a teacher with career ambitions might suddenly find the approach to professional learning of a new head teacher emancipating. Compare, too, on a larger scale, the isolated individual teacher with another who is part of a community where there is a clearly defined framework of aims and values; where research evidence into childhood and learning is widely distributed; where the curriculum is carefully defined; and where studied enquiry is the norm.

Cultural contexts provide the setting which mediates motivation and help to explain that qualitative differences can be expected, for example, between a school that has a history of success and a clearly articulated pedagogy and one that might be spurred to action, perhaps with little enthusiasm, by an unsuccessful Ofsted inspection. Given continued concerns about the gap between disadvantaged pupils and their peers (e.g. Hutchinson et al., 2020), a child's cultural context may affect whether they attend school or arrive on time, for example, and if they are hungry or living in poverty, this can impact directly on their motivation to learn. Removing barriers to learning, those factors that prevent self-expression, curiosity and enjoyment, for example, has a critical role in a system of education.

The constant dynamics and interrelationships expressed through the *voices* in a system mean there is, at the very least, some conflict or dissonance. Assigned roles, individual psychologies and personal histories (Engeström and Miettinen, 1999) interplay in systems: in a primary school this would include the head teacher, senior managers, teachers, parents, governors and children and, in the wider system, inspectors, local government personnel, Academy chief executives, governors and trustees, trade unions and central bureaucracies. Each of these, individually and collectively, brings a particular perspective or 'voice' reflecting their experiences, attitudes, values and interests: potentially a rich energy of socially mediated dialogue. The way that power is distributed and voiced helps to explain why systems and their components take different pathways, why resulting differences occur. The voice given to the child has great significance. A citizenship review by the EPPI Centre (Deakin-Crick et al., 2005) found that when children were actively engaged in dialogue, they developed a greater understanding of what democracy means. Recognising voices suggests, too, actively seeking out those who are disadvantaged and disenfranchised and understanding the barriers they face (e.g. Ofsted, 2009).

Systems are multi-layered with their own individualised history and knowledge is accumulated into the collective wisdom and structures through activity over prolonged periods. Archer (1984) describes processes by which activity takes place, is then conditioned into structures, followed by further structural elaboration. Sometimes, the system 'locks' into particular forms (in England note the generalist class teacher; the dominance of English and Mathematics and age-based grouping) which participants can be reluctant to alter: they are conditioned into the system along the lines suggested by Archer. These '*histories*' affect both the capacity and willingness of the system to change and the way ideas and innovations are subsequently adopted (or jettisoned). Primary education, in this sense, is an accumulation of developmental processes containing successes, failures, acceptances and rejections: in this way, each school also has its own starting point and unique trajectory (Tolman, 1999).

In understanding complex systems, the basis for change can often be found in the *contradictions* which build, emerging over time: they are key sources for innovation and development (Engeström, 2001, p. 137). When opposing forces come into contact they result in dilemmas, conflicts and double binds: in the 1970s and early 1980s, fierce arguments were generated in response to the growing progressive movement as they clashed with growing concerns over standards and were met by a call to go 'back to basics'.

Psychologically, it is in heightening forms of consciousness or awareness that contradictions are revealed and demand for change emerges. Data, for example, might reveal concerns over performance in a school, community or system. New qualitative forms of activity, or what Ilyenkov (1977) called 'breakthrough innovations', must emerge to resolve contradictions. The speed at which they spread depends upon both their relevance and currency in relation to the needs of the system or access to the levers needed to secure change. Identifying and resolving contradictions is at the heart of any change process, the starting point in a developmental journey.

Reflection point

What are the key contradictions, dilemmas and tensions that you experience in your role? What is at the heart of them? Are there ways to transcend them?

In complex systems, the development of new practices requires attention to the social (to relationships and how power is exercised), to the cultural (to the political, economic and technological meanings of what happens) and to the historical (to how things came to be and how practices became locked into system, in part, in structure) – together the socio-cultural dynamics. Most of all, solutions must relate to the practices of classrooms, to pedagogy, and the conditions must be fertile for them to thrive. It explains Fullan's (2001, p. 115) comment: 'Educational change depends upon what teachers do and think. It is as simple and complex as that'. Whether we are talking about an individual lesson, a school, Multi-Academy Trust or the system as a whole, objects, motives, cultural contexts, multiple voices, histories and contradictions provide a lens through which to look and raise questions (Table 1.1), one that recognises primary education as a complex construct formed from connections and choices and enriched when the capacity to engage participants meaningfully is realised.

Table 1.1: Micro-dynamics: Questions for primary educators

Object-orientedness	What is the focus of the system and its parts? Is it both vital and clear? Is it aligned?
Motive	Where does this come from and what is it aimed towards?
Cultural context	How is this affecting the work in this environment? Has it created any unusual effects?
Multiple voices	Whose voices are loudest? Are all of the parties listened to?
Histories and trajectories	What happened previously and why? What is proposed?
Contradictions	Are there aspects that are in tension or creating particular behaviours?

Pedagogy at the heart of change

Human activity, then, creates structures, systems and relationships; these are our cultural tools and include the concept of 'primary education' itself, as well as ideas of 'teachers' and 'learners', 'lessons', 'curricula' and schools'. Humans have not only developed the capacities to learn, they have created, uniquely, the means of accelerating, sharing and inspiring learning – our pedagogies (Leach and Moon, 2008). We are, as Dehaene says (2020), 'the species that teaches itself', and as Freire (1972) showed with the 'oppressed' in Brazil, pedagogy can be a means of liberation and transformation. Ironically, pedagogy has been an uncomfortable term when employed in English educational debate (Simon, 1981) but its usage is growing and its terminological benefit is that it supplants the (potentially) oppositional terms of teaching and learning and oft preferred English term 'curriculum' to capture the educative process in its rich complexity – its wholeness.

Definitions of pedagogy are widely debated and explored. The following definition of pedagogy was used by Alexander (2000) and underpinned his extensive study of education in five cultures:

> Pedagogy is the act of teaching together with its attendant discourse of theories, values, evidence and justifications. It is what one needs to know, and the skills one needs to command, in order to make and justify the many different kinds of decision of which teaching is constituted. (Alexander, 2008, p. 47)

Indeed, if we take this holistic, culturally embedded view of pedagogy, then curriculum, teaching and learning become dimensions within an overarching framework where pedagogy connects with our views of childhood, learning and knowledge, becoming a reflection of primary education's discourse of 'theories, values, evidence and justifications' (Alexander, 2008). Such a discourse takes us well beyond classrooms, but, of course, is firmly located and defined by what happens in them. When those interested in education ask such questions as 'what should we teach?' and 'how should we teach it?', many expect simple answers but the reality is that they unearth, once again, massive complexities in depth and definition; and at another level of attitudes and choices made. 'Whose pedagogy?' we might ask.

As a metaphor, Leach and Moon suggest that 'pedagogy is to teaching as architecture is to buildings' (2008, p. 172), and as they say, it should never be prosaic. Pedagogy, as defined above, is both theoretical (in that it encompasses beliefs and understandings about society, knowledge and learning) and a form of production emerging from practice. Pedagogy reframes underpinning questions of what and how to teach as multifaceted philosophical questions surrounding the purpose of primary education and sharply pragmatises political, societal, cultural and fiscal debates. Pedagogy, following the architectural metaphor, is more than a 'standard construction', it is much more than the prescription of models of teaching – its foundations require considerable understanding in terms of attitudes and belief systems; for Alexander, it is act and discourse (2000, p. 540). Prescribed models of teaching fail to understand the practical dilemmas faced by teachers each morning in their own particular context: a strong basis for pedagogy should be elicited throughout the education system but it needs to be debated, contested, evidenced and argued to gain practical authenticity. A key test of pedagogical debate is that it can translate theory to the instantaneous nature and immediacy of the classroom.

Accepting such an understanding of pedagogy moves beyond the observable and lays challenge to accepted frameworks by incorporating the many complex and changing variables, the psychological and cultural composites that play a vital role in restricting and enabling change in a globalised world (Leach and Moon, 2008). There is also, beneficially, the challenge laid down by using the term pedagogy in research – it demands respect to education being culturally embedded (Giroux, 1997). Daniels (2001) sets the challenge, pedagogy referring to social practices that 'shape and form' the development of individuals:

> If pedagogic practices are understood as those which influence the formation of identity as well as learning outcomes … then a form of social theory is required that will allow us to model and investigate the factors which may be exercising some effect. (Daniels, 2001, p. 1)

It must include, increasingly, the affective domain: we learned so much from Covid-19 about the pain of loss and the impact of isolation but also the value of compassion, kindness and community in society. In summary, pedagogy is a powerful, socially shaped concept embracing educational values and attitudes as well as theories and practices of teaching and learning. It is expressed in complex and multidimensional ways that include: educational goals and purposes; a view of learning; a view of knowledge; the learning and assessment activities required; the roles and relationships among learners and between the teacher and the learner and classroom discourse (McCormick and Scrimshaw, 2001, p. 40).

However, is this decision to promote and explore pedagogy as the guiding paradigm significant, or as Alexander (2000) asks, 'are we just playing with words?'. Alexander argues that the focus of educational discourse says a great deal about what matters most in education. A clear distinction between curriculum and pedagogy also needs to be made, and is done so by Pachler (2001). His is an explanatory distinction that places emphasis on the curriculum defining what the learner will be introduced to. Quoting Lemke (1990), he observes how in many curricular models the definition is of what you need to know, in which order and at what pace. In a more radical model, pedagogy has transformative potential (Leach and Moon, 2008); is learner focused, dialogic in process and inherently about the broader context, which ultimately shapes learning (Wegerif, 2013; Alexander, 2020), so what teachers 'think and do' matters greatly. As Alexander notes:

... because 'pedagogy' in both its broad and narrow senses retains an inescapable whiff of the classroom, we are constantly reminded that the real power of pedagogy resides in what happens between teachers and pupils ... (Alexander, 2000, p. 551)

Elevating pedagogy can begin to take account of the growing understanding and interest in learning theory; professional learning; the social, cultural and historical challenges and implications of empowering professionals and pupils alike.

Reflection point

Is it right to elevate pedagogy and think about it in this way? What does it say to us about the role of the teacher? How is pedagogy affected by prescribed methods such as schemes?

The meaning in systems

Education systems are the major means by which societies seek to define, replicate and ensure their national distinctiveness, to strengthen their national economies, to address their social problems, and to influence the distribution of individual life chances. (Dale, 2008, p. 188)

Dale suggests that it is this image people have in mind when considering education systems.

This leads us from our initial exploration to four interrelating questions:

1   What are our aims and purpose for primary education?
2   What values should underpin primary education?
3   How do we organise so our pedagogies are coherent and powerful?
4   How effective are we in achieving them?

The complexity of these challenges both reiterates old problems and raises new questions, demanding the development of new responses. How can the system of primary education best respond to them? Moving forwards some will call for stability and the keeping alive of tradition (and there is clearly a place for this) because the world is not the place we once knew – which, of course, may be unsettling, though likely much less so for our children who will want, as have previous generations, to master the challenges presented to them.

Primary education should not be analysed and debated purely in atavistic terms but in the context of changing economic and environmental conditions and for the children it serves today and tomorrow. Evidence suggests that the system of primary education is increasingly part of a set of complex, global socio-cultural dynamics. New questions of sustainability and regeneration are faced by modern society generally, and they apply to primary education specifically: how do we create psychological well-being, for example, or help children stay in touch with nature and contribute to the future of our planet? There are contradictions writ large: there is a growing sense that traditional organisations and structures may be less suited to these demands, yet their security and solidity does not render them obsolete – indeed, this is one of their greatest strengths.

How do we create the conditions for potential paradigm shifts in how we think about and practise primary education? As we contemplate, there are a number of themes each reflecting the growing complexity of the system of primary education:

- The range of expectations we have of primary education and what it can achieve; these are increasingly diverse and should be manageable.
- The expansion of our understanding of the world and the way this rests in creating meaningful and challenging educational frameworks.
- The range of expansive pedagogic possibilities and the choices available to those working in the system and its schools.

Apple's great innovator, Steve Jobs, insisted the best way of predicting the future is to invent it – a not inconsiderable but inspiring idea for those responsible for education systems. The challenge here, which we see from this short consideration, is that developing the system of primary education is more than the organisation of schools and classrooms; it is also, at once, political, structural, organisational, dialogic and cultural. One thing seems clear: it is in our collective interest to devote significant energy to generating *meaningful* forms of primary education fit for purpose in our changing world.

Delving deeper

The Cambridge Primary Review published in 2010 is both authoritative and wide-ranging. The main report (Alexander, 2010b) together with the companion research surveys (Alexander, 2010c) remain a rich, relevant and valuable source. The CPR also commissioned more recent surveys which can be found at https://cprtrust.org.uk/about_cprt/cprt-publications/ on themes including the digital age; autonomy, accountability, quality and evidence; diversity; vulnerable children and global learning.

Next: In the next chapter, this contextual overview of primary education is put in historical perspective – asking: How did this system come about? How did we get to where we are now?

2 The journey of primary education

This chapter is about the journey of primary education from its earliest beginnings to its current iteration. From this analysis there is an examination of whether primary education today is fit for purpose.

It explores: *the accumulations of time • periods of 'emergence, development and elaboration' • primary education as a spiral dynamic • the resistant core: 'stability, standards and subjects' • readiness for change or locked in the past*

The accumulations of time

Primary education has a significant history (see Gillard, 2019): it emerged from a series of events, large and small, running in parallel, crossing over, one emerging from another, weaving together and interconnecting, some still reverberating today. Identifying the most significant elements – including the political, pedagogic, economic, social and technological forces that created what we now know as primary education – gives a sense of what became important and what remains so now, including why some of it was and is still contested.

History is, of course, at least in part, interpretative; it can be read differently through emphasis and perspective (Aldrich, 2003; McCulloch, 2011): there are alternative explanations and multitudinous opinions, particularly as we are describing the unfolding of multiple histories (e.g. Silver, 1983). When the past is written, it tends to be from perspectives enabled by the present. Critics can easily level accusations of selectivity and bias; and many developments appeared to greater and lesser extents according to locality. The challenges of history applied to something like English primary education include its scale (see esp. Gillard, 2019); uneven, often ambiguous, processes of development (e.g. Lawson and Silver, 1973; Archer, 1984; Green, 1990); and sheer volume of ideas, thoughts and analyses (e.g. Blyth, 1967a, 1967b; Alexander, 2000). Nevertheless, history helps to illustrate why things are as they are and why people do what they do, and in this way we can understand our current selves better and see ourselves more clearly (Cunningham, 2012a, 2012b) so that when we see contradictions (disputes, arguments, disagreements) present in the system, they are not theoretical – they are the accumulations of activity over time (Engeström, 2001).

What follows is a synoptic chronology: some key historical events are identified, summarised and their current influence analysed. As they are contextually bound and have developed over time, this account employs Engeström's suggestion of 'periodisation': 'One must divide the stream of historical events into larger patterns that have meaningful characteristics of their own' (1999a, p. 32). The account describes three macro-periods of educational history in England: emergence (1100–1630), development (1650–1900) and elaboration (1900–2020); they are necessarily concise.

The case of England: emergence, development and elaboration

The first period, until around 1630, saw early agrarian themes of survival and continuity (Lawson and Silver, 1973) giving way to the authority, upheaval and, eventually, relative stability concerned with the growth of Christianity, the increasing power of the state and the beginnings of empire (Orme, 2006). Demand grew for education in line with societal and economic changes. In the Tudor period, for example, education was accelerated by charitable endowments for schools, new ideas (especially humanism), the changing concept of the state, increased use of the vernacular, and technical advance, especially printing (see Simon, 1966 and Table 2.1) leading, eventually, to 'the evolution of

Table 2.1: Emergence (1100–1650)

Period	Society	Education
1100: Beginnings	Agrarian, dominated by the seasons; infant mortality, economic survival	*Survival and continuity* – limited education through kinship, narratives, continuities (Lawson and Silver, 1973)
1100–1530: The growth of education	Norman conquest, European intellectual ideas, role of the Church, growth of Christianity, the growth of the trades	*Emergence and authority* – education through the cathedrals and collegiate churches; demand for education, e.g. guilds (Gillard, 2019)
1530–1650: The Tudors and the rise of the state	The Reformation and rise of the state, printing, humanism, charities and endowments, use of the vernacular (Simon, 1966)	*Allegiance, control, philanthropy* – founders and emergence of schools, lay governing bodies under the supervision of the state (Simon, 1966; Orme, 2006)

a system of schools administered locally by lay governing bodies under the general supervision of the state' (Simon, 1966, p. 291).

The second period of development (1650–1900) was contextualised by further scientific advance and technological capacity (Table 2.2); Britain was first among the European nations to industrialise. The development of an education system to maintain competitive advantage was unnecessary given the country's economic success; the politics of *laissez-faire* and the achievements of philanthropists and voluntarism overrode any concern that educational reform would be needed. As Green argues:

> It did not need to envision the future. Thus educational development in England was deprived of one of its historically most potent rationales. Tradition could accomplish what, in other nations, required education. (Green, 1990, p. 110)

By around 1750, a diverse collection of 'vaguely defined' schools existed (Simon, 1966). The privileged had access to education but for the masses it was not considered necessary and was largely ad hoc (Green, 1990); that which was available was provided 'by private enterprise, supplemented by philanthropy' (Lawson and Silver, 1973, p. 181).

Much of the English system emerged from voluntarism: free of state control, using independent initiative and resources and allowing voluntary attendance (Green, 1990, pp. 264–265). When eventually education was needed, the drivers were often concern about children's welfare and social control rather than pedagogy (Blyth, 1967b; Lawson and Silver, 1973), or to fit children to their station in life. The role of the state and its ambitions for mass education waxed and waned but were rarely ambitious: Robert Lowe, designer of the 'revised code' of 1862 commented, starkly: 'if it cannot be cheap it will be efficient, if it cannot be efficient it will be cheap'. It meant: 'Educationally, the poor were very much what the rich made them' (Lawson and Silver, 1973, p. 184). Blyth's conclusion was that 'English society was not built around its schools' (Blyth, 1967b, p. 20).

When in 1870, through the Forster Act, a national system of elementary education was finally agreed, it was 'a workable compromise', according to Lawson and Silver (1973) caught in battles for control between Anglicans, non-conformists and secularists (Simon, 1974). For Blyth (1967b), the elementary system was a 'preventative measure', built on religious and economic need and socially stratified (Green, 1990) along the lines of class; Alexander noted 'class-based assumptions and expectations about what children from particular backgrounds can and cannot do' (2000, p. 136) and many children simply did not attend (Timmins, 2001). Blyth further argues the resultant elementary system lacked a 'coherent theory or aim' (1967b, p. 22). Some perceive it as an educational response to the extension of the franchise aiming to hold back working-class advancement rather than an expansion of educational agency (see Green, 1990, p. 32–34), or, alternatively, as a middle-class admission of the extent of poverty and deprivation. There was a strong sense that it was utilitarian and custodial: Blyth recounts that the 'elementary schools [were] a whole educational process in themselves and one which [was] by definition limited and by implication inferior; a low plateau, rather than the foothills of a complete education' (Blyth 1967b, p. 21).

Against this backdrop was the pioneering work of Robert Owen, the founder of 'developmental' primary education according to Blyth (1967b), together with David Stow and John Wood, whose structuring and sequencing of education began to reflect children's psychological maturation and learning (Alexander, 1992).

By 1900, many antecedents of modern primary education were visible: it had been conditioned into structures (Archer, 1984). The 'elementary school' was organised largely around children's age, a teacher-led and authoritative pedagogy (too often using arid methods of rote learning, a legacy of payment by results, according to Sutherland, 1971) with a heavy emphasis on English and Mathematics (Aldrich, 2001): there was what Tyack and Cuban (1995) call a

Table 2.2: Development (1650–1900)

Period	Society	Education
1660–1750: Growing interests in pre-industrial England	Supporting 'wealth, hierarchy and masculinity' (Orme, 2006)	*Ideas and exploration* – Bacon's inductive science; wider demand for education (dissenters); the Academies; 'a system of vaguely defined schools' (Blyth, 1967b); Paine's proposal for a national system; *laissez-faire* (Simon, 1974)
1750–1840: The industrial revolution	Britain leading the world in industrialisation; urban areas growing; further stratification of society; child labour; Chartism, working-class movement; counter-ideologies	*Work, voluntarism, utility* – the monitorial system of Bell and Lancaster (the most influential innovation in the history of education in England according to Silver, 1983); pioneering alternatives (Owen, Stow, Wood, Lovett); debates about a national system (Lawson and Silver, 1973)
1840–1900: Municipalisation	Continued industrialisation; municipalisation; justice and rights; disquiet about child labour	*Bureaucracy, compromise and control* – 1839 formation of HMI; 1856 Education Department, the Newcastle Commission; Lowe's revised code (Payment by Results); 1870 Elementary Education Act ('a workable compromise'; Lawson and Silver, 1973); localised development: school boards, increasing attendance

grammar of schooling (a structured set of cultural practices, beliefs and understandings).

In the twentieth century, primary education settled and was elaborated (see Table 2.3 below): the administrative base was secured; the creation of local authorities superseded school boards; and a system that had existed on grant and endowments now had access to the 'block grant'. The value was recognised in more expansive statements of aims – for example, Morant's Code for Public Elementary Schools (Gordon, 2002) – and teaching steadily professionalised culminating, eventually, in what Lawton (1980) would call a 'Golden Age' of teacher control. The ages and stages of primary education, defined by the Hadow Committee (Board of Education, 1931), became steadfastly engrained in policy and practice: the universal offer now known as 'primary education'.

The first half of the twentieth century saw educational debates continue – attitudes to eugenics and psychometrics among them. Intelligence, often viewed as 'fixed', supported streaming and tests at age 11 for the purpose of selection (Chitty, 2007; Leach and Moon, 2008). Meanwhile 'progressive' ideas also gained traction through influential practitioners (Froebel, Montessori and McMillan, for example), 'developmental psychology' and the New Education Movement (Selleck, 1972; Jenkins, 2000). Lowndes (1969) describes the 'silent, social revolution' in our schools recognising pioneering advances in child psychology, educational ideas and approaches and their wider dissemination (Galton et al., 1980). The landmark 1944 Education Act established a tripartite system of school, local authority and central government (Sharp, 2002): 'a national system, locally administered' (see Richards, 2006). Professional autonomy was the order of the day, though one of the legacies for primary education would be the downward pressure of the 11+ examination. Studies revealed concerns about streaming and its organisation around class rather than ability (Halsey et al., 1961; Jackson, 1964); later the move to a 'comprehensive' secondary system would loosen the hold (Lee and Croll, 1995).

The largely autonomous context that emerged allowed experimentation (Cunningham, 1988): the 'progressive' ideal – the child as an autonomous individual; childhood as a unique phase (Alexander, 1992) – flourished but was not a coherent educational philosophy (Selleck, 1972), more a rejection of what had gone before and encompassed a multitude of meanings (Darling, 1986). Subsequently, Lady Plowden's landmark and ultimately controversial report (Central Advisory Council for Education, 1967) became its epitome.

What followed (economic malaise, OPEC oil crises and a 'Winter of Discontent') led to dissatisfaction: concerns about 'standards' in primary schools, the extent of teacher autonomy (Cunningham, 1998) and variations in quality (Simon, 1981; Leach and Moon, 2008) emerged and a series of Black Papers argued for a return to traditional methods (e.g. Cox and Dyson, 1971). Callaghan's (1976) landmark Ruskin College speech sparked the 'Great Debate'. Education was being linked to economic competitiveness.

Pedagogically, Dearden argued that for primary education to be based entirely on children's needs and interests was flawed and ignored much of the social construction of learning and development (Dearden, 1968, 1976).

Alexander observed of this time that a combination of ideology and pragmatism underpinned professional decision-making, rather than considered theory and research-based practice (2008, p. 43). Large-scale research such as that of ORACLE (Galton et al., 1980) and new effectiveness studies (e.g. Rutter et al., 1979) created a focus on the 'school' and the notorious William Tyndale Primary School, where the use of radical progressive methods caused controversy and intensified the argument (Auld, 1976). Who governs schools and how was added to debates about standards and economic success.

Reform was imminent. Thatcher's Conservative government saw traditional values override progressive ideas; the people over the experts (Chitty, 2014). There were six themes: (i) the establishment of a national curriculum, (ii) the control and accountability of teachers, (iii) assessment and inspectorial arrangements, (iv) parental choice, (v) devolution of control from local education authorities (LEAs) to schools, and (vi) strengthening the roles of head teachers and governors (Ball, 2008): the Education Reform Act of 1988 remains symbolic of political intervention in education. The role of the Local Education Authorities was reduced: Local Management of Schools gave power to head teachers and governing bodies counterbalanced by increased regulation and accountability and the era of school improvement was born (Hopkins, 2007). Revisions to create a widespread school inspection system saw the formation of Ofsted, the cue for Woodhead's so-called 'reign of terror': inspections without 'fear and favour' created a culture of apprehension and low confidence in the profession (Brighouse, 1997). The National Curriculum, applied to all schools offering 'access and entitlement', became the 'common basis of trade' (Ball, 2008), particularly when new tests for 7- and 11-year-olds came on stream. It proved largely unmanageable; a 'dream at conception, a nightmare at delivery', according to Campbell (1993). In the ORACLE follow-up study (Galton et al., 1999), the curriculum was increasingly subject-based and tightly timetabled with an emphasis on teacher talk as a means of covering the extensive curriculum material in the programmes of study: restoring a grammar school curriculum was Ball's (1994) conclusion.

New Labour's election victory of 1997 brought little respite from change despite an initial welcome from a profession suffering 'reform fatigue' (Campbell, 1998). Reynolds and Farrell's (1996) 'Worlds Apart' report generated new concerns about how well the education system was performing, while Barber set out arguments for an education 'revolution', describing 'a sense of crisis' (1996, p. 27) and a deep concern about standards of literacy and numeracy. 'Excellence in Schools' (DfEE, 1997) set out an ambitious modernisation agenda, focusing on 'the many, not the few'. There was a commitment to bring education spending in line with the OECD average and, as the Cambridge Primary Review reports, 35,000 additional teachers, 172,000 teaching assistants and a 55 per cent increase in teachers' pay (Alexander, 2010b). The National College for School Leadership was the high-profile vehicle for modernisation. It was, however, the large-scale National Strategies that were the *fin-de-siècle* focus for primary education as attempts continued to 'raise standards', supported by workforce reform and leadership development. These controversial, unprecedentedly large-scale strategies with their targets and high stakes testing focused predominantly on literacy and numeracy: Richards (2002) described the movement to an 'instructional, officially approved teaching model'. Opinions vary (Webb and Vulliamy, 2007; Sammons et al., 2008; Chitty, 2014; Tymms and Merrell, 2010): outcomes from national tests clearly improved (Hopkins, 2007) but Alexander (2004) suggests teachers began to use a more didactic style of pedagogy with an emphasis on short initiation response sequences with limited extended discussion (see also Galton, 2007; Wyse et al., 2010). Ultimately, new education minister, Charles Clarke, recognised that the sheer weight of expectation was unproductive and in 2003 the ameliorative 'Excellence and Enjoyment: A Strategy for Primary Schools' (DfES, 2003) was introduced.

Table 2.3: Elaboration (1900–2020)

Period	Society	Education
1900–1944	Stabilisation; catastrophic global conflagration, child welfare	*Consolidation, profession, key ideas* – universal education; 1902 local education authorities; 1904 Morant Code and HMI contributions; teacher training and the rise of the National Union of Teachers; Progressives (the New Education Fellowship) and psychometrics (Cyril Burt); consolidation through Hadow (primary education) and the 1944 Education Act – a national system, locally administered
1944–1975: Post-war consensus	The permissive and consumer society, increased personal wealth; mass media and time-saving technologies; immigration	Post-war consensus; influence of the 11+ and streaming; experimentation and innovation; CACE report (Plowden) 'At the heart of the educational process lies the child'; informal, flexible methods
1975-2020: Dissatisfaction and reform	Economic malaise, oil crises, dissatisfaction; neo-liberal ideas; links made between education and the economy	Reactions to progressivism – HMI Primary Survey (1978); Black Papers, media coverage. Local management of schools; a national curriculum; testing and inspection; National School Improvement Strategies; increased proscription; centralisation but with autonomy for schools – Academies and Free Schools

For the coalition government elected in 2010 economic austerity and Oates' (2010) critique 'Could do better' formed the backdrop for a revised national curriculum in the 2010s, reflecting Hirsch's (1999) theories of powerful knowledge, it was interventions allowing schools to opt out of local authority control and seek autonomy that most caught the attention and stoked controversy (Benn, 2011; Mansell, 2016). Academies (independent, publicly funded state schools) were the basis of a New Schools System reconstructing the 'ownership' of primary education from democratic oversight to private institutions (see Thomson, 2020). It put those seeking 'freedoms' more firmly in control, technically exempt from intensified curriculum demands, but still highly accountable through continued pervasive and public 'high stakes' performance measures and inspections. Multi-Academy Trusts emerged quickly bringing, according to their advocates, economies of scale and innovation (Carter, 2020) while the concept of a profession-led 'self-improving system' gained traction (Hargreaves, 2010) (see pp. 46–47). The transfer of power from the post-war tripartite of profession, local authorities and state was almost complete: teacher unions and local authorities cited as the cause of systemic inertia, the so-called 'middle-tier', now much diminished. Finally, for now, as the second decade of the twentieth century concluded and with Britain consumed by Brexit, financial constraints (Britton et al., 2019) bore down heavily on schools, moving Ofsted to report (Ofsted, 2020a).

English primary education seen in this light is a complex responsive system that reflects an interplay of dialogue and ideas, one view or approach reacting with another; while one or more may have the ascendancy at any given point, the others remain in play, creating contradictions and dilemmas that provoke debate, argument and action: those recognisable from this account are recorded in Table 2.4.

Table 2.4: Historically framed: some challenges for primary education

Productive tensions

- Traditional versus progressive understandings concerning the relationship between teacher, learner and knowledge
- Opposing psychological beliefs about the innate educability of children, including issues of achievement for all
- Integrative versus classic, subject-based beliefs about the nature of the curriculum
- Professional versus political views of leadership and ownership of the system
- Minimal, reductive, instrumental versus expansive and creative approaches
- The pressure of accountability measures, especially assessment in the system versus the information they provide formatively to stakeholders

---

Reflection point

There have been many changes throughout the history of primary education. What are the main legacies and remaining tensions from your perspective? Which of these are most in need of revision?

Primary education as a spiral dynamic

The socio-cultural dynamics that created this chronology have left a lasting imprint on English primary education: an evolutionary process that continues. Clare Graves (1970) suggested that human development is 'an unfolding, emergent, oscillating, spiraling process marked by progressive subordination of older, lower-order behavior systems to newer, higher-order systems as man's existential problems change'.

Rather than a pendulum, history is an evolving 'spiral dynamic' (Beck and Cowan, 1996) – as life conditions change, new educational challenges are generated producing changes in consciousness and behaviour. Beck and Cowan (1996, p. 29; with my paraphrasing to reflect education) argue that:

1 Human nature is neither static or finite, it evolves as the conditions of our existence change.
2 When a new level is activated, we change our psychology (and in primary education our pedagogies) and rules for living to adapt to those conditions.
3 We live in a potentially open system of values with an infinite number of pedagogies available to us. There is no final state to which we must aspire.
4 An individual teacher, school (group of schools) or education system can respond positively only to those principles, motivational appeals, educational formulae or legal/ethical codes that are appropriate to the current level of existence.

New levels of development are activated when living conditions change – they are captured in 'value systems' that are combinations of levels of psychological existence; beliefs; and ways of organising (Beck and Cowan 1996). Essentially illustrative, neither discrete nor rigid and in constant interplay, one with another, they provide another lens through which to view the history of primary education.

Table 2.5: Primary education as a spiral dynamic

	Structure and language	**Some educational examples**
SurvivalSense	Loose bonds: survival, instinctive, automatic responses	Tradition – narratives, stories
KinSpirits	Tribes: join together, animistic, magical, mystical	Transmission (e.g. of religious belief) through schools of 'Song and Grammar'; educational movements based in ideology (aspects of progressivism, e.g. Alexander's (1992) 'Shibboleths and Sacred Cows')
PowerGods	Empires – personal power, dominance, egocentric, exploitative	Cult of leadership, head teacher as hero; failing/sink schools; the Academy Trust when constructed as an empire
TruthForce	Pyramids – order, right/ wrong, absolutes, certainties, obedience, purpose	Mass education, local authorities, elementary education (1870), public administration and bureaucracy, 1944 Education Act, national curriculum, Ofsted, efficiency
StriveDrive	Delegative – improving things, autonomy, achievement, strategic, ambitious, individual, enterprise	Local management of schools, performance management, performance tables, widespread testing, National School Improvement Strategies, Academies/Free Schools
HumanBond	Egalitarian – well-being, equity, community, relational, pluralism, consensus	Comenius, Robert Owen, New Education Movement, developmental psychology, aspects of progressivism (Plowden), professional learning communities, governance, self-improving system

Based on Beck and Cowan (1996).

The spiral described by Beck and Cowan (1996) begins with an ancient survivalist phase – SurvivalSense – a primitive existence, not entirely recognisable today with our complex multi-layered lives. It was a time when experience was dominated by subsistence and life was lived through instincts and habits. Educationally this value system had a theme of continuity, slowly evolving; ways of living passed down through the generations, often in family groups. With traditions passed down orally the power of story emerged and has retained an omnipresence in primary education still relevant today (see Willingham, 2010).

As 'survivalism' waned, there was a move from largely individualistic lives towards social or collective formations: Beck and Cowan (1996) gave this the title KinSpirits. Here we see the emergence of tribalism joined through mysticism and spiritualism with the beginnings of cathartic religious practices. People came together for safety, developed new understandings of the world but mostly lacked scientific understanding; beliefs were often based in mythology. Some forms of spiritual/religious practices used educational processes to proselytise or for moralistic functions – we might see early religious schools of 'Song and Grammar' or the 'chantries' (Gillard, 2019) reflecting KinSpirits. Education still creates community allegiances that can remain 'tribal' and we might see a residue today where schools or some parts of the system seek to promote, preserve or defend particular interests. At times, particular groupings in the 'progressive' movement may have exemplified KinSpirit. Alexander's (1992) classic work shows how 'sacred cows and shibboleths' of primary education (which might be described as powerful images with very limited evidential base for their use) inspired and created collective energy. He reminds us that:

> All the sacred cows and shibboleths – the resistance to subjects, integration, thematic work, topics, enquiry methods, group work and so on – must be subjected to clear-headed scrutiny … (Alexander, 1992, p. 194)

The third shift signified a return to the individual in powerful ways – the term associated with this value system is PowerGods. It is exemplified, spearheaded even, by powerful individuals exerting their power over others: historically it is associated with the time of empire, great and small. Many examples of it played out in the period of the Reformation and the industrial revolution. There were major societal upheavals and in England this signified both personal and national expansion in power and influence. Educationally this was at the expense of the poor and often affected children negatively: there was very little education for those with little. The value system of the PowerGods is not always negative, since power can be used for good and can be a motivation for philanthropy and benefaction – today, those involved in 'turnaround' contexts may use it effectively. A moderate, constructive expression emerged in a plethora of leadership initiatives associated with the National College of School Leadership. Today, we might observe its negative excesses in a power-driven secretary of state, uncompromising 'super head' or acquisitive Multi-Academy Trust chief executive. The weakness of such an approach can be its inability to organise and create long-lasting change.

The deprivations and excesses of the PowerGods generated a movement to what is termed TruthForce. This generates the energy to create stability, tending to create forms of bureaucracy and means of government/governance, organisation and regulation: TruthForce tends to operate on a much larger scale than its predecessor memes. In England, as the industrial revolution progressed, thinking began to turn towards municipality and education systems that would serve the masses.

> Elementary education grew in response to piecemeal pressures from the needs of industry and commerce, the real or conjectured dangers of crime, the extension of the franchise, the demands of religion or the promptings of conscience, all of which made increasingly large dents in the frontier of non-education. (Blyth, 1967b, p. 24)

The Factory Acts were passed, there were the innovative 'monitorial' systems of Lancaster and Bell (Silver, 1983), the system of 'payment by results' was established and the Elementary Education Act came to fruition (see Gillard, 2019). School boards, established to develop elementary education beyond the 1870s, reflect in this meme. New educational bureaucracies were created, established and for periods of time sustained. Modifications occurred, of course; the construction of the LEAs, the various Hadow reports and 1944 Education Act all reflect the desire for stability, structure and authority typical of this meme. It remains a strong presence in our education system: the regulatory effects of Ofsted and an entitlement-based national curriculum also reflect forms of TruthForce.

While TruthForce, in its most positive forms, creates stability and order (think also safeguarding), it can, in some bureaucratic forms, be stifling and limiting. A new ambitious value system (StriveDrive) emerges out of the eventual, at least perceived, inertia. Elements of it were present in Victorian England but it has been most apparent explicitly in education reform since the 1980s. This target-driven, achieving value system remains strong and acts as a driver of our current system. Dissatisfaction has driven a new form of individualism: neo-liberal ideas proliferated and were applied to education now constructed as a market with a performance-focused culture and entrepreneurial leadership.

> The demands for ever higher levels of achievement, intolerance of failure, and, in some countries at least, concern over the remaining inequities that characterise the system, mean that schools are increasingly being set demanding goals requiring innovation. (Muijs et al., 2010, p. 6)

It is seductively powerful: who could argue against a more stringent approach and the accountability that goes with it, particularly if 'standards' do rise! Autonomy through delegation is an essentially StriveDrive concept, theoretically allowing the entrepreneurial leader to dispense with restrictive forms of TruthForce. The Achilles heel of individualistic StriveDrive is inequality (e.g. Chitty, 2014). Driving forwards for the many may be at the educational expense of equity: note the concept of 'sink' schools. This together with the continued and draining pursuit of externally constructed targets is not widely satisfying; particularly for a teaching profession whose motivation often stems from concern for the child and a new value system sees a shift to the communal. Labelled HumanBond, it echoes the return of a wider view or what might constitute a developmental education. It has a long ontogeny (Comenius, Owen in New Lanarkshire, the New Education Movement, in aspects of Plowden and progressivism, and also in Piaget and developmental psychology; see Blyth, 1984). HumanBond recognises diversity and the varied needs of children and has a long-maintained presence in English primary education but has only partially been in the ascendancy. The metaphor of the 'Family' might exemplify HumanBond with developments in distributed leadership, values-based cultures, collaboration and the engagement of parents. Sometimes HumanBond, though, has lacked well-evidenced, pedagogical justifications when in progressive form (see Alexander, 1984) and too often (as Plowden exemplified) the difference between what is espoused and what is realised can be stark (see, for example, Alexander's 1995 Leeds study).

Spiral dynamics help in exploring and explaining tensions, dilemmas, conflict and change. Each value system has affordances as well as constraints, they exist (sometimes uneasily) side by side, and the extent to which each is visible varies individual-by-individual, school-by-school, locality-by-locality and across the whole system in complex patterns.

Reflection point

The idea of the spiral is to illustrate that continued changes in 'life conditions' affect primary education. What changes have taken place recently (as a result of austerity, the rise of social media and, of course, Covid-19)? How is primary education adapting to those conditions?

The resistant core: 'stability, standards and subjects'

Primary education remains underpinned by the stability of structures and relationships that create its foundation: its concern for children and their well-being are rightly lauded (Alexander, 2010b), yet key questions should always include how well primary education is doing (e.g. Smithers, 2013) and whether it is fit for purpose.

The view of England's inspectorate was that 87 per cent of primary schools were good or better (Ofsted, 2020c); other authoritative accounts support this positive picture: the independent Cambridge Primary Review and its associated research surveys were collated around and just after the turn of the twentieth century. From the main report:

> primary schools may be the one point of stability and positive values in a world where everything else is changing and uncertain. For many, schools are the centre that holds when things fall apart. (Alexander, 2010b, p. 488)

And from their surveys:

> It is our view that a typical pupil starting in Reception and moving up to Year 6 has a good quality of life in school, and learns to read well and to get on with fellow pupils. Of course the quality can be improved ... (Tymms and Merrell, 2010, p. 455)

International evidence from TIMSS (Trends in International Mathematics and Science Study) and PIRLS (Progress in International Reading Literacy Study) suggest continued and improving achievements of England's primary-aged children against international comparators – with caveats, complexity, nuance and not without space for improvement (McGrane et al., 2017; Richardson et al., 2020). The outstanding concern, however, would be that despite 40 years of reform and significant change, concerns about the under-achievement of a proportion of England's children remains a recurring motif for the twenty-first century (Smithers, 2013; Hutchinson et al., 2020): there are still on-going challenges that are yet to be fully resolved.

The outcome of long tracts of policy for primary education remains a traditional, subject-delineated curriculum with powerful forms of accountability introduced in the 1980s; teaching, most often, is by the 'generalist' teacher in age-delineated classes who progress through prescribed ages and stages: it remains heavily focused on so-called 'standards' in English and Mathematics – Curriculum I as Alexander (1984) called it – with foundation 'subjects' to be found outside of this in Curriculum II. This curriculum exists, at least in statute, as a typology of firmly delineated subjects rather than the more holistic inter-disciplinary model some may prefer and practise. Schools continue to be judged, primarily, by a narrow and relatively limited range of indicators and repertoire of methodologies despite well-articulated alternatives (e.g. Cambridge Primary Review: Alexander, 2010b). Primary education still, too, catches in the authoritarian pressure for 'back to basics' (Campbell, 2001); as Alexander pointedly enquires: 'Does the mantra "back to basics" (always back, never forward) convey the right message for the times and world we live in?' (Alexander, 2010a, p. 1).

It is, overall, an object that might be summarised as being of 'standards and subjects' and through inspection and narrow testing has rarely been weakened in recent years, though it was reappraised in the light of HMCI Amanda Spielman's (2018) most recent interventions. The new inspection framework has attempted to lessen the focus on limited measures of attainment (Ofsted, 2019). Claxton (2021), though, describes the recent emergence of 'direct instruction, knowledge-rich' (DIKR) approaches reflecting what he terms a 'neo-traditional' pedagogy. The construction of curriculum currently is congru-ent with a strong classification of subject knowledge that frames pedagogic practice and is testable. It proposes a particular relationship between teacher and learner: the teacher is expert passing knowledge to children, meaning that their learning can be tightly controlled, at face value reflecting Kelly's (2004) point that schooling when interpreted in a purely technicist sense may be mech-anistic in manner.

In practice, the pressures of 'standards and subjects' create a complex and problematic context beyond simplistic imperatives for primary schools: leaders and teachers must reconcile competing demands with their beliefs about what matters for children and how they learn most successfully. The reality is that the curriculum is often based in something broad and rich (exemplified in Myatt, 2018). Alexander (2008) cites Ofsted's own survey evidence going back to 1978 (DES, 1978) that a well-rounded, broad curriculum is more likely to be associated with better outcomes than a narrower one. 'Standards and subjects' is far from a complete representation of the whole of primary education: a view well understood and successfully transcended by a very significant number of schools.

The core issue with the ideology of 'standards and subjects' is that questions of how to define and delineate, describe, assess and measure have generated the controversy, debate and activity about primary education far more extensively than questioning the logic that powers it. As funding tightens, the risk could be, as Alexander observed in 2000 and which could still obtain, that:

> English primary education in 2000 is nineteenth century elementary education modified – much modified, admittedly – rather than transformed. Elementary education is its centre of gravity … Elementary education is the form to which it most readily tends to regress. (Alexander, 2000, p. 147)

Reflection point

Is 'stability, standards and subjects' still fit for purpose? How does it need to develop into the future? What will be the biggest barriers to change?

Ready for change or locked in the past?

Is primary education ready for change or locked in the past? Answering this question in a system that is universal and complex is difficult. Nearly all adults have experienced primary education and there is a tendency to resort to anecdote and experience rather than evidence: we project our perceptions onto it. Moreover, the emergence of primary education over centuries leaves generational, residual imprints on our thinking, leading to many unquestioned assumptions about what it should be like – assumptions which should, at least, be surfaced and debated, particularly in times of economic and social change which demand we reconsider what we want and expect from primary education. Nor should changing the system of primary education be underestimated: as a whole it is 'heavy duty', huge in scale, cost and resource and significantly shaped by history (Table 2.6).

Table 2.6: Primary education: Nine observations from history

1. Our ideas about education and about children and childhood have evolved but pedagogy and views of learning are still framed by culture and history (Miettinen, 1999).
2. The scale of educational endeavour in England grew enormously in volume and complexity as its value and importance became increasingly understood across the social spectrum; however, for long periods the needs of some social groups and denominations were not fully met (Lawson and Silver, 1973).
3. The emergence of primary education was influenced and shaped by the changing economic, social and technological context of England – and the nation's place in the world (Green, 1990): they influenced attitudes to primary education.
4. Primary education was not always something aspired to because it was intrinsically valuable: other motives helped create the conditions for change (Blyth 1967b); the national education system provided structure and stability, led initially by social changes, latterly most influenced by concerns around economic competitiveness.
5. Many ideas and opinions continue to shape and inform long after their immediate appearance; the early traits are still visible to the discerning eye according to Dearden (1968) – sometimes the system loops back to those earlier ideas and practices, e.g. 'back to basics'.
6. Many structural features of primary education are heavily embedded: the 'generalist' class teacher; vertical grouping and finance rest on long-standing assumptions (Aldrich, 2001); minimal, state-funded elementary education retains a strong hold (Alexander, 2000).
7. The relative importance of various interest groups (political, professional, religious) has waxed and waned; the balance of educational influence and power from state direction (policy, fiscal structures and strategies) has been both centralised and delegated as the middle-tier has been diminished (Brighouse, 2012) – this balance continues to shift.
8. The concept of educational 'leadership' has emerged powerfully as a result of reforms over the last 40 years but contrasts with what Woods and Jeffrey (1998) describe as the 'colonisation' of teachers' time and space by the prevailing accountability systems (see also Woods et al., 1997).
9. A fully extended, expansive and carefully articulated pedagogy of primary education remains elusive as primary education is powered by the 'logic' of 'standards and subjects'.

In 2020, England saw the most profound change in daily life for over 70 years as the Covid-19 epidemic impacted upon everyone: it created new dynamics unthinkable in 'normal' times, prompting practices deemed, perhaps, unnecessary in more stable times. Deep-seated and fundamental belief structures were tilted causing us to question everything. In the light of Covid-19, 'standards and subjects' was under powerful threat as communities came together and teacher collaboration formed a powerful response to the 'unprecedented' changes in 'life conditions' – it was enabled by a dedicated professionalism, a renewed emphasis on well-being and the adoption of sophisticated information and communications technologies. Ideas and possibilities were debated and made real, in particular, through social media. Could primary education make a vital transformation beyond 'standards and subjects'?

In truth the system of primary education was also running another risk: that more and more was demanded of it, largely through external drivers and that this would eventually prove dispiriting reflected in the sense that there is no place to go, the absence of a developmental future and the feeling that demand, no matter what the pace of change, can never be satisfied. For those looking for creativity in its trajectory, the possibilities lay in deconstructing the powerful frames that dominate the system: in effect, in greater systemic differentiation and meaningful leadership in schools and communities. How to create the frameworks of aims and values to sustain and give purpose to what is great about primary education while further creating optimism, energy and therefore even better schools for children summarised the challenge of Covid-19.

Perhaps the inherent weaknesses in 'standards and subjects' are some deeply limiting beliefs and practices that, at times, reduce the joys and possibilities of learning. There is a need to apply the Bakhtinian idea of a 'space of authoring' to generate further consideration: thinking about primary education needs to recognise complexity, celebrate possibilities and find ways that make it relevant and vibrant, something creative and enabling for its children which requires continued change. What might transcend 'standards and subjects' that will not keep us locked in the past, but build upon it for the changing world in which primary children are growing up: is there a catalyst for re-evaluation of primary education?

If stability along with 'standards and subjects' provides the dominant frame for primary education, how does this reflect in the current context for primary education and the thinking underpinning it? Is it fit for purpose, or ready for renewal? There are possibilities: alongside coronavirus and the pressures of 'catch-up' were the power of relationships at the heart of learning, connections with local communities, innovative uses of technology and a recognition of the value of a 'rich' primary education.

Delving deeper

The website 'Education in England' (http://www.educationengland.org.uk) offers a comprehensive repository for those seeking to delve deeper into the history of English primary education. It not only provides a detailed historical account but access to many key publications and original source material. Lawson and Silver's (1973) account remains a credible and engaging account of education history.

Next: In the third and final chapter of this section, the focus turns to the wider socio-cultural environment in which primary education is embedded. It explores the global influences and policy priorities which continue to shape its identity.

3 Global driving forces and contemporary issues for primary education

This chapter is about driving forces and contemporary issues currently facing primary education. It takes account of the global patterns and political priorities to examine where there is energy for the further development of primary education.

It explores: *the political context • the global context • international influences and research • accountability • knowledge • autonomy • the self-improving system • teaching and the teaching profession • social justice • powerful productive forces*

Where the previous chapters have created a framework from which to view how primary education came to be, this chapter looks at the driving forces currently at play. In takes the position that, in socio-cultural terms, people's actions contribute to changing their environment but they are, in turn, critically mediated by the culture, history and context that surround them – the environments people inhabit shape them just as they shape those environments (Wertsch, 1998). This is the principle of 'mediated action' where all human action, be it on the individual or social plane, is socio-culturally situated and shaped by constant dialogue.

Political context

The tone of educational change is the colour and hue that is cast upon it by governments, the media, corporate institutions and other groups through the language they use to describe the nature of the problem to which change is the solution. (Hargreaves, 2003, p. 90)

History illustrates many arguments about primary education – about access to it, around standards and effectiveness and, recently, autonomy has been an ascendant concern: newly elected governments now recognise education as a vital strand of policy (Chitty, 2014). Of late, questions for politicians have been anchored firmly within a larger policy narrative of neo-liberalism whose political aegis is rooted in approaches aiming for a minimal role for the state, spawning practices that remove unnecessary regulation, bureaucracy and reducing intervention (see Plant, 2010). They sit alongside a pro-active shift in direction: the drive for achievement and better outcomes from primary education. Justifications for change play out through the language of autonomy, choice, diversity, equity, accountability and excellence (Brighouse, 2011) – sometimes, avoiding the weight of pedagogical evidence (Alexander, 2008). The argument extolled that the education system was sluggish with too many barriers in the established interest groups to allow radical change, thus change forces were brought to bear. Those forces interplayed creating changes in rule systems, organisation and resources, and in cultural advancement as set out in Table 3.1.

Such systemic development is rarely perfectly formed and always mediated as it is implemented in practice through what Lave and Wenger might describe as the 'socially negotiated character of meaning' (1991, p. 50). Adversarial educational politics and media fall-out have often been the accompaniment to education policy as teachers faced what Ball (2008) described as a 'discourse of derision'.

Change on a large scale is a highly complex process, particularly in a system as extensive as primary education. Fullan's (2011) analysis of system levers shows how if the wrong drivers are chosen, development will be less effective: these include an overemphasis on accountability; focusing on individual teacher and leadership quality; uninformed technology adoption; and fragmented strategies. In addition, change is influenced by unforeseen events: with confidence in modern politics depleted, events such as Birmingham's 'Trojan Horse' controversy (Kershaw, 2013) and the Black

Table 3.1: Productive forces in English primary education in the twenty-first century

Change to:	Examples
Rule systems	Governance, accountability (testing, Ofsted), national curriculum
Organisation and resources	Demise of the local authorities; Academies and Free Schools; Multi-Academy Trusts; supporting infrastructure
Cultural advancement	International influences; evidence-informed practice; autonomy, social justice; self-improving system

Lives Matters movement were powerful, from the 'ground up', productive forces that put values, democratic accountability and equity firmly in the educational spotlight.

Global context: the networked society

System change in primary education is a complex process and the intricacies of our globalised world are increasingly compounding this. Today, globalisation, environmental concerns and socio-economic change forces increasingly frame and influence education, qualitatively changing the filters (see Forrester and Garratt, 2016). Across the world societies are restructuring as interrelating and rapidly shifting forces affect social relations, financial and economic security, as well as individual identity with effects on employment and demands upon the workforce (see Castells, 1998, 2000; Friedman, 2005). The hegemony of competitiveness, economic prosperity and entrepreneurialism (Martin et al., 2018) forms the narrative: authorised, seemingly sensible and in Bourdieu's (1977) language now part of our 'categories of thought'. This is 'globalisation' and descriptions and analyses abound, problematically so as these definitions and interpretations have distinct meanings in different contexts; Apple (2013) describes it as a 'sliding signifier' to illustrate the ambiguity. Some see it as the maturation of the capitalist system, extended across the globe with extensive trade dominated by the world's leading private corporations that now continue to move incessantly across national borders (Friedman, 2005). Economic power has moved beyond the traditional 'West'; the BRIC (Brazil, Russia, India, China) nations are increasingly taking their place at the head of the table. It seems increasingly, too, to be a world of rich and poor and where some argue that the financial sector and the dominant elites are now beyond scrutiny (Apple, 2013). This historical period is characterised by widespread 'destructuring of organisations, delegitimation of institutions, fading away of major social movements, and ephemeral cultural expressions' (Castells, 2000, p. 3). What makes it so significant for educators is that globally dynamic forces are exerting major pressures on all aspects of people's lives. One of the most striking effects for education is the erosion of people's identity. Castells (2000) notes that this is not a new trend; identity has always been at the roots of human meaning but he argues that it is now becoming a prime source of distress; the effects being felt particularly in well-being and mental health.

In education the reassuring certainties and hierarchies of bureaucracies have been restructured or reduced in the move to technocratic approaches where highly specified versions of pedagogy through curriculum and measures of performances dominate and where, increasingly often, autonomous Multi-Academy Trusts are the means of delivery. This process continues and Castells (2000) describes the recent rise of the 'networked society' whose social structure is predicated on the speed, power and explosion in the use of information and communication technologies; powerful networks emerge alongside existing structures, then interact and shape societal organisation and communications. At their heart is what Castells (2009) calls 'communication power': when those engaged are able to take an active and critical role in creating meaning from new ideas and practices, they have huge potential for empowerment.

Global networks have their place in history but the new networks are qualitatively different; in particular, there is movement towards those that are 'decentred'. There is movement from prescribed *bureaucracies*, through descriptive *technocratic* approaches to that which is, in the language of Victor and Boynton, *'co-configured'* and involves 'building and sustaining a fully integrated system that can sense, respond, and adapt ...' (1998, p. 195) (Table 3.2). The intention is a system that is actively constructed, self-organising, inclusive of multiple viewpoints with pedagogies that are dynamic and meaningful: 'co-configuration work never results in a "finished" product. Instead, a living, growing network develops ...' (Victor and Boynton, 1998, p. 195).

Table 3.2: Movement towards co-configuration

	Bureaucratic	**Technocratic**	**Co-configured**
Object	Prescribed	Described	Actively constructed
Motive	Fixed	Coordinated	Self-organising
Cultural context	Controlled	Shared	Negotiated and connecting
Multiple voices	Hierarchical	Visible	Exchanging / multiple viewpoints
Trajectory	Defined	Precise	Dynamic
Roles	Determined	Data rich	Expert / creating meaning

Reflection point

To what extent do you believe political and global forces are shaping primary education? To what extent do you recognise the bureaucratic, technocratic and co-configured (networked) aspects of our current system?

While some evidence of co-configuration can be seen in the system that is English primary education, 'stability, standards and subjects' still acts as a powerful constraint. However, powerful effects can be seen within the system of English primary education from seven drivers (international influences and research; accountability; knowledge; autonomy; a self-improving system; teaching and the teaching profession; and social mobility): the impact, potential and especially the energies of those dynamics are explored now.

International influences and research

The rise of data, enabled by new technologies, coincided with growing confidence and expertise located in the 'school effectiveness' movement with its abilities to factorise and produce quantitative research that increasingly identifies correlations between learning outputs and teaching strategies (e.g. Hattie, 2009). Meanwhile, global 'policy speak' echoes around the world as many educational ideas have become international as much as local (see Plank and Keesler, 2009). Education policy has a powerful international community moulded by global organisations, including the World Bank, the Organisation for Economic Cooperation and Development (OECD) and international consultancy companies. The OECD (2015), in particular, has been at the forefront through the Programme for International Student Assessment (PISA) and Teaching and Learning International Surveys (TALIS). Reports from the consultancy company McKinsey, including 'How the world's best performing school systems come out on top' (Barber and Mourshed, 2007; see also Mourshed et al., 2010), fuelled debate. In England, think tanks like the Policy Exchange (e.g. Fazackerley et al., 2010) promoted extended neo-liberal ideas.

International educational comparison rose to the fore. How to respond to the plethora of studies using varying methods describing differential performance of education systems (Alexander, 2000; Crehan, 2016)? Should we look east to successful jurisdictions in Shanghai or Singapore perhaps (Alexander, 2008; Jensen, 2012); west to the USA for its charter schools; or nearer home, the high-performing Finnish system (Sahlberg, 2011)? It is inherently problematic: issues include 'cherry picking' ideas regardless of 'fit'; inaccurately identifying what is needed; and inappropriately setting proposed changes within the overall aims and purpose of a different system. Our current national curriculum illustrates the controversy: heavily 'knowledge-based' as justified by Oates (2010), yet contemporarily critiqued by Pollard for being too linear and lacking an underpinning theory of learning (2012), while other alternatives can be found across the world (see Priestly and Biesta, 2014).

While ILSAs (International Large-Scale Assessments) provide insights into how a country's education system is performing (PISA, for example, tests 15-year-olds), they are not without controversy. Although PISA assesses the extent to which the skills needed for 'economic success' are present in each nation's children, Alexander cautioned: 'PISA tests what it tests' and should not be seen 'as a proxy for the whole of a child's education' (Alexander, 2012, p. 8). Smithers (2013), meanwhile, advises that comparisons of primary education are affected by which countries are taking part, while Whetton et al. counselled: 'Direct evidence on the performance of primary school pupils in England from international surveys is sparser than might be expected ...' (2010, p. 480). However, TIMSS and PIRLS, organised by the International Association for the Evaluation of Educational Achievement, do survey 9- and 10-year-olds in England and offer opportunities for comparison (McGrane et al., 2017; Richardson et al., 2020).

It was, in part, international influences that framed Michael Gove, as education secretary in 2010, committing to 'autonomy' and new providers entering the education market, to curriculum freedom but with schools being 'properly accountable' (Chitty, 2014).

Energies

Learning from research and international comparison can provide vital stimulus: it can shape pedagogy. Alexander (2000), for example, identified 'talk' in England when comparing primary education across five cultures leading him to investigate and champion 'dialogic teaching', now evidenced through systematic evaluation (Alexander, 2020). This is an international movement where powerful understandings and practices centred on oracy have collectively developed (e.g. Mercer et al., 2020), despite it never being a political priority in England. Perhaps the time has come to recognise international collaboration as a successor to international comparison.

Bridges between research and practice, arguably limitations of early school effectiveness studies, are now being built (e.g. Hattie, 2009). Innovative works are taking place: the Education Endowment Fund has supported a system of randomised control trials and in their Teaching and Learning Toolkit summaries of international evidence can be used to inform school-based decision-making. Yong Zhao cautions us to be mindful in that there is still much for educators to learn from the study of side effects in medicine (Zhao, 2017). It is still an embryonic field with risks (e.g. Cordingley, 2009): research must provide practitioners with reliable and relatable evidence; maintain credible independence; and avoid solely focusing on instrumental 'high stakes' performance measures. Socio-cultural theory also provides a reminder that the processes of interpretation, adaptation and implementation are likely to be as important as the evidence itself.

Accountability

Progressively, as responsibility has been devolved to schools, control of quality has been externalised: testing and inspection signify school success. 'Performance' matters as much as ever; instrumental as it may be, few primary schools can ignore how they will be judged and so under pressure to raise standards they must, to some degree, teach within those parameters (Troman et al., 2007). We should not be surprised if the curriculum is skewed to what is tested and inspected (both in terms of value and time), and that sometimes reactive, superficial and tactical change overrides deeper development: the technocrats' 'field of judgements' (Ball, 2003) prevails and, as Nichols and Berliner (2007) have explained, by attaching 'high stakes' to test scores, a corruption and invalidation of the measure can occur.

In the accountability system of England, Ofsted have a powerful and controversial role as they judge school effectiveness. Furthermore, their inspection frameworks have had the effect of colonising the educational space, their criteria invasively imposing themselves in the psychology and practices of the system (Altrichter and Kemethofer, 2015). Note the dramatic effect of HMCI Spielman's changes to the framework in 2019 that reinvigorated processes of curriculum design: most schools now, very successfully and understandably, design self-evaluation and/or quality assurance systems based on the latest version. Critiques abound though: Coffield (2017), for one, has argued that Ofsted have been allowed to operate without appropriate validation, to cause undue distress and with a confusion of purpose. Others are concerned about the reliability of inspections and that the residual effects of inspection have significant consequences. An 'outstanding' judgement can positively affect a school or head teacher while special measures or serious weaknesses usually leads to 'academisation' (and loss of jobs for some). Singularly concerning is evidence that primary schools in the most deprived contexts are more likely to receive poorer judgements (Education Policy Institute, 2016).

Advocates of testing and inspection argue they are in the public interest and, not without some justification, point to inconsistency prior to their introduction. The question is: are they are fit for purpose? Undoubtedly primary education is stereotyped by the prevailing performance criteria often leading to a remorseless improvement drive that can create self-doubt and anxiety as demands increase. The pressing danger is that teaching becomes a performance: a game necessary to be played in order to be able to survive, driven by proxies for achievement which do not equate with our understandings of learning.

Energies

With foresight, Lawton (1987), as early discussions about a national curriculum gathered pace, recognised that in 'cutting the curriculum cloth' what is tested (and inspected) will, inevitably, drive what is taught. Rescuing self-evaluation from the clutches of inspection and testing and then setting it within aims and purposes that are clear and widely understood (the product of sustained political, professional and stakeholder dialogue) and placing it alongside rigorous teacher moderation of achievement could have powerful professional effects.

Assessment is one of the most powerful tools in the pedagogic repertoire (Black and Wiliam, 1998) and should support the aims and purposes of the system, recognising the breadth of a child's education; when it informs their learning and development it has a purposeful hue. Wiliam (2010), citing Resnick (1987), suggests that there is a case for exploring the idea of 'tests worth teaching to'. Advances in the sophistication of testing techniques offer many opportunities to focus on their formative affordances: they can increasingly offer diagnostic and adaptive capacity. The system could increasingly reflect MacBeath's assertion that:

> It is an index of a nation's educational health when its school communities
> have a high level of intelligence and know how to use the tools of self-evaluation
> and self-improvement … It is an unhealthy system which relies on the constant
> routine attentions of an external body … (MacBeath, 1999, p. 1)

Knowledge

Knowledge has become a central concern in curriculum debate and is without question important: a knowledge-rich approach is strongly influential in England (for different perspectives, see E. Hirsch, 2006; Young et al., 2014; Claxton, 2021). It is often in definition that it becomes problematic. The design of content knowledge for an education system, for example, will always be demanding: how to create substantial, challenging yet meaningful syntactic structures organised in ways which are developmental is a not inconsiderable challenge (Shulman, 1987). Hirsch offers one formulation; another, as Bruner (1996) argued, is that it can be developed in knowledge constructs through the idea of spiralling. However, knowledge as prescribed in curriculum frameworks often has tight boundaries and distinct emphases, and whose knowledge matters in an education system has long been the subject of sociological argument. Critics suggest the system values knowledge sets differently according to culture and class. Anyon (1981), for example, demonstrated how school knowledge embodies particular sets of values in classified and certified forms that dominate prescribed curriculum frameworks. Her work raised questions about inducting children into particular, favoured knowledge: disciplines that confirm (or otherwise) the dominance of particular groups. She wrote: 'By situating school knowledge in its particular social location, we can see how it may contribute to contradictory social processes of conservation and transformation' (Anyon, 1981, p. 38). Historically accumulated, school knowledge, Anyon argued, creates class conflict, pointing to the relationship between the absence of power and the presence of apathy.

There is much to be addressed in the way in which school knowledge is constructed and structured and from whose viewpoint it is presented, particularly in our diverse, multicultural society. If pedagogy is merely translation and transmission, the problem might be, as Blatchford et al. (2010) explain:

> … differentiation by ability/attainment has been associated with limited
> access to knowledge by some pupils, domination of pedagogic practices by
> teachers, preferred teachers for 'elite' pupils and enforcement of social
> divisions among pupils. (Blatchford et al., 2010, p. 581)

Energies

This is not an argument against a framework of knowledge: in science, for example, key concepts such as space or velocity are unquestionably accelerated through a well-designed curriculum. Evidence suggests that the disciplines of enquiry are a vital part of human thinking and that 'subjects' (however defined) are vital as part of children's conceptual development (see Shulman, 1987; Gardner, 1999).

The teaching of knowledge can interact with conscious experience, ideally through a process of return, where discourse enables children to connect their own experience with the established bodies of knowledge. In terms of science, for example, Wegerif (2013) suggests the subject is often taught as a body of fact and knowledge but could rather be seen as a wealth of knowledge including enquiry and an 'argumentative discourse'. Similarly in the relationship between subjects rather than seeing them in isolation, they are in relation, one with another, bringing versatility for the learner. If 'knowing' is a crucial and valid intention of pedagogy, then this has significant importance by shifting the emphasis towards the learner. For Dewey (1910), learning alone was not wisdom, nor does the presence of information guarantee 'good' judgement (cited in Higgins, 2009). In his meta-review of learning to learn, Higgins (2009) emphasises the difference in the 'quality' of knowledge achieved through purposeful activity on the part of the learner.

Autonomy

At the heart of Gove's reforms in 2010 was creating the conditions that would allow new ideas and innovation: the product was Academies and Free Schools (the New Schools System). This was a policy driven by leaders of the type Ball (1994) called the 'policy entrepreneurs'; notable in their combination of the areas of improving performance and the affective domain, thereby securing the emotional resilience for an outcomes driven culture (Conroy et al., 2010). The neo-liberal loosening of the traditional institutional architecture (especially local authorities), which provided a feeling of protection and of certainty for many, was seen as a necessary dynamic of change. There were cogent critiques by the New Visions for Education Group and coordinated opposition from the Anti-Academies League, the Local Schools Network and the teacher trade unions. Benn's (2011) account of 'School Wars' told of those campaigns, the demise of local democracy and favouring the locally accountable community school. Such arguments were met with the 'discourse of right' (Ball, 2008); oppositional arguments were rarely refuted through extended explanation and evidence.

Academies were part of a new framework of regulation removed from local authorities and their democracy (see Clayton, 2012) and subject to contract law on the basis of an agreement between the secretary of state and the school proprietor. The New School System was essentially professional and depoliticised. Some welcomed the affordances of Academy status and the opportunities it offered them: leadership of more than one school, for example, was the 'promised land' for the ambitious and entrepreneurial. A new group of leaders in the education sector emerged, given 'credentials' that allowed them to function in the newly constructed environment. In 'good' and 'outstanding' schools they were National and Local Leaders of Education with organisational designations such as National Support or Teaching School. The chief executive and the executive head teacher were a new phenomenon. Sometimes policy needs cover and professional legitimation provided the vehicle.

Proponents of the New Schools System illustrate it through the power of collaboration, economies of scale (capacity), stronger governance (especially in the form of Multi-Academy Trusts) and the success of most Trusts (e.g. Carter, 2020), and by May 2021 there was significant momentum: 37.6 per cent of mainstream primary schools were Academies (DfE, 2021a). Multi-Academy Trusts, too, grew quickly in size and number: 298 were listed under primary education by the DfE on their 2019 school performance tables (DfE, 2021b).

While some enjoyed the available spoils, others were left feeling insecure and unsure of their place, especially those under pressure of becoming a 'sponsored' Academy. A new infrastructure, running parallel to the local education authorities emerged in the form of regional schools commissioners and the Education Funding Agency, leaving the configuration of primary schools in England as a curious mixture of types of schools in varying forms, differentiated further according to geography, some standing alone, others part of large, potentially monolithic organisations. Concerns continued about funding, probity (Mansell, 2021) and the 'corrupted practices' that Thomson (2020) explores, together with the not insignificant salaries of Multi-Academy Trust chief executives.

How the school system will be synthesised and brought to coherence without hierarchy and inequitable access to resources and influence must be resolved. However, in the midst of such change it should not surprise us to see contradictions abounding as old and new collided: the aim is innovation but renewal is a complex process. In his account of the Greater Manchester Challenge, Ainscow observed of system leaders in new environments:

> ... many of these leaders seemed to be very active networkers and entrepreneurs. Sometimes, these traits were coupled with rather conservative leadership and management practices, relying on traditional hierarchies and involving high levels of monitoring aimed at promoting consistency. (Ainscow, 2015, p. 105)

Energies

Arguments will continue about the merits and demerits of the New Schools System as it continues to evolve. The New Visions for Education Group (2012) argued, subtly, that: 'All institutions should have the maximum level of autonomy consistent with the wider public interest'. Isolation, self-interest and corrupted practices should concern us, yet it is possible to transcend these challenges: Glatter (2017) argues that schools should be seen as institutions in preference to organisations. The point being that the former carries with it both public and private interest with multiple purposes: he uses the term 'civic institution' where the school takes 'responsibility beyond its own students to its local community and wider society and would demonstrate a strong commitment to democratic processes in decision making' (2017, p. 33).

A self-improving system

In a series of commissioned papers for the National College for School Leadership, David Hargreaves (2010, 2011) focused on the concept of a 'self-improving education system' emphasising the teaching profession (or, at least, head teachers) in leading developments. An endogenous approach where the improvement of the system comes from within where it would appear to have greatest possibilities: a potentially powerful, if asymmetric, form of innovation. It can be readily illustrated: Matthews and Hill (2010) reported on school-school support, Hutchings et al. (2012) on the London Challenge, while Ainscow (2015) reported on the capacity-building taking place between schools in Greater Manchester.

Hargreaves (2001) proposed a model of human capital where the specific skills, experience and capabilities possessed individually and collectively within the education system connect in order to develop together. He offered an alternative to top-down models of change believing that since the birth of school improvement in the 1980s, there have been significant gains in the quality of school leadership and that networks and partnership offer an opportunity for further change. He identified:

> ... four building blocks of a self-improving system: clusters of schools (the structure); the local solutions approach and co-construction (the two cultural elements); and system leaders (the key people). (Hargreaves, 2010, p. 2)

These are already partially in place but would need to strengthen. Hargreaves offers a systemic approach, not an antidote to the increasing pressure for outcomes. The tension is that politicians will need to see that embedded within self-improving systems are mechanisms that will improve outcomes: for professionals, it will depend on the extent of the 'space for authoring' allowed to them.

Energies

For some, the response to conformity can be along the lines of what Hargreaves and Shirley call 'the path of effervescence', where 'Teachers interact with teachers, schools learn from schools, and the strong help the weak' (2009, p. 41). Hargreaves and Shirley caution that this, for some, may be fun – but the benefits are short-lived, the pleasure, as they describe it, momentary, the effervescent high. The analysis is acute: Hargreaves and Shirley argue that profound satisfaction can best be provided by taking on deep-seated but fulfilling challenges that transcend narrow performance frameworks, in essence meaning a commitment to addressing collectively the most significant educational and social challenges that are identified in any context: this is the truly challenging work at the heart of a self-improving system.

Teaching and the teaching profession

According to a report from the McKinsey Institute: 'the quality of an education system cannot exceed the quality of its teachers' (Barber and Mourshed, 2007): teaching is the most significant factor in children's achievement (Hattie, 2009; Hanushek, 2011). Jeffrey and Woods (1999, 2003) recognise the power and emphasise the creativity of teaching as it responds to children's emotions, engages their interest, stimulates their imaginations, respects individuality and brings out their critical reflective capacities.

Hoyle (1974) asked whether we prefer professionally restricted or extended teachers: some favour teachers as technicians, operatives delivering the curriculum, while others prefer highly skilled, autonomous professionals. What kind of professional discipline should we emphasise? Commonly it is sub-divided into craft (repertoire and mastery), art (responsive, creative, sometimes improvised) and science (principled, informed and evidenced): extended professionalism is all of these (see Pollard, 2010; also Alexander, 2000, p. 272–276, Alexander, 2008).

The durable motive, particularly for primary teachers, remains their connection to children; it is a highly moral, conscientious profession and one proven in implementing reform. Doyle and Ponder (1977) described the 'practicality ethic': the clear obligation that circumscribes teachers and teaching, an unwritten societal expectation that constrains and binds them. Yet high stakes accountability individualises teachers who develop higher levels of anxiety and concern as they are constantly judged: it becomes harder for teachers to articulate a philosophy that offers them satisfaction within their value constructs. Teaching is changing too: Webb and Vulliamy explain that when aspects of their role prevents teachers from giving children the 'time, attention, care and experiences' they ought to have, 'they then lose enthusiasm and commitment to the detriment of the profession' (2009, p. 18). This loss of residual energy was deeply concerning for Galton and MacBeath (2008). It is these, and factors like them, that mean there is a continued and significant problem with retaining teachers within the profession.

New forms of teacher organisation are emerging – the Chartered College of Teaching, for example – while networked organisations such as ResearchEd,

CollectivEd and Teacher Tapp demonstrate how knowledge can increasingly be developed collaboratively and distributed horizontally. However, when the profession has had greater autonomy this has tended to act as a conservative force, as Alexander (2013) exemplified through the continuation of the system of generalist class teachers. The current reality is difficult to assess (Gunter, 2007): there have been too many initiatives for teachers to come to terms with (Burgess, 2010), preventing a critical appraisal of the profession; nevertheless, the logic of building its collective capacity could generate significant system energy (Fullan, 2011).

At the height of the Covid-19 epidemic when many schools were feeling huge pressure in the face of unprecedented change and there were demands for them to adapt their approaches, many responded valiantly, determinedly and selflessly, as they and their trade unions, in particular, were subject to a discourse blaming them for putting obstacles in the way of schools opening. The profession of teaching needs to be constructed so that it is respected, meaningful and motivated. It is a point extended by Bangs and Frost, who argue that: 'the concern for improving teaching and learning, and the concern to enhance the environment in which teachers operate, do not have to be in opposition' (Bangs and Frost, 2012, p. 8).

Energies

Teaching should be of consistently high quality and high status, undertaken by skilled and imaginative professionals, contextualised in a broad vision of education with a clear purpose and theories of action that are intellectually and rationally grounded (see MacBeath et al., 2018). It is time for the science of teaching in an enquiry-based profession to come to the fore: principled, informed, evidenced (Alexander, 2008). Arguably, it is teachers' overarching, deep-seated development of pedagogy that will make the difference using a wide body of professional knowledge, requiring substantive professional enquiry so that teacher leadership is at the heart of the matter. As Fullan puts it:

> Just as learning will go nowhere if educators do not have a deep theoretical understanding of the first principles of learning, improvement will not happen if leaders and others do not have a deep theoretical grasp of the first principles of change. Theories of pedagogy and theories of change must be integrated again and again in each action setting. (Fullan, 2001, p. 268)

Social justice

In an article in 2010, Estelle Morris recognised a concern that the intended reforms of the Coalition government would leave the vulnerable and disadvantaged as potential losers. According to the Sutton Trust and the Social Mobility Commission (2019), social mobility remains low in England and is not improving, large parts of the country lack opportunity and there is a sense they feel distanced. Wilkinson and Pickett (2009, 2019) observed that while a largely happy place, the UK has many poor people; inequalities and divergences of experience are much greater than they need to be. Much remains to be done: the Cambridge Primary Review's conclusion was that the 'economic prognosis for Britain's "long tail of underachievers" was poor unless social inequalities could be reduced' (Alexander, 2010b, p. 59). Research by the Education Policy Institute on primary schools suggested it would take a very long time for the gap between advantaged and disadvantaged children to narrow (Hutchinson et al., 2019). Remarkably, during the Covid-19 epidemic, it took the public intercession of a professional footballer (Marcus Rashford) to highlight the plight of many economically deprived children through the vehicle of free school meals (BBC, 2020).

The weakness of some school improvement and effectiveness models is that they are devoid of expression of values and the need for political action; school improvement has been steadily 'decontextualised' (Watkins, 2010), addressed only partly by increased funding in the form of the Pupil Premium. A cautionary note on the part of Michael Apple (1998) is apposite. He illustrated that the emphasis on educational excellence in the US reforms of the 1980s was focused on the relationship between education and increased productivity: it did not sufficiently recognise larger societal effects, including growing inequalities. Primary education must attend to diverse demands as some children live a life of affluence and choice while others struggle with hardship and necessity (Alexander, 2010b, p. 93). The Cambridge report (Alexander, 2010b) identified the danger of vulnerable children becoming what it terms a 'professional euphemism' with excuses made for them as 'nuisances' or somehow 'incomplete'. Their schools may be labelled negatively too through inspection reports leading to the concern Park (2013) raises in terms of children's anxiety about them. The lens is often narrowly defined through 'outcomes' of groups of pupils and to particular localities where the features of society create the biggest challenges – these become associated with educational failure. Somehow these become the targets for extended intervention and self-fulfilling prophecies come to bear.

Numerous approaches to address this have been tried: Social Priority Areas, Education Action Zones, 'Every Child Matters', Sure Start, extended schools, Pupil Premium funding and Opportunity Areas among them. 'Narrowing the gap', 'social mobility' and 'levelling up' are part of the associated language. Social mobility became a theme of Conservative education policy. Reay (2012) argues that a socially just education system will allow people to be what they are: it is not a system that allows some to get ahead of others. It does not seem right if an education system only gives some children a chance against a tide of economics that creates poverty in the first place. Social justice is where self-esteem, connection and confidence come together, recognising too that schools control only some of the influences on achievement (Gorard and See, 2013; Gorard, 2018): the challenge must involve galvanising the collective energy of government, local services and communities.

Energies

Who champions social justice and inclusion? Arguably this is a role to be undertaken locally, a point at which everyone becomes focused on the needs of those most likely to be excluded from educational success: this could be the single and most important purpose and focus of collective strategic organisation and planning. It will need the exercise of agency not compliance: so that in working together people can 'learn, be creative, share in the excitement of exploration, and find better ways forward' (Groves and West-Burnham, 2020, p. 137).

Reflection point

Which of these – international influence and research, accountability, knowledge, autonomy, a self-improving system, teaching and the teaching profession, social justice – do you believe to have most possibilities for developing primary education? What is it that is so potentially powerful?

Powerful productive forces

This crossfire of productive forces has created a new, often expedient discourse that has sometimes challenged and sometimes reinforced the established norms of primary education: in practice, neo-liberalism is competing with those whose basic starting points tend to social justice (e.g. Fielding and Moss, 2011) and in Spiral Dynamics this is labelled Human Bond (where well-being, equity, community and consensus come to the fore). The interplay raises significant questions of educational value. For example, if the outcome of the cultural conditions and political context is one which focuses on the short term and immediate where only what is measured seems to matter, then creating deep-rooted, sustainable communities of learning will be challenging to achieve. For many this complexity is experienced as uncertainty: 'Those searching for correctness in a complex education system that is involved in substantial change will inevitably experience ambiguity and a lack of understanding of the direction and purposes of the change' (Ainscow, 2015, p. 115).

Table 3.3 takes these seven areas (international influence and research, accountability, knowledge, autonomy, a self-improving system, teaching and the teaching profession, and social justice) and considers the challenge they provide to primary education, the debates they engender and the potential developments associated with them.

Table 3.3: System contradictions, debates and potential development

Area	Emergent challenges	Debates about ...	Potential developments
International influence on education policy	How best to use research evidence from education systems to inform pedagogy?	Debate continues about what primary education is for, particularly in a changing, culturally diverse country What constitutes valid evidence and how to apply it to the benefit of primary education	Research informed and evidence developed through enquiry
Standards and accountability	How to create an intelligent accountability system?	Debates about what should be assessed and inspected and how: moving from that which is measurable to that which is valuable and informative	A coherent set of well-articulated national aims supported by formative, diagnostic and adaptive assessment which supports school self-evaluation
Knowledge	What knowledge should be taught? How does it connect to the experiences of children?	Exploration of what lies at the core of the curriculum Whose knowledge is being taught?	Balancing a core of knowledge with a curriculum that builds on the wealth of knowledge in children's experience and locality
The case for autonomy	How much autonomy should schools have? How to ensure equity of access to resources and opportunities for schools of different types?	Discussion about the structure of primary education; debates about the ownership of schools; and the degrees of autonomy desirable in an education system Concerns about new providers in the system and whether some providers have differential access to resources and opportunities	A strategy for school self-evaluation that allows autonomy but in a variety of collaborative forms, is geared to the interests of children and families and is demonstrably fair The notion of the school as a civic institution

(Continued)

Table 3.3: (Continued)

Area	Emergent challenges	Debates about ...	Potential developments
A self-improving system	How to create the conditions for collaboration where schools, on an equal basis learn from each other? What is the balance of political and professional decision-making?	On-going shifts in the extent of political intervention in the education system and debates about the leadership and governance of a modern education system	An emphasis on collaborative approaches to educational decision-making; with an appropriate balance of national and local initiative grounded in evidence
The teaching profession	Resolving the contradiction between demanding more of the teaching profession balanced with empowering them to lead the system	Extended debate about the role and effectiveness of teachers, their professional development and their role in educational strategy	The development of the professional capacity needed to deliver a twenty-first-century pedagogy
Social justice	The balance between the general performance of the population and the best education for the lowest-performing groups	Debates about pedagogies which support achievement for all children, ensuring that the system is wholly inclusive Exploration of approaches to partnership which engaged closely with wider communities	Education system resources for pedagogies that connect with children Design of the curriculum balancing depth in key areas with a locally contextualised curriculum and children's agency and voice

Table 3.4 converts these debates and suggestions into a framework of emerging possibilities that will take us in the direction of a co-configured system of primary education. Some of these are in train and carry forwards, others need greater fuel to truly ignite their potential. These aspects chime with a pedagogy that must recognise the loss of identity observed by Castells, increasingly encompassing acceptance and respect, together with recognition of uniqueness and difference, in order to be inclusive and contribute to social justice.

Table 3.4: Ways forward to a co-configured system

- Principled, evidence-informed pedagogies underpinned by research and evidence
- Aims and purposes agreed and clarified through sustained dialogue
- Accountability systems rooted in rigorous teacher moderation and school and systemic self-evaluation
- Schools as civic institutions committed to an extended role
- Knowledge and children's agency combined in powerful forms of pedagogy
- Fulfilling pedagogies that connect with children
- A teaching profession engaged in powerful communities of enquiry focused on advancing pedagogy and building capacity
- An educational focus on agency at all levels: teachers, children and communities
- Strategic organising and planning focused on meeting the needs of localities with a commitment to social justice and equity

---

By way of conclusion, Ainscow (2015) is optimistic describing the changes in the Greater Manchester Challenge and how in a number of cases local dissatisfaction created the energy for change, sometimes resulting in individual enterprise but also in compelling examples of positive community action. Approaches such as these depend on a systemic sense of moral purpose based in constructive relationships:

> Organizations ... are centers of human relatedness, first and foremost, and relationships thrive where there is an appreciative eye – when people see the best in one another, when they share their dreams and ultimate concerns in affirming ways, and when they are connected in full voice to create not just new worlds but better worlds. (Cooperrider and Whitney, 2005, pp. 20–21)

Delving deeper

There are many and varied books focused on education policy-making that will give the reader deeper insights. Forrester and Garratt's (2016) *Education Policy Unravelled* explores developments in the modern era, while Chitty's (2014) *Education Policy in Britain* explores why education policy matters.

Next: This section has looked at primary education through a range of lenses and offered a series of perspectives. A summary of this exploration is provided in the conclusions which follow.

Conclusions

The three chapters in this section represent a journey comprising a broad consideration of primary education: from a socio-cultural perspective, through a whistle stop tour of its history, and concluding with a consideration of contemporary policy issues in a changing, increasingly networked world. It seems that in a time of rapid change, sustainability should also be a watchword.

It is time to return to the power of pedagogy: to the energy of socio-cultural dynamics, its motive and its capacity to transform children's lives. The process of re-scoping pedagogy remains one demanding attention to our current realities and, of course, there remains the possibility in a rapidly changing world that primary education could be catapulted forwards by significant events. Pedagogy in this sense is plural and dynamic: it should have multiple identities and be constantly changing, evolving to meet the context it finds itself in, propelled by the productive capacity and energy in the system.

In this section, pedagogy can be seen as the product of the complexity of an environment including: (1) the orientation of the system (its purpose and direction); (2) the structures embedded in the system (institutional forms); (3) the organisation of curricula; and (4) the support of teachers (adapted from Chronaki, 2000). The frame, therefore, through which we look needs breadth. Kipling said:

> I keep six honest serving-men
>
> (They taught me all I knew);
>
> Their names are What and Why and When
>
> And How and Where and Who.

Table P1 uses these words to frame a set of panoptic questions that frame a socio-cultural version of the pedagogy of primary education. Increasingly this places the emphasis on quality and this demands interpretation; is less easily defined and consequently more open to debate, and thus multi- rather than singularly voiced, but it may well be more relevant to a fast-changing world, something which is interpretive and multi-faceted, more complex than the milestones and measurement of the technocrat's dream. The Cambridge Primary Review recognised something similar – commenting that:

> Improving education is not likely to be realized through a single approach. There is no single factor attributable for this – it is a combination. Successful primary pedagogy is likely to be that which actively reaches out based in mutually supportive, respectful, tolerant relationships. (Alexander, 2010b, p. 79)

Quality needs productive drivers, the energy of socio-cultural dynamics: capacity-building within the teaching profession; collective solutions focused in communities; strong emphasis on teaching, learning and assessment; and synergic systemic strategies (see Fullan, 2011).

Table P1: The pedagogy of an education system

Question	Pedagogical theme	Orientation, organisation, structures and support
Why is primary education as it is? What is its purpose? (Values and aims)	Purpose	• What is the purpose of primary education and what aims and values underpin this? • Is primary education aligned with the country's democratic principles?
What is the identity of primary education? (Pedagogy and curriculum)	Content	• What are people's perceptions of primary education? • What is the structure of the intended pedagogy / curriculum? • Is primary education equitable?
How effective is primary education? (Quality and provision)	Quality	• What constitutes quality in primary education, and what is the corresponding system of accountability? • How is the system organised to provide primary education? • How well are children doing?
Where do partners come together? (Contexts)	Partnership	• Where do partners within the system come together to meet children's needs? • What is the relationship between partners in this process?
Who has agency within the system? (Agency and voice)	Voices	• Whose voice is listened to and who has agency in creating the pedagogic process? • How does the system support the inclusion of children?
When does pedagogy take place? (Structure and timings)	Time	• When are the processes of primary education taking place?

If pedagogy is envisioned so that in Leach and Moon's (2008) words 'unlocking the creativity of our minds' is dependent on creating rich, vibrant and dynamic educational contexts, the answers to these questions will require particular principles and values: democracy, kindness, honesty, justice and equity among them so that well-being, learning and children's varied achievements combine through energy, creativity and determination. Hargreaves and Fink conclude that 'imposed, short-term, target driven standardisation is ultimately unsustainable' (2006, p. 14); we can see, socio-culturally, that emphasising sustainability within primary education has a vital resonance and may well emerge in combination with what Jean Anyon (2005) calls our 'urgent realities' and the search for meaning:

> Sustainable educational leadership and improvement preserves and develops deep learning for all, that spreads and lasts, in ways that do no harm to and indeed create positive benefit for others around us, now and in the future. (Hargreaves and Fink, 2006, p. 17)

Sustainability may be an age-old concept but it has never been a principle of more value.

Next: Part 2 is an extended and deeper exploration of a number of themes which have emerged as important in this account: learning and childhood; pedagogy; leadership; and collaboration and the self-improving system. They draw on a range of perspectives but the socio-cultural in particular.

Part **2**

Connecting Primary Education: Through the Looking Glass

> **This section** will take you on a journey into primary education viewed through a socio-cultural lens. It moves steadily wider from a beginning in children's learning and childhood, through the pedagogies they experience and on into leadership and then the wider landscape through collaboration and the self-improving system.
>
> **It explores:** *learning • thoughts on the changing context of childhood • approaches to pedagogy through a socio-cultural lens • the importance of leadership • reflections on collaboration and the self-improving system • an approach to 'systemness'*

Where should I go? That depends on where you want to end up.
— Lewis Carroll, *Through the Looking Glass*

The connections and complexities, the socio-cultural dynamics of primary education are what provide its verve. Those dynamics recognise a child's development is influenced by their environment (their family, community, school and wider socio-cultural patterns); it understands that pedagogy and curriculum shape them as do the leadership, networks, partnerships and structures of the education system. In this section, I borrow from Bronfenbrenner and Morris's (2006) 'bio-ecological systems theory' to explore this further. They believe that development occurs through progressively more complex exchanges between the child and others – the constructive potential of social relations. For illustration, these are often depicted as a series of concentric circles: they capture the connectedness of the cultural context that is primary education. The model builds in this way as the section progresses.

Chapter 4 begins by looking at learning and the significance of instruction before consideration of the child (the learner) in relationship with their world. Chapter 5 explores this through the pedagogies of primary education, while Chapter 6 looks to the leadership and governance that in turn create and enable successful primary schools. The wider system – the relationship between primary education, the so-called 'self-improving system' and the national context – is the focus of Chapter 7.

Figure 1: Connections and complexities in children's experiences

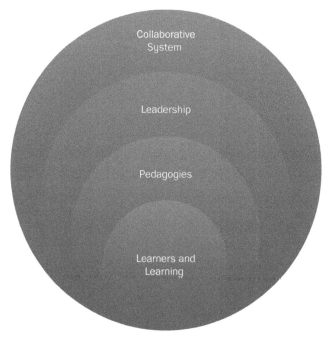

Next: The first chapter in this section explores learning and childhood in greater depth.

4 Learning in a changing world

This chapter is about children's learning, their lives and contemporary childhood.

It explores: *perspectives on learning • Piagetian and Vygotskian ideas • developments in cognitive neuroscience • children's agency and the making of meaning • thoughts on the contemporary context of children's lives • a family and community perspective • the global and digital context • the core needs of children*

I know who I WAS when I got up this morning, but I think I must have been changed several times since then.

– Lewis Carroll, *Through the Looking Glass*

Perspectives on learning

This chapter starts with learning before contextualising children's lives within the cultural context of our fast-changing world; an exploration of those 'urgent realities', to borrow from Anyon (2005), that surround today's educational context.

Learning is everywhere: witness the great civilisations, scientific discoveries, medicinal breakthroughs (Covid-19 vaccines and treatments included) and the inquisitive and creative endeavours of the very young child grappling with their world – Engel describes the sense of curiosity found in the 'hungry mind' (Engel, 2015). In Wells' (2009) studies of young children learning to talk and talking to learn, he coined the term 'the meaning makers' to describe their highly active processes of learning. For the young child, learning is purposeful; as Bradford and Wyse (2020) powerfully demonstrate in work co-constructing writing with 2- and 3-year-olds, curiosity abounds. In socio-cultural terms, the formation of goals, however small they may appear, is central to generating purpose.

Learning, however, is a complex and problematic concept, one that has been studied and approached from a range of perspectives (e.g. behaviourism, developmental psychology, cognitive psychology, social constructivism). Contemporaneously, genomics, neuroscience and epigenetics are all revealing the importance of our relationship with the world. Recently, controversial research by Plomin (Asbury and Plomin, 2014; Plomin, 2018), for example, has offered a radical revision to our thinking about ability, arguing that genetic inheritance has a significant effect on children's outcomes (see also Rimfeld et al., 2018). Yet he too points to our distinctiveness and argues in favour of active learning that is personalised to recognise genetic propensities and interests. In the process of pedagogy, then, it is not just 'what' children are learning, it is also 'how' they are learning and 'who' they are learning to be.

When learning, children imitate, attend, explore, observe, connect, problem-solve and hypothesise; they engage in dialogue and make meaning; they interpret, form concepts, develop moral and ethical frames; and engage in imaginative action with growing self-awareness. Children are often highly resourceful and adaptive in their learning capacities: they switch between systems so that rather than looking at learning as a single process, there are several processes, some of which will be active, others passive at particular points in time: learning is layered and there are different ways of 'being' in the same person. It is hard to define: more than a cognitive process, it is sensory with affective and physical dimensions and ever-evolving as the world changes. According to Perkins (1993), learning is 'person-plus' and threefold: (1) physical, through the artifacts we use in everyday life (mobile phones, tablet computers); (2) social, through the dialogue and interactions in which we engage; and (3) symbolic, in the language and thought systems we use to communicate. Kahneman's (2011) concept of 'thinking, fast and slow' recognises both conscious learning that is self-aware and unconscious learning without self-knowledge; humans also establish habits and routines that allow them to deal with much of what is experienced at an operational level, while a more complex set of capabilities (a generative capacity which often operates below the level of consciousness and appears instinctive and partly perceptual) offers capacities for problem-solving and creativity.

Learning is most powerful when children recognise the need to acquire new knowledge, anticipate they need particular skills or wish to participate in a learning community; here their energies multiply. Learning emerges when:

- disequilibrium exists and existing knowledge or previous understandings are challenged or come under threat, meaning they need revision or reconstruction;
- the learner becomes conscious of wanting to learn in a new area and actively pursues this, creating a concerted level of cognitive activity; and
- there is a dialogic process at play, of which schooling should be the epitome, which exposes the learner to new understandings developed through social constructions.

Our understandings of learning continue to grow rapidly as advances in science enhance our knowledge of the complexities of cognition. For example, the brain, we now know, has multiple ways of organising and we know that while human brains have many 'architectural' similarities, each has its own individualised topography (Dehaene, 2020). The functional modules of our brains connect and interconnect – and while cognitive neuroscience remains a developing field (there is caution because our understandings remain partial), applications to our pedagogic context are vital with advances likely to include:

- the knowledge which we have of the process of learning and how it occurs for individuals and through social contexts;
- our understanding of the growth of knowledge itself and how we access it; how this is constantly being revised, for example, through new theoretical advancements in science which provide challenges to deep-rooted assumptions;
- understanding of how pedagogy can encapsulate these advances and the implications for our organisation and presentation of learning.

Our full human capacity is more likely to emerge from awareness of these growing understandings and when education is designed inclusively from a range of perspectives informed by them.

From Piaget to Vygotsky and beyond

From the perspective of children's learning and development in primary educa-tion, two of the key influencers of the twentieth century were Swiss developmental psychologist Jean Piaget and the Russian psychologist Lev Vygotsky.

Piaget (1896–1980) broke significant new ground by making systematic studies of children's cognitive development and his ideas have been both extended and challenged. Piaget's work (1926, 1928) in cognitive psychology suggested, in summary, that children's thinking is qualitatively different from that of adults, developing through adaptive processes of assimilation (where new ideas are established alongside existing schemas) and accommodation (where new ideas shape and influence those schemas) and in discrete stages (which he labelled sensori-motor, pre-operational, concrete operational and formal operational). Focusing as they did on conceptual thought and processes of learning, these ideas informed pedagogy, featuring, for example, in the ratio-nale of Plowden (Central Advisory Council for Education, 1967). Piaget's stages have been criticised for proposing ceilings on learning: Hughes and Tizard (1984) and Donaldson (1978) argued convincingly that young children are not so egocentric or limited in their deductive reasoning as Piaget claimed. The idea of 'readiness', for example, sometimes expressed in the view that at the right developmental stage children will be able to learn things for themselves, arguably shifted expectations of learning to the child rather than the professional responsibility of the teacher (Glasersfeld, 1989). These criticisms notwithstanding, recognising Piaget's contribution to thinking about intermental activity involving the active negotiation of meaning, as well as the psychological structure of thought, have been influential (e.g. Silcock, 2013). Slowly, our understandings of learning have moved beyond seeing progress in defined stages: avoiding the Piagetian pitfall of underestimating children's capacity for higher-order learning, for logical reasoning, perhaps, or their capacity for abstraction (see Alexander, 1984). Optimistically, it seems that teaching some cognitive aspects associated with stages of development such as successive processing skills may well be beneficial (Das and Naglieri, 2001), while Egan's (1997) interpretation through modes of understanding and cognitive tools (somatic, mythic, romantic, philosophic and ironic) coalesce as they support the user's 'requisite variety', their nuanced repertoire of strategies (MacBeath et al., 2018).

Vygotsky (1896–1934) placed greater emphasis on the social context of learning; his treatise focuses, too, on educators facilitating learning that outpaces development. Vygotsky is seen as the creator of the cultural-historical paradigm of 'social constructivism', where knowledge and understanding emerge and are constructed in the interplay of experience and language. For Vygotksy (1962, 1978), language is central to the pedagogic process: shared meanings between adult and child, child and child, depend upon it – dialogue is the fundamental element. The 'zone of proximal development' (ZPD; some prefer potential to proximal) is what leads to the acceleration of learning as emergent understandings are developed within the mature forms of thinking of the surrounding culture (of scientific knowledge, for example): so that what a child can do with assistance today, she will be able to do by herself tomorrow (Vygotsky, 1978, p. 87). Howe and Mercer (2010) report classroom-based research that suggests the expression of difference is a key component in learning or, perhaps, in a process of argumentation: humans, from this perspective, need the perspective of others to be themselves. Dialogue enables sharing knowledge, challenging ideas and exploring possibilities with powerful cognitive resonance. Yet this insight, for some, also means the ZPD, the point through which children learn constructively, can impinge negatively on them and their identity – 'on a Vygotskian premise they become more rather than less vulnerable as they age and "internalise" cultural mores' (Silcock, 2013, p. 325); Silcock's point suggests pedagogy must engage with values of belonging, acceptance and respect.

A Vygotskian pedagogy is interventionist, guiding children through established bodies of knowledge while recognising that active, dialogic engagement in learning is essential (Wegerif, 2013). These understandings brought into pedagogy aim to expand children's perspectives on the world, recognising that there are many different ways to look. A Vygotskian interpretation, therefore, points us to a social rather than a mechanistic view of learning: the ZPD can be used as a space that opens children's minds, to construct meaning through dialogue and inquiry (see Wells, 1999; Littleton and Mercer, 2013). Teaching, in these terms, working through the space of the ZPD can be transformative: it brings new understandings, bridges between forms of knowledge and creates cognitive anchors that secure concepts and understanding.

Where Piagetian and Vygotskian pedagogical influences come together is through 'play'. Piaget recognised it as central to cognition: play enables young children to make meaning from their environment and a significant contribution to its educational recognition and value are part of his legacy; from a Vygotskian perspective, the value of play lies particularly within its social dimensions. Children develop understanding of the world and, in particular, the way it is governed through comprehending rule systems, morality and language (see Theobald et al., 2015). Play is central to socio-cultural theory: it tends to be voluntary and self-motivated and while seen by some as trivial or spontaneous, it can be intensely focused, structured and involving and is, unquestionably, a vital part of development (e.g. Lewis, 2021). In young children, play often promotes dialogic processes and can assist children in coming to terms with their environment, particularly social situations (e.g. Sahlberg and Doyle, 2020). It is also associated with the development of adaptivity and organising as the variables of social life are explored leading to children's self-realisation (Henricks, 2014). It is a way to manage stress and become resilient. And it is not just the province of our youngest children – electronic gaming is a feature of older children's (and many adults') worlds. Most children navigate, usually successfully, between real and virtual worlds where the dominant rules systems vary.

For primary education, learning is its heart. Piaget, Vygotsky and the very considerable work of many others (Froebel, Dewey, Bruner, for example), together have generated significant insights informing pedagogies to this very day. Socio-cultural theory recognises that learning and development is an active search for meaning. The experiences of young children are highly important, particularly in language learning in a form that is modelled by those with greater experience and skill: through what might be called the 'proximal processes' (those reciprocal interactions between person and their environment imbued with power, form and content) providing the 'engines of development' (Bronfenbrenner, 2005).

These insights are being extended and exceeded by the insights into and growth of understanding of the brain as the twenty-first century progresses.

Developments in cognitive neuroscience

Cognitive neuroscience is among the latest areas of human understanding to contribute to our pedagogic knowledge: it is an expanding, fast-moving, vital field and its insights about education continue to grow, emerging from different scientific perspectives through the multitude of innovative groups studying learning, cognition and the brain (Greenfield, 2016). Creating a map of the neural functions associated with higher cognition is on-going and increasingly fruitful area of study. Neuroscience confirms that the human brain is unquestionably complex, interconnected and specialised, and in the interrelationship between mind, spirit and body shows how significantly the brain is interconnected (what is termed cross-modal binding) and its functions integrated with our senses. One day we might be able to monitor the brain with scanners to see how well children are learning and identify specific errors, but for now we simply know that we are dealing with a highly complex organ – some have argued the most complex known to man, paradoxically also one that can be all too fragile.

If young children's brains have broadly the same neurological structure and learning algorithms (with some differences in strengths and learning speeds) as those of adults (Dehaene, 2020), then much of the difference between adult and children's thinking lies in experience (Goswami and Bryant, 2010). LeDoux states: 'the ability to be modified by experience is a characteristic of many brain systems, regardless of their specific function' (2003, p. 304). Neuroscientists are finding that young children's synaptic morphologies reflect this and adapt as the world they experience envelops them in new contexts. Le Doux explains: 'the particular way those neurons are connected is distinct, and that uniqueness, in short, is what makes us who we are' (2003, p. 303).

There is much still to be learned. If we are not careful, of course, the result could be simplistic understandings leading to what the OECD called 'neuromyths' (OECD, 2008), where assumptions have been extrapolated beyond their scientific justification (Ferrari, 2011). We can see possible contradictions in the debate exemplified in the view purported, on the one hand, that much brain development is irreversible by the age of 3; which contrasts with a further understanding that slow gradual changes in brain plasticity can occur in response to environmental conditions. There seem to be some over-generalisations too: for example, different hemispheres of the brain relate to particular types of learning, that plasticity in the brain is only available during particular periods of development and that the process of synaptogenesis must coincide with educational interventions if they are to be effective. Nevertheless, the idea that the brain is (somewhat) malleable through its neuroplasticity has powerful educational implications; a description perhaps preferable to those who might begin to see it as perfectible (see Doidge, 2007). This is educationally optimistic: children can develop skills associated with successful brain function, such as attention regulation or perspective-taking, through the careful design of pedagogies.

What follows are five areas of interest (with the humbling caveat of trying to extrapolate a series of key ideas from a hugely complex area) that are emerging with significant pedagogical implications.

First, our ability to learn involves a dynamic connecting process (e.g. Gibb and Kolb, 2018). The brain is incredibly complex, consisting of billions of neurons which connect together; a range of possibilities so enormous that we can create complex constructions and higher-order thought that are potentially unbounded. Our knowledge of the functions of the pre-frontal cortex suggest that it operates as a key working space where information is filtered and stored (short-term) and which accesses information from elsewhere in the brain so that connections enable strategies devised by the mind to be put to work. Experiences (teaching included) are central to these connections as they draw heavily from one another; in instructional terms there has been a resurgence of interest, for example, in 'memory' and 'retrieval' (Barenberg and Dutke, 2019); processes such as interleaving (Rohrer et al., 2015); and the power of narrative, metaphor, analogy and visual representation (see Bisra et al., 2018). *Implication*: Teaching needs strong frameworks of 'content knowledge' exemplified by detailed progressive conceptual frameworks and understandings of how to support the structuring, sequencing and connections in children's learning.

Second, our ability to learn effectively is regulated by our emotional states. Damasio (1999, 2010) argued in the 'somatic marker hypothesis' that the beginnings of emotion in the brain are experienced through the senses and the brain uses these to create the feelings that influence our decision-making. Much of our understanding develops at a deeper level that may not be entirely apparent to us: new imaging technologies are mapping the energy that is being produced in what might be described as the deeper reaches of the brain (Greenfield, 2016). For example, it is now generally recognised that understanding often emerges after the event. Much too is being learned about the cognitive significance of feelings and emotions (Um et al., 2012; Seli et al., 2016). Our capacity for empathy, our ability to feel, is important but will depend on seeing mind and body as an integrated system rather than separate components (Immordino-Yang and Damasio, 2007). Feelings, those things that are experienced sufficiently strongly to create emotion within us, become personal by connecting to our previous experience. It appears that emotional attachment matters hugely in our perception and orientation to the world and capacity to learn (Tyng et al., 2017): our 'emotional thoughts' (Immordino-Yang, 2016) are the rudder that steers our reasoning and decision-making. *Implication*: Teaching should connect the socio-emotional dimensions of learning: creating climates that are warm, supportive, respectful and experiential (Immordino-Yang, 2015) and that stimulate well-being.

Third, learning involves multiple integrating systems and multi-sensory processes. Neurosciences connect our nervous system and molecular biology indicating that they are fundamentally interrelated through complex processes involving hormones and neurotransmitters. This processing depends on our level of sensory awareness and attention, both conscious and sub-conscious, as our body experiences both internal and external stimuli. The functioning of our senses is so integrated that our body is a critical aspect of our psychology. There are complex feedback loops which process information flow from the nervous systems, which monitor and integrate and are where the connection between psychological, physiological and cognitive functioning is made. The key pedagogical understanding is about the larger dynamic of educating across a rich terrain of interconnecting experiences and should include a strong attention to sensory combinations. *Implication*: Teaching engages a repertoire of instructional strategies selected specifically and precisely for what is being learned, engaging all of the sensory capabilities and mediums (e.g. drama, art, dance, film).

Fourth, experience has a 'sculpting effect' (neurogenesis) on the brain through the learning process. The concept of neuro-plasticity (Geake, 2009) recognises that through learning the brain grows, changes and reshapes and though it is most flexible in the earliest years, research suggests that we continue to make new synaptic connections into old age. Goswami and Bryant (2010) argue that children do not (automatically) have the capacity for self-regulation and cognitively complex tasks; that comes to them as they experience life often through imitation (and the exploratory and social value of play), learning particularly through the power of language. Young children learn language differently from older learners but if experienced in a rich form, their synapses will connect, allowing them more readily to develop particular capacities: a richness of linguistic environment gains importance. *Implication*: Rich linguistic experiences underpin learning while the sculpting effect also suggests the need for teachers to actively address misconceptions: it demands high-quality dialogue and diagnostic feedback to children.

Fifth, adaptive learning is enhanced by the development of executive functions. Executive functions are a combination of skills (working memory, self-regulation and flexible thinking) that combine to create a management system in the brain that is critical to decision-making. 'Executive functions, in short, make practical thinking and reasoning possible' (LeDoux, 2003, p. 178). The importance of actively teaching learning dispositions has been highlighted by researchers; as LeDoux comments, this involves juggling mental items, for example, 'comparing, contrasting, judging, predicting' (2003, pp. 177–178). Executive functions include being able to screen information for that which is most useful, to plan ahead, to retain key information in working memory. Integrating teaching logical memory with category perception and self-regulation might be given greater attention as ways of building cognition. Executive function is critical to subject- or domain-specific learning. Some suggest that its development with young children could be vital for future educational success (Blair and Diamond, 2008). Both the Teaching and Learning Toolkit (Higgins et al., 2015) and Hattie's (2009) meta-analyses recognise meta-cognitive control and awareness as factors in effective learning. Described differently, the Cambridge Primary Review argued that three challenges of pedagogy are to provide: 'meta-cognition' – the ability to think about one's own knowledge and ideas; 'theory of mind' – the awareness that other people have minds which may differ in thoughts and feelings from one's own; 'self-regulation' – the ability to monitor and control thought and action, for example, by setting and abiding by rules in play (Alexander, 2010b, p. 98). *Implication*: Teaching needs a repertoire of methods or 'didactics' (activating through explaining and questioning, for example) to extend children's meta-cognition (see Quigley et al., 2018).

Cognition operates on multiple layers, suggestive of pedagogy based in generating meaning in context: perhaps this is why Shulman (1986, 1987) places such significant emphasis on a teacher's 'pedagogical content knowledge', and Gagné's (1985) classic text emphasises both the condition of the learner and sequence of instruction. Rather than downplaying the demand for automatic operations, the ability to read fluently and recall mathematical facts is emphasised, for example. Indeed, it seems to be a symbiotic process: the more something has been committed to an automatic level, then the less 'load' there is on the executive function. Solving a mathematical problem requiring recall of number facts is easier if these have been committed to memory. These skills benefit from repeated practice but where motivation is high and the process enjoyable, needing both time and skilled instruction (see Mccrea, 2017). New understandings of the implications for teaching and learning are reaching deeper, exploring children's cognitive capacities: Sweller's (1988, 2011) 'cognitive load theory' refers to the type and volume of information that can be processed at any one time. Approaches such as 'interleaving' and 'spacing' (Weinstein et al., 2018a, 2018b) and the Rosenshine principles of instruction, for example (Rosenshine, 2012), also provide powerful heuristics.

This brief journey through Piaget, Vygotsky and some aspects of cognitive neuroscience observes learning as a complex and holistic process: in the socio-cultural sense, learning involves the formation of identity through engagement in relationships where meaning is actively constructed from experience.

Table 4.1: Observations on learning

- Dialogue is at the heart of learning
- Learning is actively constructed, adapted and elaborated as new understandings shift our conceptual bases, advance our skills and newer representations replace others that become outmoded
- Learning is the active process by which the individual adapts to or transforms the context in which they find themselves
- Learning can be thought of as an integrated system with 'synaptic networks devoted to cognitive, emotional, and motivational functions' (LeDoux, 2003, p. 258)
- Learning is situated and shaped by context, including family, culture, community, school and the wider world

---

We should be cognisant of the changing neural patterns as the species evolves. Perhaps, though, the most optimistic educational insight is that research across a range of domains is converging in recognising that ability is not fixed and is expandable (Geake, 2009; Zull, 2011) – this is too compelling for education to ignore.

An invitation to agency: the mediated action of making meaning

Pedagogy does not just optimise cognitive development but recognises what it means to be human in its widest sense, recognising that children have different predispositions and personalities (Frazzetto, 2013): its variety should engage multiple means of expression (to demonstrate what they know), engagement (to mirror interest, challenge and motivate) and representation (Meyer et al., 2013). Where developmental psychology, social constructivism and neuroscience converge is to reveal learning as a complex process responsive to a range of pedagogical qualities we know to be beneficial (e.g. experience, dialogue, enculturation). Two illustrative concepts help here: mastery and appropriation. The former involves developing a deep, long-term and secure understanding; the latter embraces making something one's own and creating personal meaning from it (Blanton et al., 2000). Children's agency (Kuczynski and de Mol, 2015) moves to the centre.

In Tough's (2012) accounts, qualities such as 'grit', perseverance, curiosity and optimism – what he describes as 'character' or 'inner resources' – are critical to success. Dweck (2000) pointed to the importance of the locus of control in a child's psychology, their 'growth mindset': if children see behaviour and learning as something they can control from within themselves, they are likely to be motivated (see also Deci and Ryan, 2008); conversely, if they feel it is not, then they may be discouraged by the absence of power to influence their lives. Significant energy will be expended when children find a connection to key goals and when they believe they can succeed (see Muijs et al., 2014). The classroom climate matters because when thinking genuinely occurs, it is an uncertain process. For the teacher, this means the intersubjectivity of 'handover' – passing the responsibility for learning to the child while guiding their journey: dialogue becomes central in converting learning processes into knowledge as learning moves from the social to the individual.

However, curiosity and desire do not necessarily appear universally – they can be selective rather than general and as children's personalities, interests and dispositions vary, so pedagogy must connect, recognising and removing barriers. Within the pedagogic process children must feel they have the power to achieve, to become self-actualising and for some children transcend their limiting beliefs about being involved in education successfully. In this way, we also explain the power of the expectation that adults have of children. For children, an investment in learning, by return, should provide for the development of one's self and one's well-being as a learner. Purkey (1978) has described a pedagogical approach that he calls 'invitational': an approach which actively seeks engagement with Matthew Arnold's (1869) 'best that has been thought and said' and provides consideration and respect for the learner.

Those who believe their intelligence is fixed tend to experience greater disappointment when they fail at a task and subsequently avoid taking risks for fear of the outcome, whereas those who have a developmental view tend to be more optimistic and accept challenges (Dweck, 2002). Dweck (2006) also suggested that a child's self-image can be altered by feedback and importantly their beliefs about their own intelligence are changeable. In the Learning without Limits model at the Wroxham Teaching School, there was a planned choice for learners giving them decision-making power over their learning. This freedom resulted in them increasingly pushing themselves forward and when in control in this way they were able to demonstrate their existing knowledge and understanding more effectively (Swann et al., 2012).

The more children learn, become autonomous, independent and self-regulating, the more they learn to control and manage their environment and see larger, meaningful patterns, learn to solve problems accurately and grow their working memory, allowing things to connect in the mind. Learning happens through the vehicle of children's agency: to coin a phrase, an education system cannot exceed the desire and capabilities of its children.

Reflection point

How do the theories presented here match with your lived experiences of children's learning? Is there one aspect that you could develop further in your professional context?

Connecting contexts

For children, their learning and development are always relational, always in context and the extent of their agency varies. This chapter continues now by drilling deeper, recognising the many changes invading many aspects of children's lives; sometimes these rhythms and patterns are ephemeral and unstable where a number of aspects of experience, such as elements of social media, tend towards the instantaneous and disposable.

Among the many issues surrounding primary-aged children, there are four areas for deeper consideration:

1 The *contemporary context* of society including debates around community, inequality and creating an education system which connects with children.

2 A *family and community* perspective which recognises England's diversity and the impact for some of poverty and disadvantage.

3 The *global and digital context* with its powerful means of communication yet also the associated loss of identity and a concern that children could be in touch with everybody but themselves.

4 As Rogoff et al. (2003) have argued, the idea that schools could possibly be cut off from the practice and social contexts of the changing world, from *the needs of children*, if they were caught in an unchanging educational ideology with atavistic pedagogies.

Today's learners: contemporary context, changing world

Arguably childhood has been the subject of as many longstanding debates as primary education itself (Jones, 2015) with opinion oscillating and often situation-specific, while many long-established values and beliefs still hold and changing legal protections apply.

Today's learners are growing up in a changing world, a world that cannot be explained easily and where stereotyped but seemingly contradictory images of children themselves emerge: one might bemoan their selfish attitudes; another portray them as victims of a society some see as toxic (Palmer, 2006); another will praise their concerns for the environment or charitable activity, while another will point out they are the unprecedented beneficiaries of wealth and health care beyond anything imaginable by our forebears. Perhaps this is a result of the power of scientific advance and media and communications technologies that extensively permeate our lives, the latter creating a reflection of our multiple realities.

While their life expectancy is increasing, today's learners are also considered by some to be at greater risk: they are no longer as mobile (in some respects the urban landscape is particularly changed) and they find their immediate environment less accessible, despite the fact that they are more likely to have travelled abroad than any other previous generation. Children's access to information and media is unprecedented. New language to describe it is constantly emerging: 'power browsing' and 'information foraging', for example. Meanwhile, the media readily presents children with images of war, conflict, terror, famine and environmental disaster from around the world: they flood consciousness, sometimes overwhelmingly – we are drowning in advertising, exposed to violence, yet somehow immune and distant from it all. When protestors entered the White House in 2021, children were watching. These images contrast with other attracting images of wealth, fashion and celebrity. When Covid-19 emerged, it created uncertainty, concern and, for some children and families, a greater sense of disenfranchisement. Most schools were temporarily closed and a lack of access to technology provided a significant barrier to learning for some.

Among the most concerning effects for educators emerge when children feel powerless, insecure, socially isolated and marginalised (Castells, 2000; Elliott, 2000). Castells wrote, tellingly:

> In a world of global flows of wealth, power and images, the search for identity, collective or individual, ascribed or constructed, becomes the fundamental source of social meaning. (Castells, 2000, p. 3)

Thus, children's well-being (Seligman, 2011) and mental health present powerfully as modern-day issues for primary education. Of particular concern are the effects of stress and adverse childhood experiences (Lacey and Minnis, 2020), which seem to weaken the architecture of their developing cognitive structures. Wilmott (2002) argued that the loss of attention to the spiritual, moral and emotional needs of children had been the most significant effect of the changes of the past 40 years.

Today's learners: family and community perspectives

For today's learners, their family, peer group and community significantly impact on their engagement and development within school. As Gorard (2018, p. 205) noted: 'educational participation and outcomes are strongly linked to era, place, social class, sex and family background' (see also Desforges and Abouchaar, 2003; Wilkinson and Pickett, 2009, 2019; Gorard et al., 2012).

Family life for today's learners is changing; the structure is more varied than at the end of the Second World War, for example, evidenced by lower (though not consistently so) birth rates and greater instability and variability of relationships. Compared with half a century ago, there has been a rise in single-parent families, step-families, atypical working hours, longer working hours and, more often, both parents working (see Muschamp et al., 2010). These changes in working patterns and child-care arrangements have created qualitative differences in processes of parenting (Alexander, 2010b, ch. 4). And child poverty is on the increase: a rise of 500,000 children in 5 years, most notably among working families, according to the JRF Analysis Unit (2018). According to Rice (2006), 1.4 million children in England live in poor housing! The gap between rich and poor is increasing: the level of distress and anxiety experienced by some children is, at least in part, a product of socio-economic policy-making.

In an analysis for the Cambridge Primary Review, Muschamp et al. (2010) illustrated clearly how living in poverty impacts negatively on a child's health, their well-being and therefore their ability to connect successfully with the educational process. Evidence suggests that when disadvantaged children start school, they are often behind their better-off peers (Minogue and Moore, 2013): they may never catch up. For those experiencing poverty there is a correlation with low educational performance that tends to be located in challenging urban areas and more intensively in some than in others (Cassen and Kingdon, 2007). Moreover, there seems to be evidence that the concentration of disadvantage in particular schools is growing (e.g. Harris et al., 2006). According to Lupton (2006), this revolves around poverty (including malnourishment), children with lower starting points, a wider range of learning needs and greater emotional need resulting in more reluctance to participate. In these contexts, we should be conscious of a tendency to the language of deficit. Expectations of children from such backgrounds are of significant importance (Allard and Santoro, 2006; Gazeley and Dunne, 2007). Reay's (2006) work showed how in an inner city multicultural primary school there emerged a clear hierarchy of children based on perceptions of achievement, noting that children had to adapt their identities to meet their school context. In this context, our attitudes to learners matter (Goodman and Gregg, 2010): in denying, disrespecting or stigmatising particular backgrounds or lifestyles we can unwittingly create further educational disadvantage.

Bourdieu (1974) theorised that children develop the skills and habits of the cultural group from which they originate but it is the dominant group members who are most valued in education, and that it is the middle classes who are best equipped to exploit the educational market (Bourdieu and Passeron, 1990). It is not just a matter of economics. Literature and the written word dominate primary schools and for today's learners language experience and vocabulary acquisition can be important determinants of their capacity to succeed (see Maguire et al., 2006). Exposure to books, for example, varies considerably and correlates with literacy, numeracy and ICT skills (Sikora et al., 2018). Studies show striking variations in the acquisition of vocabulary in different contexts (Gilkerson et al., 2018). Some children, depending on their circumstances, may have less access to 'school knowledge' and this can be exacerbated by particular orientations to the curriculum: if, as some have suggested, aspiration for the types of learning associated with school are lower for some children than others, then the importance of connecting and engaging them attains huge significance. Pedagogy must have a key role in creating and sustaining a sense of meaning and belonging, rich in language and experience.

England's cultural make-up has changed too: today's learners are part of a society where there has been a growth in the number of children from ethnic minorities, so that today about one-fifth of primary-aged children are Black, Asian or minority ethnic (BAME), with a resultant increase in bilingualism and multilingualism. Many children now move across and between languages as part of their daily lives, often benefiting from these affordances in conceptual understanding (Cummins, 2000), though this can sometimes be hidden from school (see Ainscow et al., 2010). The tendency towards concentration of ethnic groups in particular areas reminds us that diversity is not evenly distributed: our communities can be segregated and across them values, beliefs and experiences differ so that understanding by children of one another's worlds represents both opportunity and challenge. A child's background can affect how they are perceived in school. Weltman (2008) warns that when our conceptions of race, class and gender are 'frozen', it can be at the expense of understanding patterns of social change. Kerr et al. (2014) point out that some areas in which today's learners live do better than others – describing this in terms of 'neighbourhood dynamics'. We should be concerned to actively address the achievement of identified groups of children and geographical areas.

In many senses we might reach the seemingly contradictory conclusion that the quality of children's lives is both improving and declining at the same time. Our educational priorities must include the significantly vulnerable, for whom education has never been more important but the issues are wider than education: families face increasing pressures from, for example, rising food and utility costs. Power is revealed through dialogue: connecting to a child's environment outside of school is critical to their ability to successfully participate in the educative process. Today's learners will test their own worlds in the context of what is expected within classrooms; as Bakhtin argued, much is revealed by who is speaking, in what context and for what purpose.

Today's learners: global and digital perspectives

Today's learners live in a 'globalised' world, the effects of which, especially forms of social media, are challenging our existing norms, creating uncertainty, and accepted forms of knowledge and communication are being transformed (Tapscott and Williams, 2007). The extent of consumption and production of knowledge in multitudinous forms is remarkable: given this ubiquity, it is perhaps as Lyotard (1979) argues, that 'knowledge ceases to be an end in itself'?

The digital revolution is powerful in accounts of the 'globalisation' process (Castells, 2000) and in the lives of today's learners: social media, the internet, smart phones, wireless communications grow endlessly – ever accelerating, never abating. Web 1.0 speeded up personal interactivity (email and internet), Web 2.0 enabled unbounded global social interaction, while Web 3.0 proposes a new dynamic where so-called intelligent machines pass information between them, joining up what some have called the 'semantic web'. And, potentially, apocalyptically, technological development may only be in its infancy! Hawking raised concerns about a time when digital intelligence surpasses that of humans: the alarming concept of singularity (Web 4.0?); alternatively, emergence of nanotechnologies has led to the concept of trans-humanism and the idea that silicon can help to create the 'improved' human being.

Already our interconnectedness is creating new challenges. The mass media is now being replaced (or, at least, regenerated) by new sources (the so-called blogosphere) that provide immediate, highly relevant content, while many children generate and produce their own content; social media also creates images of 'perfect lives'. 'Fake news' is symbolic of the overwhelming proliferation of information and communications in our times: criticality (understanding the provenance of information, for example) becomes important pedagogically. The search for 'truth' was powerfully illustrated by Alan November (2001) through the example of a boy researching the holocaust and the implications of the materials that, during surfing, he first stumbles across and then is influenced by. This powerful anecdote in which the adult interlocutor provides teaching both about the curriculum content and about specific focused knowledge demonstrates the dangers for children but also the power of pedagogy. Questions of knowledge have been central to debates about the curriculum recently and, pointedly prescient, as the Black Lives Matter movement gained momentum. The question of what knowledge is taught also needs to consider 'whose' knowledge we are teaching and how it connects to and empowers learners. Abundance of information will not guarantee depth of understanding: making meaning and identity emerge in both the cognitive and affective domains.

Humans are increasingly technology dependent (person-plus) and capable and this can be both convenient and enabling (note the adaptation to online learning demanded by Covid-19). Already technology use, some argue, is rewiring our minds, making our attention spans shorter, reducing depth of reflection (Carr, 2010). For children immersed in such environments, some are now concerned that their experience is intense but lacks 'feeling' as raw sensation takes over, while Stone (2009) describes a state of 'continuous partial attention'. Here we lose our traditional identities and it seems that children's immediate realities are changing; the psychological challenge, of experience being faster and faster, will require important pedagogical consideration, and should provoke deeper questions going beyond merely introducing more technology into schools. Search engines change our behaviours by allowing us to trigger thoughts and retrieve information very quickly, what Collins calls 'conversational thinking' (Thompson, 2013), and along with social media can enrich our cognitive possibilities. As a result of the ubiquity of information and the prevalence and availability of learning, some argue that today's learners are more intelligent than their parents and grandparents (see Flynn, 2007) and while this is a point of argument, perhaps it should be recognised that today's learner has never known the analogue world. The irreversible growth of a global network of communications has marked effects on how today's learners engage with the world.

Significantly, today's learners will access a huge amount of the digital revolution from outside of school: the move to online learning environments as a result of Covid-19 suggests greater future emphasis on 'where' and 'how' learning is happening. As far back as 2002, Downes identified that learning in the home is often powerful but qualitatively different from that which takes place in school, arguing:

> The blurring of the processes of play, practice and performance ... contrasts strongly the dominant pedagogical approaches in schools that continue to separate learning and doing, or practice and performance. (Downes, 2002, p. 48)

The pedagogic relationship between education and technology will need constant revision. 'Remote learning' during the coronavirus epidemic was illustrative: access to technological resources was limited for some pupils, while the absence of 'proximal' pedagogical processes appeared as a cause in studies finding educational gaps were widening (see Worth and Faulkner-Ellis, 2021).

Kirschner's (2015) suggestion is that it may not be outdated teaching methods that challenge us as much as our changing cognitive functions. Pedagogically it will demand attention to how we keep up with things when the sheer weight of information is beyond comprehension and consideration and when, for example, technology raises 'meta-pedagogical' questions: for example, how to enable physiological relaxation when overloaded psychologically by the environment.

Finally, another perspective on global communications is that it is generating a world consciousness that sees our challenges interconnecting and that collective action can resolve them (see Risvi and Lingard, 2006). Today's learners will need to understand what it means to be a so-called global citizen, which will depend as much upon one's interpretation of the narrative and the pedagogies brought to education amidst burgeoning technological development: pedagogy must consider 'how' as much as 'what' (Higgins et al., 2015).

The needs of children

For educators, Kellmer-Pringle's account of the needs of children remains resonant 40 years later. She proposed four needs: (1) the need for love and security upon which the balanced development of personality and identity depends; (2) the need for new experiences that are the basis for growth and understanding; (3) the need for praise and recognition that create social and emotional resilience when sustained over time; and (4) the need for responsibility met by growing independence and realised fully in a concern for others (Kellmer-Pringle, 1980). Since children make meaning from this world as they experience and live it, primary education is a vital existential experience and means by which they can make sense of it: the challenges associated with their childhood have qualitative differences from those experienced by their elders. They are certainly different from Victorian times: when the elementary system was envisioned, the immediate challenges were 'infectious disease [notwithstanding Covid-19], malnutrition and inadequate hygiene' transformed today to 'obesity, diet, lack of exercise', in part the products of 'affluence and choice' (Alexander, 2010b, p. 93). Buckingham (2005) coined the phrase 'prosperous majority', which reflects the benefits an advanced industrial nation has provided for many children through successful schools, increasing disposal incomes and improved environmental conditions but it reveals, by implication, a minority blighted by poverty and its concomitant difficulties, better understood through exploring the combinations of overlapping systems (thereby the concept of intersectionality; after Crenshaw, 1991).

A global viewpoint sees the world as interconnected and interdependent, increasingly integrated as people 'reach' around the world through developments in transport, communications and data processing (Chawla-Duggan and Lowe, 2010). There is much that will exercise our children: fundamentalist ideologies; consumption associated with continued economic prosperity; ecological and environmental crises; food and water shortages; production of energy and the continued effects of climate change. Some argue that the patterns of development are not qualitatively different but rather the rapid accelerations of existing emergent patterns. Indeed, ancient ideas resurface: concerns about the loss of democracy, for example, reignite Ancient Greek concepts of decision-making or the civic ideals of the humanists; when concerns emerge about our environment then we recall attitudes to Earth from the Sioux Indians, for example. Today's learner grows up in a fast-changing, fragile environment; as many children have great concern for our humanitarian and environmental challenges, increasingly pedagogies must help them make sense of this, and an emphasis on sustainability emerges again. Collectively this is a reminder that pedagogy is a situated and connected social and cultural educational process.

Reflection point

What is your experience of children's changing lives? Are there stereotypes of children that need disentangling? How best do we support children to be the strongest versions of themselves?

Conclusions

Collectively, culture, families, communities and schools surround children with messages, values and power relationships (Feldman Barrett, 2017) exerting powerful psychological effects. Primary education is positioned in relationship to the myriad complexities of a child's life from where their development emerges through a continuous process of meaning-making. Pedagogies that encourage children's agency, well-being and deep learning and reflect Anyon's (2005) 'urgent realities' recognise local contexts and are responsive to the wider aspects of children's lives.

The effects of globalisation are pushing boundaries – seemingly moving the emphasis from 'knowledge' to 'knowing', emphasising the need to explore new approaches and challenge our current epistemological assumptions.

It brings us to pedagogy. Increasingly, studies of 'Learning to Learn' (meta-learning; e.g. James et al., 2007) have influenced pedagogy; for Claxton (2002) this is 'building learning power' and the development of valuable 'dispositions' (Claxton et al., 2016) that help to create flexible, resourceful and adaptable learners: the capacity to learn in this way enables children to be able to adapt to new contexts and challenges. Coupled with essential knowledge, this provides an essential vehicle to make sense of our world.

Many debates about primary education assert the power of the human spirit: notably, the Cambridge Primary Review reported (Alexander, 2010b, p. 56) that where primary schools addressed children's concerns through gathering relevant curriculum experience and approaching specific issues, they were able to generate a more positive outlook. While Cheang and Goh (2018), in a Singaporean context, suggest that children have greater agency when connected to social resources rather than acting in isolation: these connections contribute to well-being and resilience.

The socio-cultural dynamics of primary education in the twenty-first century are rooted in a fast-changing and rapidly developing world (Castells, 1997, 1998, 2000; Singh, 2002, 2013): knowledge is being restructured and society is increasingly diverse in form. The effects of globalisation on primary education are only just beginning to be felt: technologies permeate the teaching and learning process, but they have not yet radically restructured the relationship between the teacher, learner and knowledge. As they do, a culturally sensitive pedagogy will need to harness children's sense of agency in contexts that are relevant and real for them, developing their contributions to sustainable forms of society.

Delving deeper

There is a rich literature surrounding children's learning from a range of perspectives. Dehaene's recent book *How We Learn: Why Brains Learn Better than Any Machine ... for Now* (2020) is an engaging introduction to the field.

Next: This exploration of learning and childhood has recognised the complexities and challenges in creating an 'education' in the twenty-first century. It leads now to a focus on pedagogy exploring it from a socio-cultural perspective.

5 Socio-cultural dynamics of pedagogy

This chapter is about pedagogy viewed through a socio-cultural lens.

It explores: *the pedagogical messages of different classrooms* • *a socio-cultural approach to pedagogy* • *the importance of children's agency (self, connections and the world)* • *the pedagogic mix (approaches and repertoire)* • *five domains of pedagogy*

It's a great huge game of chess that's being played – all over the world – if this is the world at all, you know.
— Lewis Carroll, *Through the Looking Glass*

Pedagogical messages: shifting sands

Education is the most powerful weapon you can use to change the world.
— Nelson Mandela

Right here, right now is where we draw the line. The world is waking up. And change is coming whether you like it or not.
— Greta Thunberg

The pedagogical ecosystem is beginning to reveal its interrelationships: diverse and nuanced contexts; the power and complexity of learning; children's agency; and an instructional repertoire that should be precise, adaptable and fit for purpose. Equally powerful, embedded deep within pedagogy, are values – interplaying, revealing themselves in policy and practice, tangible, for example, in how the government portrays teachers; the content chosen for the curriculum; how inspection activity is conducted; how teachers think children learn and why they choose particular methods; and in children's attitudes to the classroom. Do we orient the classroom primarily for learning, organisational or behavioural purposes, for example?

Pedagogy is the mediated action of education, it carries messages and what form it takes has long-lasting implications; it is innately caught in its socio-cultural context. As Jerome Bruner put it: 'How one conceives of education, we have finally come to recognize, is a function of how one conceives of the culture and its aims, professed and otherwise' (Bruner, 1996, pp. ix–x). Those choices will have a distinctive influence on how education is perceived by children. Consider the difference between lessons where teachers simply 'deliver' knowledge compared with those where the process is actively designed and co-constructed with children. Importantly, differing contexts (individual primary schools and their classrooms) do matter: they are nuanced, when children and teachers in action create meaning, they are where values interplay in their most visceral form. Many of our mental models of effective and ineffective teaching tend to endure, so how the education system views its children, seeks to include them, listens to their voices, addresses their needs and orients teaching eventually will leave powerful educational, social and cultural residues.

Pedagogical values reflect beliefs about education (ethical, moral, professional) acting as guides for choices and decisions: the pedagogies we choose are infused with them. Values and beliefs become engrained in educational orthodoxies: there is ebb and flow, minor shifts, and sometimes those of significant proportions; some, albeit in generalised form, can be recognised as a 'type'. To illustrate, here are five brief caricatures drawn specifically to illustrate some contrasting possibilities.

1 Beginning in a late nineteenth-century elementary classroom, the power rested indubitably with the teacher, the classroom was tightly controlled and a strong divide existed between teacher and child: what was to be learned, the 'basics' of an education, was not negotiable and its teaching followed a narrow, prescribed instrumental formula, probably considered now as unpalatably controlling and lacking a compelling theory of how children learn.

2 Advances in developmental psychology and increasing breadth in the curriculum lead to a classroom, perhaps, *c.* the 1978 primary survey (DES, 1978). It offers a wider repertoire of subjects but children, ironically, while placed in groups, often work individually through tasks 'matched' to their ability and with limited extended classroom interaction. In this classroom, children spend significant amounts of time on written activities.

3 In contrast, a visit to a progressive 'child-centred' classroom shows the children in control, making choices reflecting their interests with high levels of self-direction. The teacher acts as facilitator; however, much attention is given by teachers to caring for children with less emphasis on accelerating academic progress. Simon (1981) used the descriptor 'exaggerated individualism' and the level of self-direction might now be considered unrealistic.

4 Compare again, this time with the expectations of primary classrooms that emphasise 'achievement' and 'standards' with their culture of 'high

expectations'; differentiation tailors the curriculum to need and teaching allows individual expression from the child. The focus on the individual means recognition emerges predominantly from comparison with external outcomes. Data, because performance matters so much, informs what is taught and how learning is measured.

5 A fifth version of the primary classroom offers a much greater sense of community. There is a collaborative culture and a strong sense of agency: children are active in their learning. Adaptable and skilful they switch readily between different modes of learning, as does the teacher. Children's achievements retain their importance but are balanced by their contribution to the communities of which they are part.

Each example, albeit stereotypical and simplified, carries its own values and beliefs and theories of how children learn: a child may experience elements of a variety of approaches during their school experiences and each has their purpose (phonics teaching will have different features to a dance lesson, for example). Pedagogy is never simply a list of approved teaching methods simplistically described and is much more likely to be successful when it is inclusive of a range of approaches, a multiplicity of voices, when carefully crafted and tailored into an approach which reflects the learning needs of children, communities and localities.

If primary education faces imperatives of equity, supporting children's well-being and agency, as well as sustainability in a fast-changing world – how do we translate these challenges into pedagogy? The fifth description above reflects responsiveness to many of these challenges; while not losing the importance of children's achievements, it depends upon having learned many of the lessons about effectively achieving high standards but securing them within a powerful sense of social responsibility where teacher and children now share agency, building towards a better world. Primary education here is justifiable in its own right. Great pedagogy in these terms is combinatory: a strong emphasis on knowledge and learning dispositions, a values-base where tolerance, community, collaboration and citizenship are to the fore, one where active, engaged learners meet creative and skilled teachers who are sensitive and adaptive to their context.

Characteristics of a socio-cultural educational approach

In a study exploring the relations between school and other learning, Resnick (1987) argued three important points: first, most effective learning has features characteristic of out-of-school contexts, involving shared intellectual activities where learners gain meaning when jointly completing tasks; second is an element of apprenticeship in activities, allowing skills to be built gradually; and third, most activities recognise bodies of subject knowledge and develop associated specific skills. New pedagogies are reflecting these understandings, including the Project for Enhancing Effective Learning at Monash University (Mitchell et al., 2016). There are also the productive pedagogies of Hayes et al. (2006), whose intention is to produce children capable of helping one another respectfully, understanding others' perspectives attentively, and intelligently adapting their position in the light of experience.

Wells and Claxton (2002) explored the premise for a socio-culturally based pedagogy from which I focus on five principles here (see Table 5.1).

Table 5.1: Five characteristics of a socio-cultural pedagogy

Characteristic	Description	Evidenced in:
'A mind to learn'	Active, curious, creative; meaning-making; mind, spirit and body; meta-cognition concepts and ideas; well-being	Core skills and higher-order thinking; challenging learning
Enculturation and transformation	Complex and significant ideas; apprenticeship; structure of knowledge; creating products – 'the improvable object'	Depth of understanding, carefully selected subject knowledge (connected and deeper)
A communicative core	Dialogue at the heart; socially purposeful; collaborative; highly literate environment; precise feedback	Variety and volume of talk; diagnostic assessment and feedback; rich literary environment
Cultural relativism	Non-judgemental, diverse and responsive; connecting and contextualized, building on what children know; sense of belonging	Mutual respect and widely inclusive; contributions welcomed and valued; authentic, real-world context and audiences
Communities of practice	Guided participation; a focus on community; civic engagement; bridging to the home; enabling and empowering	Collaborative and connected; inclusive and meaningful; social support for children's achievements

First, there is an argument that education is centrally about fostering '*a mind to learn*', explicated in the relationship between learning and social practice. Wells and Claxton argue that the way that a mind develops is not, fundamentally, through what they call 'didactic instruction and intensive training' but rather through

> ... a more subtle kind of learning in which youngsters pick up useful (or unuseful) habits of mind from those around them and receive guidance in reconstructing these resources in order to meet their own and society's current and future concerns. (Wells and Claxton, 2002, p. 2)

Second, they describe a 'process of simultaneous *enculturation and transformation*'. In a socio-cultural approach, culture plays a significant role in shaping the development of mind; children learn through critically engaging with the values, beliefs, ideas and bodies of knowledge that have built up over generations, perhaps evocative of Matthew Arnold's (1869) famous statement, 'the best that has been thought and said in the world', thus generating 'a stream of fresh and free thought'. Rogoff's (1990) perspective on pedagogy describes an *apprenticeship* where children are supported in learning the identified tools of the culture, a key part of which is accelerating their induction into powerful knowledge (Young et al., 2014). Stetsenko and Arievitch (2002) believe that it is by using cultural tools around them that learners find out about their purposes in society. The term 'apprenticeship' fits well with ideas of agency, implying involvement, responsibility and goals.

Knowledge in socio-cultural terms does not just exist in people's minds, rather it is something that can be created and improved, an active and social process where the intention should be to produce something of value (Scardamalia and Bereiter, 2006); transformation emerges from the idea of an 'improvable object' (Wells, 2002). The original products of children's studies – an object/artifact, a presentation, an art-work – create opportunities to engage with audience, acting as a celebration and endorsement of children's creativity. Rogoff's (1995) term is 'participatory appropriation'. Wells and Claxton believe that alongside children absorbing their cultural heritage they also, through their contributions are transforming, even if only slightly, the culture as a whole (Wells and Claxton, 2002, pp. 7–8).

Those first two principles can only soar through a rich tapestry of language and dialogue, for as Alexander (2020) shows language is the foundation of learning. Vygotsky (1962) would concur: thought and language are inextricably interrelated, coming into reality through participation, suggesting classrooms should be structured around dialogue (Alexander, 2020) thereby giving pedagogy our third principle, a rich *communicative core*. Language and literature, particularly through the power of narrative, are able to combine the cognitive with the social, emotional and physical aspects of education (Willingham, 2018): it sits well with approaches such as reading for pleasure (Cremin, 2020; Kucirkova and Cremin, 2020). Language is both the heart and soul of a powerful primary education.

Wells and Claxton (2002) debate the fourth principle, *cultural relativism*: they argue that education can be neither 'culture free' nor 'teacher proof' (see Doyle, 1979, 1983). A centrally planned pedagogy or curriculum 'delivered' uniformly cannot meet the needs of the range of educational contexts; contrast rural and inner urban contexts by way of example. They are concerned when 'situated complexity and idiosyncrasy' (2002, p. 6) is ignored, believing that decision-making must respect local needs and the concerns of children and their communities. In Reggio Emilio where parents as well as teachers are central to the learning process (Leach and Moon, 2008; Fielding and Moss, 2011), for example, community is vital to both the purpose and process of education. The 'third space' approach pays great attention to building on children's existing identities and 'funds' of knowledge (Moll, 2019). Bourdieu's theory of cultural capital articulates educational failure not resulting from linguistic deficit but in the extent of connection with the cultural mores that children bring to school. If primary education is to progress, in a rapidly changing and complex world, teachers must see learning through the eyes of children – this matters, socio-culturally, because the classroom is a place where children's motivation meets not just professional knowledge and expertise but the attitudes and beliefs of teachers. As Vygotsky puts it: 'through others we become ourselves' (socio-culturally also expressed in the term 'intersubjectivity' (Wertsch, 1998).

This leads to the fifth principle: Wells and Claxton (2002) propose pedagogic *communities of practice*, where development takes place 'through active participation in purposeful, collaborative activity' supporting social responsibility. Teaching here is a deliberate and skilled practice, allowing children to 'master' and 'appropriate', demanding contexts where the goals are shared and the purpose is to find solutions to the problems encountered as part of learning processes: Rogoff (1995) uses the term 'guided participation'. The climate that ultimately prevails will be key to success: particularly in the opportunity to make mistakes and take risks; where negotiation, interaction and collaboration take place in authentic contexts; where we foster the 'dispositions' of learning (Perkins and Salomon, 2012). Wells and Claxton argue that children can also contribute differentially according to their expertise and learn from the skills, values and dispositions that they see in the contributions of others (2002, pp. 6–7).

A socio-cultural pedagogy, too, must have a critical edge to deal with what it uncovers at particular points. Pollard (1985), for one, demonstrated how, in the social construction of pedagogy, assumptions which negatively stereotype working-class children can become embedded and need to be confronted.

Other aspects are problematic and need further clarification. Context is important in a socio-cultural approach, yet followed to a particular conclusion, the argument that pedagogy is context-specific has its limitations: when it leads to justifications of 'it's common sense' perhaps; to low expectations; or approaches where everything and anything might be claimed to work; or some schools 'sitting this initiative out', for example. Of cautionary note is Blatchford's (2012) research on the efficacy of teaching assistants. The evidence appeared counter-intuitive, that additional adults in the classroom might not lead to improvements in pupils' achievements: uncomfortable as this might be, it called for open-mindedness, rigour and studied insight. To enable context-specific approaches pedagogy needs to edge towards an evidenced and increasingly scientific approach where it is subject to scrutiny and justification. By allowing context to matter, it means clear and precise decisions must underpin well-chosen, carefully articulated, evidence-based approaches.

Reflection point

Which of the five characteristics of socio-cultural pedagogy resonates most with you? How can they be used in the design and evaluation of pedagogy?

Agency: self, connections and the world

Above all, children are both active and agentive in a socio-cultural approach. And, as Bruner (1996) argued, 'Pedagogy is never innocent. It is a medium that carries its own meaning'. Consciously or not, educators are always teaching values, attitudes and skills: they are better made explicit.

For Dewey (1900, 1916), education had the potential to bring about change, for *self* and others, so that democracy, potentially, could become part of the fabric of pedagogy, demanding though a much greater emphasis on social values, citizenship and cooperation. If, somehow, collective responsibility has been lost (Apple, 2013), this points us back to an inclusive, participative approach; the teacher has a key role in making *connections* in the lived realities of classrooms. Education is essentially human in spirit. There is now much greater attention to the forces of change in the wider world: among them environmental-scientific and community-led social changes which some such as Facer (2012) and Fielding and Moss (2011) have argued are of great importance: they include the demand for collective citizenship, including a developing view of the *world*. This recognises, too, the frenetic, often anxiety-inducing context surrounding us: to learn calmness and to identify with others and ourselves suggests a need for a much greater focus on awareness and the richness of our experience (Kabat-Zin, 2013), which will enable us to understand and reflect better on the impact of our human activity. Biesta (2020) suggests education is also about living life well, reinforcing the existential importance of 'how' to live in our pedagogies. In the socio-cultural paradigm, helping children navigate themselves to 'become' something, to be themselves and to understand their actions, is exemplified by the educator who transforms the experience of children who say 'I cannot'. Drawing on the Cambridge Primary Review (Alexander, 2010b, ch.14, p.237–278), pedagogies of primary education thus promote a sense of self (through well-being, participation and independence) through connection to others (through collaboration, reciprocity and empathy) and within a contributory active citizenship for the world (through respect, contributing and leadership): focusing on who children are and how they are provides an architecture for the riches of the curriculum (Table 5.2).

Table 5.2: Architecture for the curriculum From Alexander (2010b), Ch 14

Self	Connections	Global
Well-being	Collaboration	Respect
Participation	Reciprocity	Contribution
Independence	Empathy	Leadership

In designing a socio-cultural pedagogy, we can begin to define this (again with the Cambridge Primary Review as its key referent) so that:

- *The self enables ways of knowing*: through emotion, feeling and intuition; through curiosity, imagination and creativity; through logic, memory and argument; through faith, culture and language.
- *Connections enable access to forms of knowing*: through the established disciplines (the various arts and literature, mathematics and science; technologies) and through folk and religious forms as well as the moral and ethical.
- *The world provides us with perspectives on knowledge*: through our gender and race; through positions in relation to religion, culture and history; and through education and economics.

Reflection point

How important, relatively speaking, is developing a child's sense of self, their connections and understanding of the world for the children you educate? Should the approach vary according to developmental stage?

The pedagogic mix: insights, approaches, repertoire

Shulman (2005b) introduced the phrase 'signature pedagogies', which bridge the gap between theory/practice and global/local considerations. They develop out of the complexity and challenges of specific contexts requiring considerable personal/organisational reflection, collaborative problem-solving and deliberation creating positive approaches attuned to need. Signature pedagogies as a concept suggest an adaptable, carefully chosen and precise repertoire. Cybernetics uses the concept of 'requisite variety' (after Ashby, 1958), which translates well to the demands on pedagogy: in short, it means having a repertoire of responses for the challenges faced, that is the greatest flexibility of pedagogy to the demands of creating well-rounded learners.

A socio-cultural perspective on learning recognises multiple integrating approaches are needed: it is through skilful integration of a repertoire of purposeful approaches that quality emerges. From the understandings described thus far: pedagogy deepens and accelerates learning; uses experience and all of our senses; it is participative and dialogic; involves skilful inquiry; and supports the formation of identity and a sense of belonging – it is a deliberate and cumulative process. Pedagogy takes many different forms, evolving in practice; it makes links and connections, is rich in language and experience; applies learning in new situations and, in its highest form, moves to the abstract.

Ideas of diversity and respect are writ large, as are ethical and moral considerations: the individual and the collective are important in the design of a coherent pedagogy. A socio-cultural perspective can point us to a series of domains to support the design of pedagogy (Table 5.3).

Table 5.3: Five 'design' domains for a socio-cultural relationship between learning and pedagogy

Insight into learning	Pedagogic approach	Pedagogical effect
Learning involves the direction of skilled others and adopting, adapting and internalising established ways of knowing	Learning as an accelerative apprenticeship	Inductive – teaching for understanding and progression; fluency, mastery and appropriation; dispositions for learning
Learning appears twice: first, on the social and then on the personal plane, critically enabled by dialogue –	Learning through a guided participatory and dialogic process	Dialogic – communicative, participative, citizenship, other perspectives
Learning demands critical sense-making opportunities and experiences	Learning as a rich multi-sensory, experiential and creative process	Creative – meta-cognitive, criticality, enrichment
Learning involves mastery and appropriation in contexts where understanding is externalised	Learning as organised, skilful and critical inquiry	Collaborative – problem-solving, social responsibility, real-world contexts, applied knowledge
Learning is holistic and connects together, combining mind, body and spirit	Learning supporting the formation of identity through a sense of well-being and belonging	Identity – building character, love of learning and balance of life, connecting

Learning as an accelerative apprenticeship

Whether they are defined as subjects, domains or disciplines, there is relatively little argument against children learning key elements of the main bodies of knowledge of our society, after all this knowledge has been amassed through history: such 'powerful knowledge', according to Young et al., supports learning 'if it predicts, if it explains, if it enables you to envisage alternatives' (2014, p. 74); it takes children 'beyond their own experiences' (p. 7). Appropriating the tools of our culture, the core 'literacies', with a highly skilled teacher, an 'accelerative apprenticeship', is an essential element of primary education.

The idea of an apprenticeship is long-standing, suggesting the process of learning with or from a practised expert (see Resnick, 1991); Bruner uses the term 'initiation'. In its way it characterises elements of the teacher-child relationship where there is a clear asymmetry in experience: skilled guidance helps children to participate and deepen, to go beyond and accelerate their learning (Myatt, 2018, 2021). Acceleration, however, is not headlong coverage of content: children's learning moves through plateaus as their neurological understandings build cumulatively. For some learners, solutions do not appear immediately but may emerge sometime later without apparent conscious attention to them (Howe, 2010): analytic and generative dimensions of learning can take time (Wegerif, 2013). Value comes from curriculum plans where children re-experience key concepts presented in more complex and coherent forms (spiralling), where task demand spurs neural activity and deepens learning with different tasks activating the brain to create valuable connections. Science, for example, can be learned, in part, intuitively, but benefits hugely from the affordances of teachers with advanced pedagogical and subject knowledge. Harlen (2011) explains that the way a scientific inquiry is carried out will influence the emergent conceptual understanding. Staying with science, Wegerif (2013) suggests the subject is often taught as a body of fact and knowledge rather than as a wealth of knowledge developing through enquiry and through an 'argumentative discourse'. Each child will assimilate knowledge and understanding uniquely dependent on their neurological frameworks: thus the learner needs not only to be connected to established bodies of knowledge but be apprenticed in how to engage with the ways of a skilled historian, artist or scientist.

When aiming to accelerate and deepen understanding, the diagnostic role of the teacher becomes vital: a child's concept (for example, of light or sound) may be incomplete or inaccurate providing a barrier to progression. Powerful teacher instruction and content knowledge matched to children's development become essential (Coe et al., 2014). Instruction includes feedback that must address and provide correctives in key conceptual areas to generate neural change, helping the child to wrestle with their understandings. Hattie, in his extensive meta-analyses (2009, 2011), recognises positive reinforcement, helping children to improve and to clarify their goals combined with feedback on processes as part of tasks and self-regulation. Pedagogically, for him, this is significant because it 'was only when I discovered that feedback was most powerful when it is from *the student to the teacher* that I started to understand it better' (Hattie, 2009, p. 173, original emphasis). This means teachers seeking feedback from children about what they know and understand and, importantly, where they make errors and have misconceptions. When this is present, 'teaching and learning can be synchronized and powerful. Feedback to teachers helps make learning visible' (ibid.). The pedagogic balance lies in the teacher accelerating a child's learning within key bodies of knowledge, expanding their horizons while allowing their 'learning dispositions' (Claxton, 2021) to flourish.

Learning through a guided participatory and dialogic process

Our development as a species has been between people (Christian, 2004). Interaction studies confirm how growth of knowledge comes from the socially participative and communicative nature of learning (Mercer and Littleton, 2007; Howe and Mercer, 2010). In this sense, dialogue is an essential element because it opens up possibilities in the zone of proximal development. Alexander's (2000) study of five cultures led him to theorise that talk is one of the critical differences between education systems; he explains the significance:

> Language and thought are intimately related, and the extent and manner of children's cognitive development depend to a considerable degree on the forms and contexts of language which they have encountered and used. (Alexander, 2008, p. 10)

Alexander (2000) pointed out that, in England, classroom talk more often had social rather than cognitive purposes, while Howe and Mercer (2010) argued that exploratory talk is insufficiently present so that what Lemke (1990) calls the recitation script (teacher-led questions requiring factual answers) predominated. One of the chief arguments against the methods of the National Literacy and Numeracy Strategies was the relatively limited discourse between pupils and teachers (see Tymms and Merrell, 2010). Alexander (2018, 2020) sets the challenge – how best to transform classroom talk into dialogue that is at the same time social and cognitive. Consider its potential: talk for thinking, learning, mastery, communicating, relating, acculturation, democratic engagement and for teaching (Alexander, 2020, p. 130). In this vein are peer tutoring (Robinson et al., 2005, cited in Higgins 2009), reciprocal teaching (Palinscar and Brown, 1984; Palinscar, 2013) and cooperative models (Baines et al., 2007) which all hinge on dialogue. Phillipson and Wegerif (2017) and Dawes and Warwick (2012) exemplify other ways through 'thinking together'. Dialogic teaching 'harnesses the power of talk to engage interest, stimulate thinking, advance understanding, expand ideas, and build and evaluate arguments, empowering them for lifelong learning and democratic engagement' (Alexander, 2020, p. x).

It is not simply a question of increasing the amount of talk but the nature of it: an elaborated conversational style, for example, will develop detail and make connections across other interplaying knowledge. Keeping information alive in discussion for longer helps it to be patterned into deeper, longer-term storage and helps children to deal with abstraction. Alexander (2020) advocates dialogic teaching comprising six principles where talk is collective, reciprocal, deliberative, supportive, cumulative and purposeful.

By its nature a dialogic pedagogy is about giving a voice (Wegerif, 2013), a voice that opens up meaning. Dialogue partners with participation in democracy: 'Democracy, we contend … must be learnt by doing, so an education for democracy must be inscribed with democracy as a value' (Fielding and Moss, 2011, p. 40) Hargreaves and Fullan (1998) pointed out that schools remain our last coherent means of building a sense of community so that ideas of civic virtue and social responsibility link well to dialogic approaches where shared values can be realised.

For children this means active citizenship. Lawton (2000) identified the key difference between active (concerned with ideas, politics, conflict and action) and passive (facts, constitutions, duties, responsibility) in citizenship models. The Crick Report (Advisory Group for Citizenship, 1998) supported a model of participatory democracy focusing on social and moral responsibility, community involvement and political literacy. For schools, within their local environments there are histories, community struggles and issues, immediate environmental concerns (parks, noise or littering, perhaps) which are often ripe for public debate and action. Interviews with local community members, visits and visitors as well as historical and geographical simulations offer wider experience. Pupil voice at its most advanced sees children involved in the collective deliberations and decision-making processes that affect the running and development of their schools and classrooms (Lefstein and Snell, 2014). Its purpose is to create a concern for the wider benefits of the community and generate social benefits through which all 'flourish' (Fielding and Moss, 2011, pp. 43–44).

Learning as a multi-sensory, experiential and creative process

Our understanding of the link between the brain and the perception and sensation of the body is increasing: experiences are part of a child's rising consciousness and their growing agency, the foundation of the prior knowledge they bring to learning. Experience enables connections; LeDoux argued that we should understand 'why we attend to, remember or reason about some things more than others. Thinking cannot be fully comprehended if emotions and motivations are ignored' (LeDoux, 2003, p. 175). Learning takes place through all of the sensory modalities. Davidson and Begley (2013), meanwhile, have shown the importance of developing the emotional side of the brain. Together, sensory and experiential pedagogies offer a therapeutic understanding that may be able to bridge the socially constructed gulf between mind and body (Orr, 2002).

Polanyi (1966) argued that creative acts are imbued with feelings and commitments and this is a significant part of how personal knowledge is developed. The expression of children's creative skill and imagination can often be the culmination of their learning. The expressive arts, for example, which could include - visual art, music, drama, theatre, dance, poetry and writing (in myriad forms) are not only intrinsically pleasurable (enriching, enlivening, inspiring) for many but combine attentiveness with a sense of audience, connecting people to the world in deep ways: through their disciplines of knowledge, skill and the dedication they often inspire. This echoes Robinson's (2010) call for education to allow children to find their 'element': those things that resonate with them and reflect who they really are (their interests and aptitude).

In a curriculum, in their plural form, each subject, domain or discipline should have distinctive value in its own right. They can connect to children, to their cultural heritage and earn their place in pedagogy. Be it through a literature 'spine', the study of great artists, inspirational cultural visits or working with a visiting poet: building rich experience into pedagogy is enabling because the ability to 'recall' seems to be situational and contextual – the more we are able to trigger it through 'cues', the better it can be used particularly in the 'real' but demanding situations that McFarlane (1997) calls 'authentic' problems, challenges and investigations. Meaning emerges also from real-life experience: from studies, for example, of local river pollution, by considering carefully both the local and global implications, which intertwine and act as contrasts in stimulating learning. When children are taught in age-appropriate ways – scientific understanding that contributes to addressing environmental challenges affecting their world, for example – they are then, in democratic terms, able to enter the debate about the impacts of choices, to understand the trends and patterns of dialogue and their various 'interests' (Wegerif, 2013). Such approaches reflect the importance of being able to savour the actuality of things and to deepen their understanding of the world. The challenges of 'connecting with' and being 'respectful of' the child's world, of helping them make links between past, present and future are part of a recurring generative process of cognition.

While pedagogies allow children experience, they need also to be creative and contributory, to help children demonstrate their skills and knowledge. Some advocate portfolio style presentations that capture individual children's interest. Experience can readily be turned into forms of production – newspapers, blogs, videos, public performances and exhibitions. The web, too, by making children's work visible to their peers, spurs some children on to produce greater contributions than the normal teacher audience offers (Thompson, 2013).

Finally, in this section, there is the pedagogical power of 'narrative' (Fielding and Moss, 2011; Willingham, 2018): stories are an age-old human form of expression bringing meaning to potentially disconnected experiences and can be about renewal and responsibility, for example. By building narratives with their children, teachers assist them in making meaning from their immediate lives and in the wider world – they bring things together. Narrative approaches, too, recognise the process of meaning-making that comes from a personal and emotional connection. Critical engagement by children helps knowledge be seen as more than the accumulation of facts – when we see our children immersed in learning, there should be opportunity for contemplation, to be able to look deeply, developing awareness and insight.

Learning as a process of organised, skilled and collaborative inquiry

Figuring out what to do under different circumstances in order to achieve your goals is what life is all about. Learning and motivation are thus closely intertwined topics. (LeDoux, 2003, p. 237)

How do we meet this challenge in forms of pedagogy that are authentically intellectually challenging and productive? How do we find ways of enabling learning in which children consciously and strategically apply their knowledge, understanding and skills? As far back as 1910, Dewey advocated an inquiry approach; meaning to 'ask' or 'investigate' by posing questions, generating problems or exploring scenarios, sometimes, but not always, in project form. It is a controversial area, maligned by some and difficult to judge for often research does not compare like with like – for example, do we mean project-based, enquiry-based, problem-led? (see Barron and Darling-Hammond, 2010) – and its incipient variety may currently make it impenetrable to randomised control trials. Nevertheless, evidence suggests judicious use of inquiry, embedded in high-quality pedagogy, offers value (Mourshed et al., 2017). It has a growing base in primary education (see, for example, www. openfutures.com).

The availability of ubiquitous information from the web adds to the importance of learners being actively taught to exercise both discretion and judgement. There is no longer a single source: the background of complex information, of multiple perspectives, of international dialogues makes the straightforward answer and simplistic solutions less likely to work. A key purpose of inquiry is that children learn intentionality; they exercise a degree of choice and explore learning where they do not know the outcome in advance. If we are looking for further justification, then Bruner (1973) argues that the aim is to go 'beyond the information given', which involves, for children, processes of explaining, giving new examples, of applying knowledge and giving evidence and defending their ideas.

Inquiry can also be considered 'unstructured' when in reality this is not the case. This is teaching at its most challenging and instructionally demanding: there is a need to manage the cognitive load which children experience; carefully introducing the skills and knowledge needed for development of an artifact, for example, and constructing what Sweller (1998) calls the 'problem space' in achievable form. Any inquiry would need to meet the demands of Wrigley (2003). He argues that teaching inquiry would need to involve, for example, concrete preparation (rich experience and an introduction to specialist vocabulary and concepts); cognitive conflict (designed to create puzzlement and discord, raising questions and thoughts); a construction zone (speculation and collaboration) where constructs that oppose one another are proposed; and metacognition (children guided into control over a task, with modelling and bridging to new situations).

If inquiry pedagogies provide a flux of positive forces by engaging imagination and creativity, and develop collaborative problem-solving skills while helping children learn the deep conceptual structures of our bodies of knowledge by connecting information together, then more exploration is certainly needed: Kirschner et al. (2018) have explored 'collaborative cognitive load theory', for example. Through inquiry primary schools can be movement-building and opinion-forming as children construct problems, explore them and propose solutions. When inquiries are sufficiently demanding they will bring children into situations where they must take heed of the feelings and beliefs of others. Here, then, inquiry learning connects back into children's worlds and life-situations. Knowledge is integrated but highly valuable as children find contextual and specific knowledge vital to their endeavour. It is as Wegerif explains: 'meaning always assumes at least two perspectives held together in creative tension' (2013, p. 4).

Learning supporting the formation of identity and a sense of well-being and belonging

The Cambridge Primary Review asserted: 'A child's "learner identity" is increasingly accepted as a key determinant of performance' (Alexander, 2010b, p. 82). Evidence suggests that learning is an active meaning-making process and that growth in the number of neural connections depends on participation, so what a child experiences linguistically, culturally, religiously and attitudinally shapes them and affects their image of themselves. In this context, developing children's identity is a deliberate pedagogic process. Many schools are adopting an approach to 'character education' (Reay, 2017). On the one hand, this means developing children's personal strengths but also, systematically, their ethical and moral thinking: the way to help children to develop wisdom (Jubilee Centre, 2017). This sits alongside fostering well-being: the human ability to learn and to grow, to heal and transform, helping to reconcile the demands of 'being' and 'doing' (Kabat-Zinn, 2013) in a world which often appears frantic. Shirley (2020b) suggests this is more than 'quiescence' or fitting with existing norms and rules, but also 'energetic' forms of well-being, healthy lifestyles, the right to 'play' and critical ways of thinking about the world.

When we make judgements in education, we often do so on two broad planes: first are the judgements we make of children's learning (and their 'work'); and second are judgements we make about the children as characters and can be based on their social circumstances. The context of the professionals working in schools can be different (in terms of social mores – rituals, beliefs and values) from those of the children they teach and is most likely to be the case, arguably, in urban environments. As the Cambridge Primary Review cautioned, 'some professionals may be too ready to assume that their values are unassailable' (Alexander, 2010b, p. 81): how people do things is the fabric of their well-being but not everything is learned in school and may not be known by school (see Nuthall, 2007). The view pupils are given of themselves colours their perception of the world: thus belonging becomes a key determinant of motivation. It is why the movement for 'curriculum decolonisation' (see Kara, 2021), for example, is psychologically powerful in every context and not simply symbolic.

In Hart's (1992) 'ladder of participation', at the highest levels children's participation is in partnership with their teachers. Lupton (2004) has explored the effects of poverty on different ethnic groups finding varied effects in the groups she studied, for example, the emotional needs of some white working-class pupils contrasted with the home responsibilities of some minority ethnic groups. Moreover, there were differences in attitude towards education, often generated by experience. Not all children will adapt well to traditional school knowledge, since it is context dependent: for some it will be problematic because their personal knowledge constructs and experiences do not map to the prescribed values or curriculum model. When they focus on belonging, schools recognise that families have different values and beliefs and these can be built upon. A school's relationship with a child's home and community may be less direct but interplays with values, customs and beliefs. Goodenow (1993) described it as 'membership' – whether children feel accepted, respected and valued. Leach and Moon refer to the Maori idea of radiating wheels, which shows how education moves beyond boundaries: 'Maori pedagogy emphasises that learning depends on these interlocking experiences and understandings being in balance – but such experiences must always be outward looking' (2008, p. 77). Perkins (2014) expansively offers the concept of 'lifeworthy knowledge' – the things likely to matter in the lives of children.

Tuning into possibilities, Brighouse (2012) uses the term 'commonwealth' to describe the rich resources which exist in localities and which can be unlocked for children's benefit. The Cambridge Primary Review uses the term 'funds of knowledge' to describe the vitality of communities and the outward-looking approach which is needed. In making connections children must feel that they are part of the same world as their peers, part of the community of learners: many schools make a psychological investment in creating personal and collective memories. It is not surprising that for children friends really matter in school. An alternative way of describing this relationship is through the idea of 'principled interdependence', which:

> ... implies a recognition of the extent to which we are dependent upon other people, wider institutions, environment and tools to be able to act in the world; and the extent to which our actions therefore also have implications for other people and their agency in turn. (Facer, 2011, p. 55)

And children, too, can be part of this pedagogic process, supporting one another (older children, for example, reading and playing with younger children). Increasingly, schools use technologies to reach beyond the school gates and combine with community learning. The Children's University has an offer of educational experiences that takes place in cultural and community contexts outside of school, with passports leading to graduation. Their seven A's resonate: attitudes, ambition, aspiration, adventure, advocacy, adaptability and agency.

Polanyi (1958) placed a strong emphasis on dialogue within communities recognising the strength of opinions and understandings in the negotiation of meaning. The aim is that reciprocally teachers and children understand each other better in an empowering form of relationship: it involves a much stronger connection than purely 'homework'. James and Pollard (2010) report on the work of Hughes who investigated home and school learning environments drawing three key conclusions:

- that there are substantial funds of knowledge embedded in cultures of homes and communities;

- knowledge exchange activities can provide reciprocity in terms of teachers understanding children's wider lives and parents' understandings of school; and
- though gains were variable, there is potential for home-school knowledge exchanges to impact on attainment.

One of the potential benefits of remote learning, through the communicative affordance of new technologies, may prove to be in enabling parents to learn alongside their children.

Identification with place matters too, in both the development of identity and to future civic engagement (Nash, 2008). As Leach and Moon comment:

> ... location focuses on the quality of social structures that enable the learner to feel central or marginal, active or passive, empowered or disempowered, in the various groups to which they belong. (Leach and Moon, 2008, p. 76)

Auerbach (2012) argues, in summary, that knowledge from family and community strengths offers great opportunities for the development of pedagogy. Among the pedagogic questions it generates are those that ask whether pedagogy is relevant and important to the children who experience it. In the way they are active in creating useful aesthetics and products, by participating in activities and events (festivals and celebrations, for example) or through digital spaces (e.g. Papert, 1996; Facer, 2011), children build on their cultural heritage, acquiring self-regulatory knowledge; in part, they are learning 'how' to be as well as demonstrating imagination, creativity and perseverance. If assessment is set within their community contexts, children begin to understand the impact of their exhibitions and performances.

Identity and belonging build bridges: through such an approach children learn a strong sense of who they are and, significantly, what they might become.

Reflection point

What are your 'signature' pedagogies? Is anything missing from the five domains set out here? How would you balance them, make them distinctive, yet interrelate them in practice?

Conclusions

There is an enigmatic quality to pedagogy, as each school will have its own interpretation: it must be deliberate, explicit, precise and intentional but, at the same time, flexible, responsive and evolving. No singular pedagogy prevails: pedagogical domains mix to meet the demands of context, best experienced by children as a coherent, progressive narrative that helps them to flourish. It is underpinned by teaching of knowledge, dispositions and understanding and, by return to the beginning of this chapter, values – perhaps those proposed by the Jubilee Centre: courage, justice, honesty, compassion, gratitude, humility, integrity, respect (Jubilee Centre, 2017).

Pedagogy cannot easily be constructed from a single centralised or rationalist viewpoint and should be considered, evaluated and redesigned on a regular basis. It should have a contemporary quality, addressing the needs, issues and challenges current to today's children; as Bruner has shown, it may require conflict with existing ideas and beliefs. Pedagogy must be actively styled, passed as it is from generation to generation, and open to development (Bereiter, 2002) – it must regenerate.

As pedagogy evolves over time, many recognise new forms will be needed for a world where advances in neuroscience, biogenetics and information technologies, for example, test our educational orthodoxies. The system can make shifts: significantly, over recent decades, there have been significant advances in the teaching of reading, writing and mathematics, for example. Innovation accelerated too in response to the situational effects of Covid-19 – the move to 'remote' learning demanded and demonstrated high levels of adaptivity while the much used 'Building Back Better' concept demands further evolution.

New technologies, harnessed effectively, offer new pedagogical potential and challenge. As Leadbeater explained: 'The web matters because it allows more people to share ideas with more people in more ways' (2009, p. 7). The 'flipped classroom' concept, alternatively, embraces the availability of knowledge and ubiquity of technology to move aspects of instruction (using videos and quizzes, for example) from the group learning space to the individual with the resulting group time transformed into a dynamic, interactive environment exploring those concepts. As our environmental conditions change, pedagogy must evolve in response to multiple aims and newly emerging goals.

In the twenty-first century, the role of teachers will also evolve: they must help children to connect with knowledge, create the tools to allow children to contribute and collaborate and have purpose and precision, particularly if it is to transform inequalities. Hattie's (2009) reminder that teaching is always a process dependent on 'what happens next' emphasises their importance: powerful pedagogy is demanding and dynamic, learning needs directive skill to create and accelerate it while deepening intentionality from the learner so that they actively internalise and externalise their growing understanding.

Developments in research and assessment could potentially be highly valuable. Using only outcomes in English and Mathematics tests as benchmarks, valuable as they are, becomes problematic when considered from a wider perspective: the challenge is to find ways to evaluate multiple purposes and pedagogies. There are key opportunities around assessment: first, to create informative, 'small' data that tells us much more about a child's wider development with informative diagnostic capacities; and, second, ways of evidencing outcomes that reflect the breadth of a child's achievement.

It is the holism of great pedagogies (a mind to learn; enculturation and transformation; communicate core; cultural relativism; and pedagogic communities of practice) that activates learning: they breathe life into classrooms, and create wisdom through considered reflection, spurring children into action. For professionals, their creation requires energy and skilful design (Table 5.4).

Table 5.4: Pedagogy from a socio-cultural perspective

Planning	• Principles of pedagogic design should embody our changing understandings of children, learning and society • Subjects and their knowledge, dispositions and understandings are specified and sequenced • Pedagogic decisions are evidence-informed and values-based • Pedagogies are co-constructed in local contexts on an on-going and everyday basis; curriculum plans are dynamic
Context	• Learning takes places in a supportive and collaborative community creating a sense of belonging • Dignity and respect characterise relationships in the school and the community, who live well together
Curriculum	• A communicative and dialogic core underpins learning experiences: children's voices strongly inform the curriculum • There are carefully designed plans for progression and continuity and links between elements • Real-world experiences and the local community are strongly embedded into curriculum plans • Subjects, domains or disciplines are valued equally, in their own right and in their rich variety
Teaching	• Teaching is highly skilled, fit for purpose and adaptive and strongly dialogic • Teachers become associated with designing learning opportunities; science, art and craft combine; there is a coherent presentation, sequence and structure unified by narrative
Learning	• Children's active pursuit of learning is supported by rich experiences and engagement with knowledge in multiple forms • Pedagogy recognises multiple representations of knowledge from which children develop their own interpretations and schemas • Curiosity, inquiry, creativity and the development of character are developed deliberately: children learn the wisdom of appreciation alongside the aspiration to go further as they develop character • Learning has surprise, awe and wonder to promote imagination and curiosity but this combines with rigour, determination and resilience to structure a holistic process • Learning can be an uneven process because it demands a growth that comes from ownership and a level of involvement that involves grappling with ideas, testing out beliefs and emerging understandings
Assessment	• Intelligent diagnostic assessments inform teachers of children's progression • Teachers assess formatively and use this to inform planning
Partnership	• Parents and children benefit from engagement and their participative voice being heard in the learning process

All of this is dependent on being able to create the conditions for a rich and enabling pedagogy to thrive in our system of primary schools. Exploring and suggesting principles of pedagogic design draws us further into the ecosystem of primary education, raising questions relating to how leadership and management of our schools bring this to fruition.

Next: The next chapter takes us into a consideration of leadership, management and governance in primary education, viewed again through a socio-cultural lens.

6 | The power of leadership

> **This chapter** is about leadership and governance in primary education.
>
> **It explores:** *what leadership is • the way leadership is framed in primary education • the idea of expansive leadership • community connections • distinctive character • collegiality • teacher leadership • perils, problems and pitfalls of leadership • governance*

What is leadership?

The journey continues, expanding now to explore the conditions that allow great pedagogy to flourish. Life in a primary school is a complex multidimensional ecosystem in its own right: this brings us to leadership where civic responsibility, stability, systems, inspiration, creativity and, ultimately, pedagogies emanate. It is leadership that fosters minds that learn, enculturation through a rich curriculum experience, a compelling communicative core, respectful cultural relativism and pedagogic communities of practice. Increasingly, governance is part of the leadership equation for it supports, inter alia, strategy, accountability and probity across the system.

Across many studies, leadership has consistently emerged as vitally important in the success of schools, second only in importance to instruction (see Leithwood et al., 2008, 2019); along the way it has become a complex and necessarily varied concept with a mountain of associated literature. When we think of it, it is often in terms of being an enabler of success (Day et al., 2010; Leithwood and Louis, 2012); the reason or basis for an institution's achievements; or, conversely, the reason for stagnation, lethargy or lack of direction. Through the lens of socio-cultural dynamics, leadership is a process; it is the flow of activity, rather than a product, enabling pedagogical development to gain momentum stemming from purpose, engagement and the creation of energy. In Engeström's concise summation, '*anticipating, mastering and steering qualitative changes*' (1987, p. 2, original emphasis). Covey (1989) created the expectation of an uneven process when describing it as a 'beginning with the end in mind'. The focus here is on how leadership makes schools better places for children to thrive by developing great pedagogy (see Robinson, 2007) that is 'improvable'.

Viewed inclusively and borrowing Dilts' (2018) system of logical levels then, leadership includes shaping the vision, identity and values that drive primary schools (relating primarily to 'object') and the capacities, practices and environment (relating primarily to action) that realise them. Leadership in these terms is combinatory: in one sense a multi-directional, collaborative process of intentional social influencing undertaken by individuals and teams; and in another, the formal organisation that structures, supports and engages the process of learning and removes any barriers. Adapting Dilts' (2018) levels creates a ladder through which the range and complexity of leadership can be seen (Table 6.1).

Table 6.1: The range of leadership in primary schools (after Dilts, 2018)

Vision	• Active strategy formation and evaluative reflection • Ambition for children and their achievements • Moral purpose, including a commitment to equity and inclusion
Identity (character)	• A dynamic and connecting pedagogical object • A deeply distinctive character • A concern for equity and a culture of inclusion
Values	• A deep concern for the well-being of everyone concerned • Ethical and moral behaviour of the highest standard
Capacities	• Empowered and highly skilled professionals • Subject and pedagogical content knowledge • A collaborative learning culture
Pedagogies (practices)	• Actively constructed, high-quality inclusive pedagogy and curriculum • Children's voices influence policy and practice • Responsive systems of self-evaluation
Environment (learning, interaction)	• Systems to operate smoothly, efficiently and safely • Home-school and community connections and engagement • A positive climate for learning

Skilful leadership builds culture through influencing vision, identity and values: Blatchford (2014) describes the 'restless' school where that culture is being 'the best it can' – the heart that drives primary education. MacBeath et al. (2018) describe a professional integrity to leadership which involves reminding people, at every opportunity, that education is a moral enterprise serving the interests of children; education professionals becoming the guardians of powerful forms of learning; taking an unshakable position on critical issues of social justice; creating the conditions from which education can grow from the ground up, that is from a child's point of view; and listening to the voices of those who have interest in the child's education. Sometimes that culture may be less than visible but often, because it is played out in the way people think and act, it is only hidden below the surface ready to emerge when needed. Such influential leadership empowers others (Earley, 2017) and Louis et al. (2010) remind us that leaders do not lose influence when others gain it. As Fullan commented: 'Ultimately, your leadership in a culture of change will be judged effective or ineffective not by who you are as a leader but by what leadership you produce in others' (2001, p. 137).

Leadership can be challenging and demanding too: when faced with resistance to change, with revitalising an object or introducing new forms of pedagogy. It is usually long-term and sometimes a process of attrition, perhaps involving what David Hargreaves calls 'swimming upstream' (cited in MacBeath et al., 2018). It is then that we hear of determination and resilience. Collins (2001) described his highest 'Level 5' leaders as those who 'build enduring greatness' through conscious 'choice and discipline'. Given the complexities of context and levels of demand it has to be substantive and grounded in this way (see Earley, 2017). Whatever one's style, both navigation and structuring are features of leadership so that success means not simply reacting but being able to build capacity, design pedagogy and harness the available resources, potentially in adverse conditions. These myriad challenges and the endless variety need what Leithwood et al. (2006) call a 'synergistic relationship'. It is a continuous process, which Southworth (2002) demonstrated when drawing on the leadership experience in ten primary schools. He found that the following were essential: working hard, as a matter of course; determination; a positive disposition (or belief); approachability; valuing team work and an on-going commitment to school improvement. In bringing this together, self-aware leaders often use the power of narrative to build a compelling strategy and recognise that the meaning of their leadership is reflected in the response they receive.

In socio-cultural terms, leadership is always present, ever emergent; its nature dialogic and situated. It depends, for example, on the challenges facing a leader: a newly appointed head teacher may be charged with arresting decline, challenging complacency or maintaining excellence. Leadership, at its best, is a dynamic, active and essentially collective process requiring 'organizational agility, joint enterprise, shared interpretation, negotiation of meaning, sense-making, deep understanding, and knowledge building' (Breuleux et al., 2002, p. 21). Table 6.2 captures some of the challenges of leadership and what is essentially demanded in response.

Table 6.2: The situated dynamics of leadership

Context and situational challenges	Essential leadership
Questions of value and moral judgement arise in social contexts	Leadership actively advocates moral purpose, champions social justice and lives its values
There are a plethora of demands on primary education	Leadership is pedagogical at heart and dependent on shared leadership: teaching and teachers' capacities are actively developed
Local contexts vary creating specific situated demand	Leadership engages with and is attuned to the specific demands of the socio-cultural context
The educational environment is constantly changing, creating shifting demands that require different responses	Leadership is responsive: it evolves and changes within a whole-school 'design'; it prioritises and plans
There is a growing body of educational research, developing in and through practice	Leadership is both theory and practice and should be evidence-informed (from research and development work); data is used sensitively and informatively
Evidence shows that only a proportion of the impact on achievement comes from within school. Learners and their identity are complex constructions	Leadership connects to identity, belonging and well-being: it engages and values learners and their communities
Each school is in a unique context but that context is situated in a global context	Leadership is contextual but connected and outward looking

It seems that interest in leadership tends always to be greatest when something needs to be done or when the system or one of its components comes under pressure. The Covid-19 challenges illustrated the vitality of leadership in primary education: the challenges were immediate, complex and adaptive for school leaders, including burdensome operational and organisational demands set within a political and media maelstrom; many primary schools reached well beyond what might reasonably have been expected, particularly for their vulnerable children, responding to changes on an almost daily basis, some of them of huge import. At its heart, educational leadership is always pedagogical. Covid-19 demonstrated strongly how adaptive and creative leaders turned around and engaged with their local communities to create, among other things, remote learning: when they work well together, innovation and change couple closely.

Responding to complexity constantly manifests itself in movement that is purposeful and agentive. As Macbeath comments:

> Conflict, dilemma and ambiguity are, of course, at the very centre of learning, individual and organisational, and it is this constant grappling with complexity that makes schools interesting and dynamic places. Effective schools, in their myriad forms, never stay still long enough to be pinned down. (Macbeath, 1999, p. 9)

Reflection point

Do these descriptions of leadership resonate with what leadership means to you in your context/role?

The leadership frame

Fullan (2010) notes that how leadership is defined depends upon context: it is situational and relative, framed in different ways in different periods and different places (see Silver, 1994). For politicians and those with system responsibilities, leadership has become an essential ingredient in applying the levers of change (Fullan, 2011) as the prevailing priorities and systemic demands have shifted.

Throughout the 1970s (and beyond), interest in leadership grew, often professionally constructed through higher-level degrees and developmental organisations (e.g. the National Development Centre at Bristol University). Campbell (1985), for example, offered a commentary and vision exploring 'collegiality' as an organising principle for developing the primary curriculum: a model based in the professionalism of teachers and illustrating the intricacies of relationships in primary schools. Subsequently, the context for leadership development was transformed. For Thatcher's Conservative government leadership focused on locally devolved administrative functions with increased decision-making for schools, often along 'managerial' lines. The leadership role, particularly that of the head teacher, changed dramatically post-1988 (Hall and Southworth, 1997) with the emergence of school improvement, including: strategic financial and staff planning, performance management, corporate style whole-school approaches and reformed governance. During New Labour's reign, 'leadership' was central to reforms. A National College for School Leadership was the subject of significant government investment providing a key means to 'radically change professional identities and practice' (Gunter, 2012, p. 3). A plethora of programmes, accreditations and research were imagined, commissioned, developed and implemented running, crucially, alongside the 'detailed deliverology' of central school improvement strategies (Hargreaves and Shirley, 2009) leading, often, to a culture of pragmatism and compliance (Alexander, 2008). Head teachers became primarily accountable for 'performance'; in part, policy consumers expected to realise the ambitions of central government. Some leaders and their schools became accredited (designated as National Leaders of Education, National Teaching Schools, for example) and some had greater opportunities (supporting less successful schools and leading teacher training, for example). A 'cult' of educational leadership grew, Gronn's (2002) 'designer concept'. Steadily, too, leadership moved beyond the head teacher and became a whole-school issue that was now both distributed and governed (Harris, 2003; Bush et al., 2019). Dominated, for Fink (2010), by the compliance of the standards agenda, some have suggested that the leadership debate did not always, in those years, emanate from the first principles of pedagogy. Notably though, Hallinger et al. (2020) conclude, from over 40 years of research, the field of educational leadership is now focused around a conceptual core that they term 'leading teaching and learning'.

In 2010, the Coalition government initiatives were based on the principle of school autonomy and a *collaborative* self-improving system. A new national curriculum and its assessment together with revised inspection frameworks maintained the pressure on primary schools, driving operational elements once again; however, new organisational forms emerged quickly, particularly Multi-Academy Trusts: pioneering new structures (with the new parlance of principals, executive head teachers and chief executives) allowing a growing and relatively significant number of school leaders to exercise wider system roles, while many others were involved in what Greany (2017) terms role-related informal partnerships. The range of responses to policy was understandably varied: the descriptions of 'confident', 'cautious', 'concerned' and 'constrained' used by Higham and Earley (2013) captures both the psychological realities and the variation in how leaders perceived themselves in the beginnings of a self-improving school system.

In leadership, powerful socio-cultural dynamics interplay and responses vary. Over time, in complex ways, some groups of head teachers might align themselves steadfastly with the government agenda embracing various opportunities; others may be necessarily compliant under pressure from accountability frameworks; while still others tacitly find their own ways of creating meaning – perhaps, flying, as Hargreaves described it, below the radar. In Scotland, MacBeath et al. (2009) summarised five forms of response to external mandate: 'dutiful compliance', 'cautious pragmatism', 'quiet self-confidence', 'bullish self-assertion' and 'defiant risk-taking'.

Leaders, to some degree, adjust to what they think the system expects of them in order to create meaning, which can be both powerful and problematic. Multiple demands ebb and flow: in any organisation the future is not entirely known, as people come to terms with those meanings that are not entirely rational and controllable and, at times, contradictory. Thomson (2009) describes the tension between the moral purpose of many head teachers and the day-to-day realities that they manage. Lofthouse and Whiteside (2020) explored, predominantly with primary head teachers, how coaching could support the intense interplay of demands on leadership: personal well-being, professional capacity, leadership identity and values. The rise of coaching, perhaps, reflecting the acute level of demand on leaders and the sophisticated support needed to nego-tiate the terrain.

Collectively, expectations and approach matter. In the Learning without Limits project, commenting on a head teacher's leadership, Swann et al. note how: 'She worked to create a learning environment where it was safe to take risks, where confidence would increase, where everybody could be caught up in the excitement of learning' (2012, p. 9).

The paradox of leadership in primary education is that, at the same time as greater power and control has been devolved to schools, significantly greater responsibilities and accountabilities have also arrived: note the responsibilities of governance in Academy arrangements, for example. Leadership in primary education is for multiple purposes and with weighty demands: much more than flotsam on tides of policy. Evidentially, in English primary education leaders have proven their ability to respond to and implement external change; it was revealed again in responses to Ofsted's (2019) changed framework and, of course, to Covid-19.

Reflection point

How can leaders in primary education turn its weighty demands into positive energy and create the conditions in which everyone can flourish?

Daly and Finnigan (2011) have cautioned against increasing the number of initiatives where intensification impacts negatively on morale creating pres-sure and subsequently burnout. Paradoxically, sometimes we can get more done by doing less as we conserve energy and use it strategically. The time may well be right to build a framework for primary education that builds on the motivation, capacity and sense of responsibility that typifies its leadership, that balances the opportunities of freedom with the commitments of obligation, perhaps, to revive and re-imagine the concept of collegial leadership. It will need thoughtful design and systemic reform to create a sustainable framework of values, expectations and supporting structures together with an intelligent, rigorous and guiding accountability system.

To understand this better, the next section steps back to look at leadership afresh in the light of contemporary challenges through a socio-cultural lens: it explores the type of leadership that might be needed (expansive); the value of leadership to local communities; the distinctive character of primary schools; and the potential of teacher leadership.

Leading expansively

A socio-cultural position theorises leadership as 'generative' – a vital produc-tive force for change, taking many forms, generated by numerous motivations (see Simkins, 2005) and constantly changing, going beyond what Bryk et al. (2015) call 'solutionitis'. Activity theorist Yrjö Engeström's research group at the University of Helsinki recognise that:

> Work organisations undergo cycles of qualitative changes in their logic of operation today more frequently than before. These changes dissolve established concepts and practices, and call for a new kind of learning.

In such times, Stevenson (2019) suggests that a plan is not enough, there needs to be strategy.

A period of rapid change means leadership must concern itself with 'what next' and discovering 'what might be'. Yet, often leadership challenges have been constructed as implementation or problem-solving and almost 'exclude the possibility of finding or creating new contexts' (Engeström, 1987). Engeström et al. believe that change, when it is superficial or narrowly systemic, leaves the conditions unchanged, meaning deep-seated issues remain unresolved and thus issues are faced time and again, recurring in aggravated forms; technical solutions, they argue, cannot fix them (2002, p. 216). Engeström (1999b) employs the concept of 'expansive learning'.

> Expansive learning is learning what is not yet there by means of the actions of questioning, modelling and experimentation (Engeström, 1987; 2001). Its core is the collaborative creation of new artefacts and patterns of practice. (Engestrom et al., 2002, p. 216)

Cycles of expansive learning concentrate on finding new approaches and ways of learning through questioning accepted practices, collective reflection and planning, culminating in transformative actions. Qualitative change through expansive learning involves finding a springboard and creating the conditions for taking a model into practice (Engeström, 1987) through 'questioning, confrontation and debate' (Engeström, 1999b, p. 402); helped by what Wenger (2005) calls 'tools for seeing'. The intention of rigorous studied endeavour is to move teachers from 'myth'-driven to 'object'-driven discourse (Engeström et al., 2002), addressing as Alexander argues, the not inconsiderable challenge of having 'a sufficient grasp of epistemological, developmental, cultural and pedagogical matters to promote intelligent, informed and purposeful debate about curriculum aims, values, structure and content' (2013, p.11).

When the object is constantly developed by collective effort and energy, then the horizons of primary education will be regularly changing and expanding (see Figure 2). For Virkunnen (2009), this means creating learning cycles that create a school improvement pathway and the 'theories of action' that underpin pedagogy (Hopkins and Craig, 2014). Thompson and Wiliam (2007) describe the balance between 'tight and loose' in their model: there is a need for clear pedagogical design principles to be held tight but these reflect context and while held close they are made adaptable through developmental processes. On the one hand, this involves 'articulation, explication and extension'

Figure 2: Expansive learning and pedagogic development (after Engeström, 1999b)

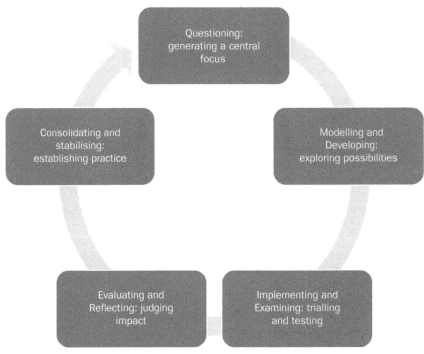

of the tacit (or implicit) knowledge underpinning pedagogy, while on the other, it is about the 'distribution, legitimation and amplification' of understandings so that new 'conceptualisations, metaphor, analogies and models' are developed (Virkunnen, 2009, p. 149). In primary schools, this needs to emerge from children's learning:

> To know and understand learning requires the studied long-term insights and analysis of teachers and pupils reflecting together, using tools and finding the language to get inside the learning process. (MacBeath, 1999, p. 4)

Building community connections

The risk in pursuing a narrow, simplistic standards agenda is that it can mask social inequality (Wrigley, 2003): where leadership finds such a challenge it must connect deeply to address the issues. Focusing on quality leads discussions in a different direction, including: cultural empathy, political sensitivity, an inclusive curriculum and desire for social justice; it connects strongly with the concept of 'cultural relativism'. Riley points out: 'schools remain one of the few shared social institutions where values and beliefs are played out on a daily basis; and school leaders are the mediators of those values' (2017, p. 140). Riley argues persuasively in favour of creating schools where the children and community belong and where they feel safe in their identity and leaders engage in 'place-making'. Parents and carers, in particular, must feel the system is just and that leadership favours their children. Civic leadership seemed to blossom in just this way during the Covid-19 pandemic – leaders responded to the pressures and challenges in their specific circumstances.

Achieving high educational outcomes is more challenging in inner urban contexts: it is harder work and likely to require more commitment, faced with unemployment, mental and physical health issues and worklessness (Wrigley, 2003; also Wrigley et al., 2012). In an inner urban primary context where poverty is prevalent, leadership is likely to be more unpredictable (e.g. Lupton, 2006) and the effect on leaders and teachers is more personally demanding. Some suggest that they may not be professionally advantageous places to work (Wrigley, 2003). Finding supply teachers, or school governors, for example, can be harder and greater community leadership is demanded according to Maguire et al. (2006). The risk of burnout is greater yet there is a need to exceed the efforts expended elsewhere. The risk, it would seem, is not being able to consistently exert all the levers necessary on a sustained basis; nevertheless, Harris et al. (2006) show some schools achieve hugely, 'bucking the trend'.

Many leaders embrace the challenge. Leithwood and Louis (2012) describe the 'critical connection' which resides foremost with the head teacher but radiates outwards from teachers who have most influence with children. A leader's influence is not always direct but creates the conditions and the climate. For example, according to Maud Blair et al. (1998, cited by Wrigley, 2003), head teachers in successful multi-ethnic schools provided leadership focused on equity; empathised with political and social factors affecting children; listened to children and parents; endeavoured to see things from their point of view and carefully built links with them.

Successful leaders taking on challenging schools often recognise the symbolism of change: how connecting with and raising the expectations of a community can be a powerful lever for development: they are symbols of 'hope' in Wrigley's (2003) idiom, their leadership then diffuses becoming an attribute of the team (Hallinger and Heck, 2011) as their schools become hubs for their communities. Apple (1996) describes a 'democratic professionalism' that builds alliances with constituencies of children and communities. Many schools have projected such a role onto children and their communities, actively seeking their voice in transforming pedagogy. Gerver (2009), in his personal account of primary school leadership, describes the process of 'selling school to our children' thereby making education 'invitational' – a compelling and intrinsically valuable experience. Chapman and West-Burnham (2010) use the term 'social entrepreneurship' and in Wrigley's (2003) version of school improvement:

'Turning around' a struggling inner-city school involves precisely that – turning around to connect and negotiate with the community and its circumstances, as opposed to building higher institutional walls. (Wrigley, 2003, p. 19)

Schools with distinctive character

Hallinger and Heck (2003) argue that each school must demonstrate its own journey of school improvement created from its own circumstances, context and trajectory: a journey that will depend on what matters most. An OECD survey (2015) found that parents valued reputation, climate and safety above academic achievement. Riley (2017) argued that the community leader engages in bridging (recognising difference while creating dialogue and relationships), challenging (setting boundaries and challenging prejudice), building (developing skills and creating capacity) and place-making (creating a sense of place). These aspects influence a school's reputation with teachers, children, parents and the wider community and relate to how a school is defined and judged and create meaning for participants. With remarkable prescience, more than 50 years ago Blyth argued:

It seems that, in age of rapid change, an autonomous culture which expresses the best within each school's capacity is more necessary than ever, especially since primary education may have the special responsibility of nourishing children's creative imagination when social pressures are often inimical to it. (Blyth, 1967a, p. 192)

Judging leadership in primary schools, in these terms, uses different perceptual 'filters' formed in the everyday interaction in and around a school to explore its impact (the difference it is perceived to make), its standing (the respect in which it is held), its sustainability (the continuity it provides) and its contribution (the difference that it makes to the lives of others) (see Table 6.3). As Bedny and Karkowski (2004) explain, meaning is 'a form of presentation of reality to consciousness'. Sometimes the reputation and trust within a school can be so strong that even a negative inspection can have very little effect on perceptions.

There are, of course, dangers in these 'filters'. When they are overly conservative, too deeply anchored or allowed to drift, they might be the very features that prevent a school from being adaptive or 'expansive'. Indeed, schools which are highly stable can be weakened or unaware of threats because they have paid too little attention to the changes in the surrounding environment and therefore to expanding object and mediated action; it is, for these reasons perhaps, that concepts such as 'coasting' were used as descriptors for schools which were not doing as well as might be expected.

Primary schools often inspire huge loyalty and commitment that is so deep-rooted that when they are subject to pushes and pulls which stretch their capacities, they provide an anchoring stability that continues to offer the basis of

Table 6.3:   Primary education: community and contextual filters

Connection	Links to the community	Key questions
Impact	... the difference it makes	Are the school's effects discernible, so that its communities (teachers, children and parents) know how well they do? Is it responsive and inclusive? Do children feel welcomed and are they successful?
Standing	... the reputation it holds	Is it well established as part of its community? Does it have resilience when things do not go well? Does it listen to its community? Will its community stand up to support it?
Sustainability	... the values it lives by	Is it committed to practices of self-renewal and does it have a foundation offering stability? Are staff known and valued?
Contribution	... the generosity it offers through its relationships	Does it shape and influence through what it develops and produces? Does it learn from others, innovate and share? Is the community able to exemplify how the school helps their children?

trust, acting as a vehicle for continued development. These deepest foundations are based in doing the best for children and are the building blocks for the future.

A culture of collegiality

As the demands on primary schools continually increase, alongside the changes in the head teacher's role, leadership has become 'everyone's responsibility'; potentially distributed, developed and/or delegated across the primary school (Harris, 2003). Earley's (2017) summary suggests focusing on collective development may be one of the most beneficial forms of leadership.

However, first, a cautionary note: some see that a number of versions of primary school leadership are now essentially hierarchical and focused on delivery where leadership and management are simply shifted downwards (see Gunter, 2001), in part – and with reason – as a means of avoiding head teachers being overloaded. Delegation, in its worst forms, according to Gunter, is a neo-Taylorist approach to getting tasks done through the auspices of individuals while portrayed as learning and development: what Hartley (2010) called 'emancipatory rhetoric'. Primary schools need both hierarchy and control, of course, as they have important responsibilities for very young children but nevertheless there are important debates to be had about what MacBeath et al. (2018) term 'positional power'. The contradiction has generated debates about devolved and distributed leadership (Hartley, 2007). Seen positively though, it is a means of building capacity within schools, sharing the demands (e.g. Harris and Spillane, 2008; Harris, 2009; Bush et al., 2019) and making the best use of a talented workforce, which complements what Ancona et al. (2008) so humanly describe as the incomplete or imperfect leader: it seems to depend on how it is done (DeFlaminis, 2013). It also finds a counterpoint in Multi-Academy Trust models of leadership (chief executives or executive head teachers leading more than one school) where the capacity emerges from the availability of staff from multiple organisations working together across school boundaries (e.g. Chapman et al., 2011).

Louis's (2015) description of the leadership of teaching is particularly apposite – the professional community she describes is intensely pedagogical with an emphasis on equity. Shulman and Shulman (2004, p. 259) see teachers, through such a vehicle, as being more able to engage in the complex forms of pedagogical and organisational practice that transform their visions, motives and understandings into a functioning, pragmatic reality.

Professional learning has a long ontology with early exemplification recognisable in the writings of Dewey on enquiry (1938), more recently in Stenhouse's (1975) version of teacher professionalism, while Wiliam (2012), in particular, has both advocated and pioneered the 'professional learning community' which generates collective enquiry. A key point is teachers feeling a sense of belonging in collegial communities which are continually learning and developing pedagogy and where emotional support is also available; however – and with Hargreaves and Shirley's (2009) effervescence in mind – they can be judged successful only when they deepen and sustain. The move to use the term community for these purposes is significant: communities are values-based, intentional, collaborative and productive, thereby collegiate in nature.

Enabling teacher leadership

There are numerous questions in a fast-changing world that relate to the role of the teacher, to their identity and purpose: the complexity of demands upon them means their contribution is vital but also that it must evolve. Expertise and repertoire, including specialism, are likely to be vital components in the advance of primary education (Fullan, 2001). As Hargreaves argues:

> Teaching is increasingly complex work. It requires the highest standards of professional practice in order to perform it well. Teaching is the core profession, the key agent of change in today's knowledge society. (Hargreaves, 2003, p. 125)

Ironically, the downward pressures on teachers have grown, yet, in a seeming paradox, Adams (2011) describes a narrowed professionalism where the prime purpose is delivery (see also Guerriero, 2017) and where meaning is diminished. Teaching is in a process of transition: Troman (2008) observed that contracts can now be short (especially for the newly qualified); workloads are recognised to be high; new career patterns are emerging in different types of schools; and practice is increasingly shared across organisations. Yet, existentially, primary teaching has identities which run deep (see Nias, 1989; Troman, 2008), partly locked in long-standing views of what it means to be a teacher (Carter et al., 2010) and often linked with the concept of being the responsible generalist 'class teacher' (Palmer, 2016). Now with a professional body, the Chartered College of Teaching, to enhance professional standing, extend quality and support teachers to lead the transformation of primary education, it fits closely with the growing call for system leadership of primary education to be drawn from within schools (e.g. Higham et al., 2009; Ainscow, 2015). Significant professional shifts of this type will need public displays of ethics, collegiality, rigorous self-regulation, serious policy activism, a commitment to building professional knowledge and a studied examination of teacher expertise (see Demirkasimoğlu, 2010; also Goepel, 2012).

Teacher development is a complex process: enabled by sustained professional dialogue around pedagogy (Hallinger, 2003; Cordingley et al., 2015), a positive whole-institution learning environment (Leithwood and Jantzi, 2005, 2008), while needing a system underpinned by trust. Teacher leadership is not co-terminus with managerial subject coordination, nor an optional extra: it is a strengthened role with the profession recognising strategic, political, public and collaborative interfaces.

Bangs and Frost (2012) note that while teachers often see it as their role to initiate and lead development within their own school, they do not believe that to be the case when beyond their specific responsibility or locality. Bangs and Frost refer to the HertsCam Network, where they demonstrate that it is eminently possible to get teachers to think in this way (2012, p. 22). Enhancing the capacity for teacher professional leadership, as Bangs and Frost (2012) evidence from their research:

> The argument that teachers should shape their own professional lives in schools, and that their professional voice should be heard both individually and collectively, is now taking centre stage. (Bangs and Frost, 2012, p. 39)

Teacher collaboration in sustained forms seems to have highly significant potential (see OECD, 2016). In these terms, as it goes deeper, the teaching profession increasingly takes responsibility for its own improvement. Professional identities matter and in part this relates to resilience; the ability to overcome the inevitable tensions, dilemmas and challenges. The profession of teaching needs to be constructed so that it is meaningful and motivated (Bangs and Frost, 2012).

The challenge is to move towards a new teacher leadership identity: understanding the potential of pedagogy to unlock learning a powerful personal psychological process and a culturally bound product of the surrounding system of teacher leadership. There are opportunities to remove the dampeners from the teaching profession's voice, but only if it chooses to grapple further with and resolve some very significant challenges: (1) becoming highly skilled in critical analysis, including of theory and research; (2) developing curriculum expertise and capacity, including understanding epistemology (Alexander, 2013) that moves beyond engrained practices, challenging deep-rooted assumption of 'standards, subjects and stability'; (3) mastering the affordances and constraints of emerging pedagogical technologies; and (4) understanding contextual nuance, particularly in terms of diversity, inclusion, belonging and identity.

Reflection point

Is there an aspect of leading expansively; building community connection; developing 'distinctive character'; a culture of collegiality or enabling teacher leadership that you could develop further and deeper? Why would you do this and what benefits would it bring?

Perils, problems and pitfalls

Sometimes when we think in leadership terms it can appear that we do not have time to genuinely ask: what is vital and what potentially is toxic? What is desirable and what is not? Most importantly there is a danger, without reflection, that in leadership terms we simply 'must', deterministically or ideologically, press on without asking those questions.

Perils

Leadership in primary education comes with a number of perils: in a system with 'winners' and losers' comes the potential for failure, often associated with an unsuccessful inspection. Challenges quickly turn into threats as too much change causes other problems: de-moralisation and de-motivation among them, creating feelings of insecurity, failure and frustration. Similarly, fear generated in such circumstances may cause detachment; as threat increases, some people become afraid to care about their work. Even in successful organisations, slowly unable to satisfy ever-increasing demands, maladaptation can allow the gradual erosion of ethical behaviour and/or create the somewhat toxic combination of high levels of accountability delegated downwards with limited ownership of decision-making. Dissonance can occur when an organisation develops internal conflict, brought about perhaps by negative feedback.

Maladaptive organisations can emerge in such circumstances and can be self-defeating: staff may feel and appear to others to be overworked and super-busy but unproductive as they attempt to react to challenges.

From time to time leadership demand outstrips the capacity within an organisation or the wider system, creating pressure and tension and a new approach becomes necessary. The level of energy in response can either appear intense to the point of explosion or, conversely, very low. Reactions to external demand might be very immediate or too tentative, uncertain and lack purpose or a sense of overload, which can lead to reliance on excessive planning and paperwork and a loss of intuitive confidence. The usually considered response of the adaptive leader goes missing as energy depletes.

Problems

Some commentators (Mansell, 2021; Thomson, 2020) have identified problems associated with the changing structure of the school system, perhaps reflecting the transition from local authority control to the new structures of Multi-Academy Trusts and their continued, often rapid, expansion (Baxter; 2019; West and Wolfe, 2018). Increased scrutiny and a focus on governance now aims to iron out issues where, for example, unalloyed ambition had not been subject to sufficient scrutiny or oversight. When problems emerge debate often focuses on the control of the all-powerful leader: the principal/head teacher or, increasingly, in Multi- Academy Trusts, the chief executive - for some, in particular, accrue considerable power. If we need to exercise caution here, Jennings' (2006) account of crisis in the world of business offers guidance, while Thomson's (2020) `School Scandals' is equally cautionary. Jennings (2006) argues that there are problems in systems when the pressure to maintain standards leads to the creation of fear and compliance; when charisma creates an energy for change which ignores real issues and sidesteps them; when people are not intelligently and rigorously held to account (where governance fails to delve deeply); and when a spirit of innovation becomes more important than what is morally right.

Pitfalls

> Leadership, in its vernacular sense, surely involves recognising the perils of the place in which you find yourselves and having some sense of where you could move to and how you might get there. (Wrigley et al., 2012, p. 205)

Given its importance, complexity and contradiction, the discourse of leadership should be debated; sometimes portrayals barely manage to rise above the pejorative or praiseworthy personification (where it becomes illusory and heroic in tone). At the individual level, we see the impact of leaders on change, for example, in the caricature of the so-called Turnaround School, transformed by a charismatic leader who is then publicly lauded. This may well be deserved but may also be short-term: the dangers in this terrain may be that it is not where sustainability thrives. Activity theorists have explored such effects.

They argue that systems, sometimes, become blinded by the dominant narrative: Wertsch (1998) calls them 'terministic screens'. The desired options are often accepted rather than scrutinised and Elmore (2008) talks of an ensuing 'default culture' where capacity for radical and sustained change is diminished.

There are concerns that some forms of cognitive bias (a tendency to think in particular ways) have emerged in relation to ethical matters: or what is considered to be right and fair within the system. Psychologists often argue that it can be difficult to recognise ethical shifts, particularly when the incentives within the system create the conditions for self-interested behaviour and obscure or hide the personal advantage to the beneficiaries. Ethics tend to fade gradually. The biggest pitfall in educational leadership would be losing sight of what is right and what is important.

Reflection point

How do we minimise the perils, problems and pitfalls of leadership? What are the features of ethical leadership and how can they be developed?

The growing importance of governance

Most leaders demonstrate integrity and would subscribe, without hesitation, to Nolan's seven ethical principles of public life (selflessness, integrity, objectivity, accountability, openness, honesty and leadership) (Committee on Standards in Public Life, 1995). Nevertheless, talk of leadership in the context of civic institutions must return to the need for governance, particularly in a system running 'pitfalls, perils and problems'; where Multi-Academy Trusts are growing rapidly (often successfully and imaginatively but with some high-profile failures); and where there is advocacy of innovation. Civic institutions caring for our youngest children need strong governance; this is both a system and process that sets parameters for strategic direction, assesses stakeholder confidence, plans for sustainability, responds to external change, ensures ethical, moral and financial probity, and monitors risk. At their best, in combination, leadership and governance create stewardship. If stewardship is defined as an ethic of care and responsible management, then part of this is searching for equity and social justice by ensuring that every child is valued and has the support needed to be successful.

Conclusions: leadership for today and tomorrow

Arguments will continue about how we construct leadership; nevertheless, what is confirmed in these debates is that leadership is firmly legitimised as critical in educational change. Above all, the focus of leadership should be pedagogical (Atwal, 2019): in their seven claims about leadership, Leithwood et al. recognise that, 'School leadership improves teaching and learning, indirectly and most powerfully, by improving the status of significant key classroom and school conditions' (2019, p. 8).

In England, leadership, in primary education, is alive and well, among the very people who practise it, even if they are caught in a complex, sometimes contradictory policy context and changing societal demands – leadership continues to evolve but still shines. For primary education, its character is suggested by the 'Learning without Limits' description of leadership at Wroxham School where the head teacher's aim was 'to create in reality their vision of an education based on inclusive, egalitarian principles, including an unshakeable bedrock belief in everybody's capacity to learn' (Swann et al., 2012, p. 7).

During the Covid-19 milieu of political argument (including the tensions with trade unions) and media fallout about 'closing' and 'opening' schools, primary education often rose above the discourse and argument creating a narrative of compassion and care: adaptive while creating meaning, clarity, space and energy. This is why leadership has such an important psychological effect. Through the socio-cultural lens, Kaptelinin and Naardi put this particularly well:

> Human beings develop their own meanings and values not by processing sensory inputs but by appropriating the meanings and values objectively existing in the world. Organisations relate to meaning. (Kaptelinin and Nardi, 2006, p. 50)

Leading the pedagogy of primary schools has become increasingly consistent with the idea of the 'prosumer' (see Toffler, 1980), a term constructed from the blending of 'producer' and 'consumer'. As prosumers, leaders increasingly engage laterally across the profession and beyond immediate boundaries to engage with research, successful practices and technological innovation. The wealth of available approaches, resources, groups and professional development has never been greater. An expansive leadership needs the creation of new pedagogies where the Bakhtinian idea of heteroglossia flourishes: that is, positively taking the voices of others and using them in the formulation of pedagogy, and in socio-cultural terms, designing and customising pedagogy according to contextual need.

Responding to context and creating distinctive character in a school may require divergence as leadership considers, perhaps especially now, how their school stands apart; how it connects to what people (especially children) care about and ensures that a feeling of esteem permeates within a distinctively positive organisational climate. Yet expect, too, convergence emerging from evidence, research and collaboration where there is synergic sharing of professional knowledge.

There is a powerful opportunity here: ideas, potentially constructed by professional groups, on the basis of emphasis, can create powerful patterns of development when they connect to wider communities, activating new energy within the system. In our fast-changing, highly demanding world, moving beyond deterministic conceptions of culture and society by accepting that individuals can shape and reshape objects raises new questions and dilemmas but can be intensely productive in terms of educational change, especially if there is an increasing sense of ownership.

It will need leaders who are the strongest, healthiest version of themselves – Brené Brown's (2018) wholehearted, brave leaders – but more importantly, evidentially, leaders focused on pedagogy (see Earley, 2013, 2017) and embracing expansive approaches with an ethic of stewardship. As time passes, new leaders will enter the system bringing diversity and further elaboration and will 'bring an energy and openness to experimentation that is different and new' (Edge et al., 2017, p. 220).

By exploring leadership it almost inevitably causes us to explore the 'relational' elements of primary education: those things that bring people together, including collaborative and community dimensions. In expansive learning and leadership, we see together the challenges of creating objects, goal-setting, resource and knowledge management, system design, creating engagement and partnerships, in relationships, in organising and in self-evaluating. Despite the wealth of knowledge now available about school leadership, there is still more to explore particularly in the causal relationship between how leaders work and their resulting impact. However, if we accept the significance of leadership, then in a socio-cultural approach it nurtures:

- 'A mind to learn' – leadership's first priorities are children and pedagogies; it inspires and celebrates learning and demonstrates ambition.
- Enculturation and transformation – leadership has high expectations of everyone; it oversees the design of rich curriculum, cultivates an absorbing learning culture, plans skilfully and responsively, is curious and continually reflective.
- A communicative core – leadership is dialogic; there is a rich oral and literary environment; it creates a secure, safe and positive climate.
- Cultural relativism – leadership is welcoming (invitational); influential and mutual; respectful, tolerant and trusting; offers stewardship; removes barriers to learning.
- Pedagogic communities of practice – leadership is catalytic; builds capacity; creates a team and connects widely; there is a powerful sense of togetherness.

Delving deeper

Curiosity and Powerful Learning (Hopkins and Craig, 2014) is one of a series of Powerful Learning manuals – the approaches are drawn from practical experience, have been tested in practice and refined over time, and explore ten theories of action, making them particularly useful to school and system leaders.

Next: This chapter has focused on leadership and management largely (though not solely) in the context of the individual primary school; the next chapter looks at the wider context exploring collaboration, the self-improving system and the concept of 'systemness'.

7 Together: a collaborative approach

This chapter is about collaboration, the concept of a self-improving education system and broader questions about the education policy context.

It explores: *a connected and collaborative system* • *the self-improving system* • *why collaborate?* • *'systemness'* • *the tangled ecosystem* • *a self-regulatory framework* • *place, democracy and communities* • *building blocks of collaboration* • *making collaboration sustainable*

'Well, now that we have seen each other,' said the unicorn, 'if you'll believe in me, I'll believe in you.'

– Lewis Carroll, *Through the Looking Glass*

A connected and collaborative system

In this chapter, the socio-cultural lens turns to the complex, often tangled and sometimes contradictory ecosystem that connects the components of primary education together: first, it focuses on collaboration between schools before turning to the environment of politics and policy in which they operate. Along the way it explores the concept of a self-improving system, forms of collaboration, system leadership and place, concluding with a consideration of the key building blocks for a system that works well together.

Sometimes debates about primary education have focused on the autonomy of schools rather than the connections, interrelationships and interactions of the system when it is those webs that characterise vibrant systems. As Margaret Wheatley (1999) put it: we live in relationship, connected to everything else. It is the degree to which this is the case that varies, how we create those connections and to what ends. From the perspective of socio-cultural dynamics, development is a collective process, realised in context and emerging powerfully from processes of dialogue and activity where generative change creates new versions of pedagogy. Many primary educators recognise this and connect together in productive activities – for example, through ITT (initial teacher training) partnerships – that are skilfully planned and imaginatively implemented, deepening the link between teaching and learning. When systems, particularly those that serve accountability, isolate individual teachers, leaders and schools, they potentially stymie such development.

The network society enables communication in new forms that, not too long ago, were unimaginable, and what Engeström (2000) describes as 'knots' of collaborators are increasingly prevalent, partly enabled by technologies that ease communication and cross the traditional boundaries of institutions and geography (e.g. WomenEd, CollectiveEd, eduTwitter, TeacherTapp). Development increasingly involves not just primary teachers and leaders but, inter alia, technology providers, educational researchers and advisers, influencers and bloggers; and increasingly in Multi-Academy Trusts (MATs), lawyers, accountants and architects. There are many other partners. These 'knots' Engeström (2000) describes as 'pulsating, distributed and partially improvised orchestration', often between those who are otherwise more loosely connected. The concept of knots enables 'tying, untying and retying' separate threads with the locus of control regularly shifting: the opportunity exists to open a new landscape of 'dispersed, fluctuating and weakly bounded community forms' (Wenger, 2007) resulting, eventually, in the production of pedagogy. In potentially contradictory form, at the same time, MATs are proliferating; these, increasingly large, formal, multi-school structures continue to grow, circumscribed by the policies of New Public Management in the form of contracts, governance and accountability (Greany and Higham, 2018). The system of primary education is asymmetrical: a combination of community schools, faith schools, Free Schools and Academies (standalone and in various multi-academy forms) under differing governance often operate in close proximity. The landscape of the middle-tier (taken here to mean the varied bodies that operate between schools and central government) is equally irregular: there are new regional structures (for example, the Regional Schools Commissioners) and newly designated and emergent organisational forms (for example, Teaching School hubs and School Centred Initial Teacher Training providers) alongside the local authorities.

The emerging challenge is to orchestrate and energise development across this complex system; for Deming, 'The greater the interdependence between components, the greater will be the need for cooperation and communication between them' (1994, p. 96). This demands more than loose networks of collaborators; Deming contends that 'The obligation of any component is to contribute to the system, not to maintain its own competitive measure' (p. 96). Fullan and Quinn (2010) call for 'collective capacity building', where the layers within the system contribute distinctively to its improvement. Fullan's (2021) descriptor, 'systemness', is apposite; when a series of goals emerge that all participants recognise as important and, partially or wholly, contribute towards: dynamic, not enervating, they become the considered province and expectation of all education professionals.

> ... collective responsibility is not just a commitment; it is the exercise of capabilities on a deep and wide scale. It encompasses positive competition: challenging the limits of what is humanly and professionally possible. (Hargreaves and Fullan, 2012, p. 142)

Many schools offered so much along these lines during the Covid-19 pandemic, sharing their knowledge and expertise freely and openly as collective responsibilities came to the fore, collaboration creating transformations to support the learning of all children.

A collaborative self-improving system

An emergent feature of the English system of primary education has been the rise in collaboration (West, 2010) through networks (groups of interconnecting organisations or people), partnerships (groups working to achieve a common object while retaining independence, sometimes on local authority footprints) and, increasingly, combinatory structures (formally connected through legal agreement and usually in the form of MATs), all of which see developments take place between and across schools. Together, various formations (e.g. clusters, federations, strategic alliances) are strongly linked with endogenous development, or the 'self-improving system'.

The principle of self-improvement, in contrast to imposed models of change, is that it is a generative process that occurs within and between schools. By inference, the self-improving system does not need assistance from the outside but has the relationships, capacity and resources within it to generate improvement. Naturally, it is an attractive notion for those working in schools for, in its purest form, education professionals have self-determination. The collaborative lens suggests the opportunity to address emerging issues, develop pedagogy and address issues particular to localities, benefiting from capacities beyond a single entity. The argument is that networks, partnerships and structures create energy, solve problems, build allegiance and create collective pools of knowledge and expertise (see Furlong, 2014).

The self-improving system might still feel ephemeral: the descriptive language, 'system leadership' or 'self-improving system' for example, has increasing currency yet retains ambiguity: they are professionally attractive concepts but difficult to define, interpreted and understood differently according to context. Networks, partnerships and structures (especially MATs), too, reflect different approaches, from informal, locally coordinated energy to regional and national MATs with multitudinous schools. In such circumstances, as Engeström and Ahonen (2001) describe, there is constant 'interpretation, negotiation and synthesising', one effect of which is that local systems are increasingly stratified (Greany and Higham, 2018). Collectively, too, they suggest the view that we have reached the limits of the capacity of the individual standalone school; conceptually at least, extended organisational forms move the focus from the individual unit to the system.

It is, however, a broad landscape: working to support a school in challenging circumstances will require different skills and capacities from those needed in a mutually constituted peer-peer support network, or the business development and organisational design skills that go along with MAT leadership (Hill et al., 2012). For example, in a study of school-school partnerships, Muijs (2015) identified positive benefits, suggesting, in particular, the benefits for schools in receipt of support. Other studies, too, point in this direction (e.g. Chapman et al., 2011). Overall, the argument is that when well-constructed the affordances of collaboration offer economies of scale and distribute capacity that may be unavailable to individual schools; opening the system enables new meanings and understandings (Bates, 2013).

The idea of a 'self-improving education system' was established, popularised and problematised most significantly by Hargreaves' reports (2010, 2011) for the National Centre for School Leadership. 'Self-improving' connected with many professionals and emerged powerfully despite being almost incidental in the White Paper of 2010. Hargreaves' vision sees three dimensions come together: professional development (through joint practice development, talent identification, mentoring and coaching, and distributed staff information); partnership competence (through social capital, governance, evaluation and challenge, and distributed system leadership); and a collaborative capital dimension (through analytic investigation, creative entrepreneurship, alliance architecture and disciplined innovation). A vision for a connected and collaborative system of primary education recognises the importance of opening outwards, laterally, based in people collaborating together with pedagogies constantly being re-worked and re-imagined (through teacher enquiry, lesson study, exploring research into teaching strategies and building them into practice, for example).

The most recent and extensive outcome of policy changes has been the proliferation of primary schools joining together to form the newly emergent MATs. They have a stronger framework than many of the pre-existing networks and partnerships: they are carefully wrapped in legislation and contractual management, removed from local democratic control with their own demanding and legally binding governance in a form of 'coercive autonomy' (Greany and Higham, 2018). They emerged from various motivations, including: the promise of autonomy; support of failing schools; and to formalise partnership. Some schools make conscious choices to change the way they are governed when they join them. Now Trusts running several or many schools through 'chief executives' and 'executive head teachers' are firmly established (Greany and Higham, 2018) in the landscape. Examples of dissimilarity are emerging, not just in scale and size, but also approach: Salokangas and Chapman (2014) conducted a case study of two contrasting MATs, where their respective cultures had led to governance and leadership evolving differently. Successful MATs have a strong focus on school improvement (Hopkins, 2016) that includes: a deep understanding of each of their component Academies; tailoring of strategies accordingly; deploying expertise effectively; using inquiry-based learning; engagement with research; learning from others; and, moreover, they can demonstrate their impact (Hill, 2016). How – and in what form – large, maturing MATs create collaborative practices within and, importantly, beyond their boundaries, will not be fully understood for some time: as they grow, they create their own architecture (see Greany and Higham, 2018). The concern would be if MATs become overly hierarchical, insular, reliant solely on central teams and focused on their own accountabilities. If they contribute to the system only on their own terms, if their governance somehow replicates the bureaucratic caricature they were intended to replace, then their critics can legitimately ask, what has changed?

If MATs provide a structural solution with strong governance, their cousins the Teaching Schools were based on a networked model. In their evaluation, Gu et al. (2014) explain that they were each able to develop highly individual organisational forms reflecting diversity of expertise and knowledge (Walker, 2017). Coupled with a powerful, almost tangible moral purpose, their alliances of schools allowed greater horizontal movement between partners. The motivation for involvement was largely based in active participative choices that emerged from the freedom to choose the level of involvement and the less exacting legal governance requirements for Teaching School partnerships. They provided, for example, subject-specific experts, networks to support middle leaders and collective induction programmes for newly qualified teachers. Sometimes, organisations networked in this way, like Teaching Schools, are vulnerable to those that prefer simple output-based measurements: their influence will be necessarily indirect at times and illustrate that sophisticated measures of efficacy are needed for this type of collaboration. When system-wide implementation is required, they could offer a vital distributing infrastructure that can take developments to scale. (*Note*: They have been superseded by a smaller number of selected Teaching School hubs.)

Networks, partnerships and MATs still generate more questions than answers: in what situation, which solution? Is it through networks that are temporary interconnections that join together to solve problems or create resources? Or partnerships that pool together resources to address challenges together, or through structures formally joining schools together? How should this happen? Is there an optimum size for new school structures? There have been a number of high-profile MAT failures, how do we avoid this? What role too for the diminished local authorities – from control to influence and a role in actively shaping local priorities, perhaps?

In 2021, given this complexity, when trying to understand concepts such as 'collaboration' and 'self-improving', we are not describing a 'single form', or a mature system; indeed, we might expect to see schools involved with a range of networks, partnerships and structures, each generated by different motives and opportunities. There is a systemic asymmetry. Stimulated by such understandings, most primary schools are already engaged in rich and varied networks: for the development of pedagogy these are fast-moving, innovative and expansive, and this may be distinctively different to the necessarily rigorous nature of the formal governance needed as part of large corporate organisations.

Reflection point

What networks, partnerships and structures are you involved with? What is your experience of the self-improving system? What benefits does it bring? Are there any drawbacks?

Why collaboration?

Collaboration offers primary education an opportunity to overcome the unequal distribution of practice where ideas travel unevenly across its topography. It provides a clear antidote to isolation where active engagement brings benefits underpinned, according to Scardamalia and Bereiter (2006), by a commitment to progress and to genuinely moving forwards, a willingness to seek common understanding rather than just agreement, and – vitally – expansion of the basis of accepted knowledge. It is about realising what can be achieved together and creating images of possibility which 'emerges when objects are represented in fields with the help of which one can depict meanings in movement and transformation' (Engeström, 2007b, p. 1).

Ainscow (2015) makes five observations, his cautionary realism recognising the potential and benefits in releasing the energy of collaboration when he suggests that: (1) schools know more than they use; (2) the expertise of school staff is largely unarticulated; (3) evidence is the engine for change; (4) working together is socially complex; and (5) working together creates relationships that make things happen. There are many possibilities. When faced with redesigning a curriculum area for the first time, even with readily available resources, accessing expertise with experience of a similar task can ease the process. The opportunities of deep learning through 'joint practice development' are often stronger than figuring out a process alone. Programmes of 'instructional rounds', for example, where teachers from a range of schools visit different classrooms and reflect together, can serve to develop powerful theories of action (City et al., 2009; Hopkins and Craig, 2014), strengthening the link between teaching and learning. Or where consistency of pedagogy, perhaps, through the considered choice of a phonics model, emerges from the studied insights of professionals deciding together. Ainscow et al. observed:

> … we saw compelling evidence of how groups of teachers – and support staff – could carry out inquiries that stimulated innovations into ways of engaging hard-to-reach groups of learners. We also saw how partnerships within and between schools helped to create the climate within which such innovations could take place. (Ainscow et al., 2012, p. vii)

The range of possibilities is immense, so it is important to recognise where the potential benefits lie.

Collaboration, in these terms, offers a basis for development that is negotiated and allows for the shared repertoire of the community to emerge through the creation of pedagogies that can become the 'signatures' of the collective. Overall, there seem to be four main fields:

- extending expertise (particularly curriculum and instructional skills, breadth of curriculum offer);
- examining pedagogy (becoming evidence informed, joint enquiry);
- pooling resources and benefiting from economies of scale (sharing costs, access to specialist services, supporting inclusion);
- distributing knowledge (spreading skills and knowledge, teacher moderation of children's achievements, community provision).

Successful schools and localities understand the complexities of their position in the education system and respond accordingly. The discourse of education is beginning to recognise diversity of context and the power of professionals working together to develop solutions through joint activities (team teaching and lesson study, perhaps). The asymmetry of the system might prove advantageous if it allows a collaborative variety to emerge. Even so, there remains a strong sense that individual primary schools can be successful, despite suggestions to the contrary, but there is widespread agreement that schools cannot thrive entirely as islands; the psychological processes of internalisation and externalisation demand engagement with wider ideas and practices.

When talk is of structure (and, of course, it is important) this is not the 'heart' of collaboration – energy, expertise and capacity generate developments in pedagogy however it is organised. Wenger (1998) described the structure of a 'community of practice' consisting of three interrelated aspects: 'mutual engagement', 'joint enterprise' and 'shared repertoire'; then, as 'movement' builds, there are (a) shared understandings, (b) powerful belief systems and (c) meaningful activity. In this sense, the self-improving system needs agency and collaborative skills to create the vision, rules, relationships and infrastructure that take innovation to scale. The features of the collaborative communities needed for powerful professional learning are set out in Table 7.1.

Table 7.1: Features of collaborative learning communities

- A strong orientation to pedagogy and children's achievements
- Flexibly organised rather than fixed
- Evidence-informed
- Designing and adapting professional development over sustained periods of time
- Active involvement from all the collaborative community
- Based in a system of mutual exchange
- Recognises that multiple collaborations are needed within and between schools
- Has lateral and horizontal structures allowing a strong emphasis on coaching and mentoring

Adapted from Engeström (2007a)

Reflection point

Do the features of collaborative learning communities (suggested above) accurately capture what is required to create successful processes of professional learning?

Primary education as a system

The recent changes to the structures of primary education and the growth of collaborative connections are so complex that they require extensive description and evaluation (see Greany and Higham, 2018). Nevertheless, the self-improving system suggests that the stronger our commitment to working together within primary education, the greater will be its overall resilience. Whichever path is chosen, collaboration is now recognised increasingly as a productive feature of growth and development (McGregor et al., 2006).

However, England's self-improving education is not a vacuum. It is encumbered by legislation and policy; managed by bureaucratic institutions (e.g. Department for Education, local authorities and Regional Schools Commissioners) and populated by a complex mix of types of schools in multifarious configurations. Primary education is a 'developmental environment' where control remains, in many respects, centralised through the powers of the secretary of state (Brighouse, 2011) and where development is often interrupted by their relatively short terms in office and rapid succession. Certainly, the idea of primary schools being autonomous professional organisations removed from system governance and regulation is not the picture in England (see, for example, Gibton, 2017).

A report by the McKinsey Foundation (Mourshed et al., 2010) argued that successful education systems establish collaborative practice between teachers, supported by a mediating layer (or middle-tier) of infrastructure. 'Developmental environments' are a product of policy decisions that are both extensive and complex with affordances that have systemic, collective, expansive and capacity-building elements and effects. I describe them below under four headings (see also Table 7.2):

- *Policy space*: the combination of policy, political priorities, funding, central initiatives and accountability measures and the architecture of the school system whose effect is systemic.
- *Collaborative space*: the systems which enable partnership, knowledge production, initial teacher education, professional development and which encourage collective impact.
- *Leadership space*: the devolution of power, the climate for professional decision-making and the extent to which independence and interdependence mesh together to create capacity.

- *Innovation space*: the way in which pedagogy is expanded: the support for research and development; for evidence-based practices; and for the introduction of new technologies.

Table 7.2: Systemic conditions for change

	Policy Space (policy, funding, priorities, systemic structuring, values, accountability, equity)	
Innovation Space (research, development, knowledge-building, innovation dissemination, technical)	**Developmental Environment (system, collective, pedagogy, capacity)**	**Collaborative Space** (partnership, sharing, knowledge production, collective impact, governance)
	Leadership Space (climate of growth, pedagogic action, innovation, continuing professional development)	

Centrally initiated system development certainly has its place, shaping those four spaces, and when coherent can impact positively. The reforms of New Labour remain illustrative: arguably the most challenging, wide-ranging and extensive educational changes ever attempted in England. They applied a wide range of policy levers that were striking in their ambition, above all, to raise standards and modernise the teaching profession. If they faltered, it was, perhaps, because of not fully anticipating the complex topography; or by not maximising collaboration and unleashing professional commitment and innovation. Perhaps, on reflection, they tended to impose models and arguably worked on too many fronts simultaneously.

Reflecting on New Labour's reforms, however, recognises that powerful systemic combinations generate energy and it is in creating ownership that change forces are most effective. Directive change can be effective but needs professional commitment (compliance will often diminish enthusiasm) while strategic direction and the allocation of resources can sustain the energy of so-called 'grass roots' development that could, without infrastructure and resource, burn brightly and fade away. Lateral developments offer commitment and learning across organisations, building 'inside out' (using inner strengths and capabilities) and 'outside in' (creating value matched to the needs of children and communities): together they serve to bind systems together. As an illustration, Brown et al. (2017) showed the combined effect of systemic leverage in Tower Hamlets, which included: clear leadership, effective school improvement models and favourable funding, while the evaluators found community development was essential to the turnaround of the district. Leaders went to great lengths to strengthen relations and engagement, citing Payne (2008), it appears that this is a vital ingredient. Development requires volition, multiple agencies and the exercise of a variety of levers (see Beckett and Wood, 2012): it tends to be localised across multiple layers.

The aim is to build what Engeström calls 'collaborative intentionality capital' (see Edwards, 2009): the system accepting both accountability and responsibility. In these terms, self-improving never means isolating: a feature of it must be active decision-making as part of wider engagement, or as West described it: the potency of local ownership and local ideas (2010, p. 96). This recognises, too, that many challenges require adaptive responses, needing new insights that are 'not amenable to authoritative expertise and standard operating procedures' (Heifetz and Linksky, 2002, p. 13).

Reflection point

Which elements of the system of primary education are effective and enabling of schools in meeting the needs of their children? Which impede schools in fulfilling their responsibilities effectively?

The system must engage with the thorny challenges for primary education, equity and inclusion among them, through the values, commitments and contexts of primary educators. If we want powerful change processes that are based in evidence, are consistent, flexible and diverse, they have to be multi-layered and multi-dimensional, and as Elmore (2004) pointed out, pay sufficient attention to building the capacity to realise them. Fullan offers a reminder: 'The solution is not a program; it is a small set of common principles and practices relentlessly pursued. Focused practitioners, not programs drive success' (Fullan, 2010, p. 59).

A tangled ecosystem: striving for interdependence

The challenge of system change is clear: where every school is successful for every child. Significant contemporary issues facing primary education currently are still caught in multiple layers of structure and require attention through the levers of policy. They include:

- International evidence that contends that successful systems are equitable where stratification between schools is lower (OECD, 2012). The segregation of the English system remains a concern (see Gorard, 2018).

- Some observers argue that current policies are creating hierarchies of schools; some have ready access to opportunities and therefore benefit from policies differentially (see Greany, 2015).
- The tail of underachievement among disadvantaged pupils is uppermost among concerns.

A collaborative self-improving system must attend to such pressing issues if every child is to flourish. Some research has demonstrated that only a proportion of educational outcomes are within a school's control, suggesting the need to explore place and the needs of communities more fully (e.g. Groves and West-Burnham, 2020). There are a number of emergent questions.

Who leads the middle-tier and what purpose does it serve? The middle-tier remains unsettled and is, arguably, a crowded space as the layers of system architecture change. If the middle-tier is less defined, has lost democratic accountabilities, and become increasingly corporate (see Ball, 2007), perhaps some of the glue has been lost? Yet, in many local authorities schools have come together to create powerful local partnerships, demonstrating both commitment and contribution regardless of school type. Even so in such an active space, expect dilemmas, tensions and contradictions to exist: the extended admissions choices of one school may detrimentally impact on another. What happens if the needs or wants of a locality are in conflict with the expansion of a Multi-Academy Trust? Who is the arbiter ensuring fairness and that the system works for all children? *New forms of civic leadership are possible to provide oversight, unite partners and focus development so they benefit children first and foremost.*

With equity and inclusion writ large, how does a school-led system address them? Systems that support vulnerable and disadvantaged children are critical, particularly in times when resources are reducing. Structuring fair access panels, resource allocation systems and alternative provision, for example, works when there is active engagement of all in deep forms of partnership that take responsibility for all the pupils in an area. *Values are central and any competitive instinct must be channelled into an ambition for all children to do well.*

What form does challenge take in a self-improving system? Our current system of accountability lies squarely with individual schools and institutions: in a collaborative, self-improving system this is timely for review. How does the system harness evidence about how well it is doing and challenge itself to make further improvements? Can it develop ways of focusing on ensuring vulnerable and disadvantaged children are effectively supported and their localities meet their needs? It implies a much more active involvement in working with the specifics of context. *Embracing challenge is the commitment to participate and explore together ways of improvement.*

Each of these questions relies on a commitment to interdependence, namely: (1) finding intelligent forms of accountability that focus on quality and champion children, potentially moving beyond individual schools as the focus; and (2) the importance of community involvement and leadership of place as the ground for action in overseeing further development within a self-improving system.

A self-regulatory framework

In a self-improving system, among the many questions are those that relate to judging effectiveness. Greany (2014) argued that there were a growing number of questions about whether or not the system of Ofsted inspection was robust and impartial – in short, fit for purpose. Typical arguments concern whether it is too punitive as a force for change, whether there is sufficient recourse when needed, and whether there is too strong an emphasis on regulation. Regardless of the answers, what is clear is that in England Ofsted has become an arbiter of what matters; the 2019 framework had as profound an effect as any with its shift in focus towards curriculum. Perhaps now, though, it needs a different outlook for as Fitz-Gibbon (1996) comments, a complex education system should not have a reductive means of accountability.

Might we build inspection into the fabric of a self-improving system, so that it mediates self-evaluation and works alongside systems of peer review following the ethos of MacBeath's (1999) *Schools Must Speak for Themselves?* Schools would enter an 'inspection' prepared to explore uncertainty or see it, perhaps, as an enquiry – currently the stakes are too high but the intended shift is from summative to formative, based in 'collaborative negotiation' that gets closer to what Park (2013) calls the 'acoustic' of the school. This movement towards what MacBeath et al. (2018) term 'multiple horizontal school accountability' shares the responsibility for improving practice. A system predicated in self-improvement needs intelligent accountability: if there is underachievement there needs to be an explanation of why.

Might inspection support the agreed vision, aims and purposes of primary education and be engaged in supporting and evaluating their achievement? If the inspection system remained impartial, able to gain the trust of the teaching profession and the public while acting as an authoritative adviser on policy, as Cunningham and Raymont (2010) suggest, this would position it rather differently to its current guise. Engaging the leadership of primary schools closely in such a system so that it acts as a motivator and driver for better practice could also bring those responsible for evaluation closer to the explanatory 'action' too. Fitz-Gibbon and Tymms (2002) suggested that broader frameworks (that is multiple indicators) offer a fairer comparison across schools, while Park (2013) also argues for multi-perspective inspection that involves valuing the perspective of leaders, staff, students, parents and inspectors rather than one prevailing group. Would we be brave enough to embrace diversity of practice, endorse cultural relativism, recognising schools in inner urban areas may differ from their more affluent neighbours and open doors for peer review? Within an accountability system there will still need to be mechanisms to challenge assumptions made by schools, for example, if they have low aspirations.

There does need to be an element of external scrutiny, and making shifts of this type will have to convince others of primary education's efficacy, including the public and politicians. Nevertheless, by learning with and from schools, rather than solely judging, the accountability system could develop understandings that support schools in pursuing their ambitions through their pedagogies. A self-evaluating system could take a position on all matters relating to education particularly within a locality, influencing and shaping: a national system integrally connected to the locality, enriching and drawing upon its resources.

Which brings us to the importance of 'places' and 'communities'.

Place, democracy and the needs of communities

Hargreaves and Shirley (2009) refer to the 'fourth way': in which there is democracy, in a very local way, and professionalism, in a public, collaborative form that serves to enhance public confidence in the education system. Hatcher (2011) argues that what is needed is a 'democracy' formed from a combination of 'elected representative democracy' and 'direct deliberative participatory democracy': a vehicle for targeted action on equity, social justice and inclusion. A public education system needs its guardians who restore the concept of an external environment that allows the local 'commonwealth' to flourish (Brighouse, 2012). Children are shaped by place, so responding to it builds the civic connections and actions, especially at a time when support for vulnerable children is diminishing and, sometimes, local governance has been removed.

It is not surprising in this context perhaps that the New Visions for Education Group (2012) recognise that democratically elected authorities must be able to respond to the educational challenges associated with place. Ainscow argues that 'school focused strategies have to be complemented with efforts to engage the wider community' (2015, p. 102) as many opportunities transcend the individual institution. It is necessary to create the conditions for effective decision-making to be established which can integrate services around the child (from the earliest age; the first 100 days where evidence suggests educational impact is most profound, perhaps), their family (what it means to grow up in the twenty-first century; working with the Living Wage Foundation, perhaps) or community (maybe through an Ashoka 'change makers' programme). It might include family support teams and consider patterns of child care and family learning. The Scandinavian tradition of 'social pedagogy' offers many insights. This extends educational development beyond school, building on cultural, sporting and youth offers within a locality. Museums, theatres, universities and businesses – all can become active in the education partnership at work in a locality, as can 'alternative' provision and early years providers. A self-improving education system should be part of a wider approach to meeting the needs of children, integrated within a community strategy, but encouraging a form of grass-roots community activity at local level will only be successful if those participating feel they can genuinely make a contribution.

Creating 'public value' in a multi-sectorial networked, open leadership framework where those participating locally define the specifics is a challenging collaborative demand, yet one that many want to be part of. In this model, contributory partnerships would be formed allowing schools to be set within and draw on the strength of their local community. Well-designed organisational forms will be needed to do this. Virkunnen et al. (2010) argue for 'collaborative communities' such as, for example, Strive Together, which combines values of community, courage, equity, progress and results. Such a community is based on shared object and negotiated value, the participants' ability to contribute, mutual trust in each other's capability, and the emergence of non-zero-sum outcomes of the collaboration (Virkunnen et al., 2010, p. 23). Creating public value partnerships means putting chances and choices for children at the heart of partnership looking at how talent can be developed in every individual, to create aspiration, helping children to become the change-makers.

The challenge is to create new co-developing partnerships so that schools remain unique organisations that meet the needs of their communities, yet committed to a wider collaborative goal that benefit from the greater resilience and capacity which comes from collective action. A partnership of this type will have many requirements: it will need the power to 'convene', contextual analysis, the skills of brokerage, access to capacity and a strong mandate. The democratic system needs to be supported by evolutionary and emergent consultative arrangements which create new developments and infrastructure which can grow, where ideas and approaches can be not just ignited but also sustained. If a system like this has public accountability, the New Visions for Education Group (2012) suggest this will need: skilled guiding governance with appropriate powers and responsibilities commensurate with the size of locality; an appropriately democratic structure; access to skills and expertise; and an agenda that serves the disadvantaged, actively seeking equity and inclusion.

The national system would focus on setting direction while a local board could interpret those aims, support innovation and experimentation, target available resources and provide accountability. The board would create the emphasis on school leaders to be pro-active in forming partnerships and dismantle barriers, harmonise around strategy and protect and strengthen the most vulnerable children and schools. The distinctive character for each institution would remain but clearly delineated in such a framework. As part of this autonomy, governance arrangements would provide children, teachers and community with an active role in decision-making. It would of course be necessary for all aspects of such a system to be transparent and accountable. It would be a system dependent on mutuality.

Developing the ability to understand one another's responsibilities means that empathy is vital but it is in the power to create and shape change that benefits lie. Such approaches will increasingly confront the choice between collective decision-making and individual autonomy: the likelihood is that the changing system is less scripted with more emergent features requiring leadership that is both responsive and creative.

Table 7.3: Features of public value education partnerships

- A strong orientation to equity and inclusion
- A commitment to interdependence
- A mandate for action and a sense of identity
- Appropriately democratic forms with multiple layers, if appropriate
- Informed and sophisticated analysis of the local area
- Consistent, clear and transparent governance
- Brokers expertise from the most appropriate sources
- Coordinates the key resources available to the locality
- Evaluates the impact of local partners on children's outcomes
- Has suitable levels of expertise to fulfil its responsibilities
- Engages multiple partners from a range of providers and services

Reflection point

How can we move forwards with the self-improving system? Can we manage the twin challenges: collaborating to improve pedagogy and working together for the benefit of localities/places (creating public value)?

Building blocks of collaboration

There remain significant challenges on primary education's journey to becoming a self-improving system with coherent and powerful approaches needed that leverage collective energies. From the analysis, it seems that definitive choices should underpin the self-improving system: an emphasis on multi-layered system leadership; a strong emphasis on evidence-based approaches; and the adoption of productive new technologies. Building networks, partnerships and structures can meet a range of systemic needs by:

- sharing professional expertise and knowledge across a wider system;
- developing resilience and strength across organisations;

- addressing issues of equity and inclusion and challenges facing a locality or clustered across areas;
- bringing together multi-disciplinary partners to meet children's needs and aspirations.

A self-improving system cannot hide behind professional cover, it must turn to the public and demonstrate its efficacy locally and nationally.

We should be cautious too: for collaboration may create the illusion of substantive change, when it is superficial and not transformational. Of course, collaboration is not a panacea, as Lektorsky explains:

> Development is collective, not individual, though it is influenced differentially by individuals, therefore, the structuring of the overall system also defines power: this is profoundly important for system design because it can both give and take away power. (Lektorsky, 2009, p. 80)

Lektorsky recognises that collaboration is dependent on how people connect; whether participants 'accept the norms of the system, challenge them, transcend or transform them' (ibid.). If motivations conflict, then tension might well emerge. These ways of working can be particularly vulnerable to 'marketisation' and can be weakened because of it, particularly if one or more members are seen to be actively pursuing particular agendas (their own self-interest or aggrandisement, for example) that may not serve the common good (Waslander et al., 2010).

Here are two conditions (trust and reciprocity), two impacts (system resilience and distributed capacity) and two intentions (sustainable innovation and expansive energy) that obtain whether we are describing professional learning communities or public value education partnerships.

Condition 1: Trust

If peers are to work effectively together across a system, they need to understand each other and feel 'trust' (see Covey, 2006). Trust-building is a key part of leadership (Handford and Leithwood, 2013) arising from activity; rarely achieved theoretically, it is an inherently psychological and human quality (see Finnigan and Daly, 2012). Stephen Covey argues not just that development is dependent upon trust but that sustainable partnerships and collaboration will progress at a pace determined by it – he calls it the 'speed of trust':

> When you trust people, you have confidence in them – in their integrity and in their abilities. When you distrust people you are suspicious of them – of their integrity, their agenda, their capabilities or their track record. It's that simple. (Covey, 2006, p. 5)

When it is absent and self-interest flourishes, there is a reluctance to take risks and an inherent conservatism can emerge, motivation diminishes and energy dissipates. In collaboration there is a need to care for each other and build energising relationships. *Implication*: Trust is built where integrity, reliability and dependability are present: trust serves to creates security and confidence.

Condition 2: Reciprocity

A core part of any successful process of collaboration is to feel part of a community: it is experiential – a landscape of reciprocity where one positive action is met with another. A young teacher, for example, might learn from expert teachers and those with greater experience in mutually enriching contexts. Among the skills of collaboration, according to Tapscott and Williams (2007), are: being open, peering, sharing and acting globally. The isolation of the primary teacher is opened up. Ainscow argues:

> In this way ambiguity sets the scene for organisations to learn about themselves and their environments, allowing them to emerge from their struggles with uncertainty in a different form than when they started the confrontation. (Ainscow, 2015, p. 115)

The principle in part is based on the idea of 'gifting': across a multiplicity of schools pedagogy is negotiated, contested even, developed, distributed and supported. Such models are less status driven and more expertise dependent and eventually, the group begins to orient towards peer group accountability. Reciprocity must be an active process, as it is this which keeps people engaged in development; with multiple contributory sources of knowledge come new ideas and the creation of hybrid models fit for purpose and context. *Implication*: Reciprocity involves mutual benefit from exchange, where positive actions flow from one another.

Impact 1: System resilience

Sustainable approaches should foster the interdependent qualities of resilience and capacity. Resilience, for these purposes, is a psychological ability within a system that allows it to face setbacks and challenges while retaining its ability to drive forwards towards its object – 'a collective activity system is driven by a deeply communal motive' (Engeström, 2000, p. 964); surely it was this that underpinned the remarkably resilient response of primary educators to Covid-19. Object creates a lasting sense of purpose, potential fulfilment and the organisational character to come back in the face of adversity. Resilient organisations have spirit and face up directly to the contradictions and disturbances that from time to time invade even the strongest of them – these are shared openly. Actively developing new approaches with others also gives a feeling of control and self-determination. When Brighouse asserts that 'a sense of powerlessness is the enemy of democracy' (2012), we recognise the value of mutually supportive collaboration. *Implication*: Systemic resilience is the combination of reliability and robustness together with the adaptive capacity of the system, primarily revealed in an ability to respond to adversity.

Impact 2: Distributed capacity

If capacity is the cousin of resilience, then it resides in the ability to effectively match the demands being faced with the available pools of physical and psychological resources. Capacity, for example, is a major factor in the challenges facing primary schools in terms of providing a rich and wide-ranging curriculum (Alexander, 2013).

Capacity-building is one of the challenges of the system – available capacity is often stretched as new demands are made on the system and those demands shift schools away from their core purpose, at times, making their roles feel, at least temporarily, unachievable. Building capacity is a means of dealing with more challenging demands, yet it should not be seen simply as a limitless pool.

Distributing capacity across schools is powerful and a major advantage for MATs. When building well-evidenced theories of action, for example, or collectively curating a new curriculum framework it not only shares expertise, it can often prove a refreshing and energising process for those involved. The aim is to amplify repertoire, transfer knowledge and distribute specialist expertise. Hargreaves (2010) suggests the term 'joint practice development' to illustrate how deeper understandings can be built between collaborating professionals. Pools of distributed capacity are built through coherent, lateral and well-structured programmes of change and development. *Implication*: Distributed capacity involves expertise, knowledge and resources generated by and accessible to multiple partners.

Intention 1: Sustainable innovation

Innovation in pedagogy is about creating better solutions through new ideas, artefacts and processes. Sometimes a local innovation is about more effectively meeting need, in which case it is caught within a problem-solving model but at other times it is catalytic, creating qualitatively new advances in pedagogy which are original and travel widely. Collaborative innovation involves curiosity and disciplined enquiry alongside others, not settling, too soon, on one particular model but exploring openly and deeply.

Innovation is a complex concept and one to handle with some care; it is not enough on its own (a poor innovation could be retrogressive) and the ideas and initiatives which make up an innovation need to meet three criteria, in part to make them sustainable (see Hannon et al., 2011):

- they are ethically sound and not detrimental to others;
- they fit well and go beyond the practices they are intended to link with or supersede;
- their introduction is sustainable and is organisationally and financially practicable.

Implication: Sustainable innovation is the adaptive development of new pedagogies that have coherence with the guiding vision and values.

Intention 2: Expansive energy

There are concerns when some forms of change have a deleterious effect on motivation. Yet, the pace of change in primary education is unlikely to slow. When it is fragmented and lacking either coherence or meaning, then it causes frustration, lack of connection and energy depletion.

A mixture of approaches is needed to create the conditions, the expansive energy, for a successful self-improving system. A compelling and engaging 'object' (vision, identity, values) can provide meaning and motivation for individuals and organisations – as we work with 'objects' they begin to affect us and stimulate a response so that exploring, interpreting and creatively responding are engaging processes. When productively collaborating together and learning from one another, further expansive energy is released. Creating this energy throughout primary education will present some of the biggest 'system design' challenges, a task described by Ainscow: 'create the experiences that turn out to be motivating because people find them emotionally meaningful relative to their values and their ability to fulfill them' (2015, p. 56). *Implication*: Expansive energy builds from a collective commitment to extend and develop pedagogy through the drive gained from collaborating with others.

Reflection point

Are these the 'right' principles and approaches for a collaboration self-improving system? How can we embed them throughout primary education?

Sustaining a self-improving system: collective impact

It is perilous to claim that practice removes ambiguity about the purposive aspects of behavior ... However, in practice we at least have an opportunity to put different interpretations into dialogue with each other, and thereby to learn more about each 'voice' in the dialogue. (Cole, 1996, p. 343)

Unquestionably the system of primary education is full of tensions, dilemmas and contradictions, most notably the competing demands and commitments of delivering 'public value' and the corporate demands of the 'New Public Management'. Currently the system of primary education is asymmetric: a combination of community schools, faith schools and Academies (standalone or in MATs of various sizes and geographies) are found in close proximity to one another. So, today, whether one feels the system is purposeful and ethical, coherent or fragmented may well depend on one's position within it or perspective upon it. If the system atomises excessively or places elements in direct competition with one another, it will lose the potential of collaboration. Nevertheless, there are many examples of the successes of collaboration and the self-improving education system. It is difficult work and moral purpose and collective commitment will continue to be necessary in driving the next stages of change.

One of the challenges lies in the extent to which the system is subject to short-termism, reflected in 5-year terms of political office and the rapid turnover of secretaries of state. Primary education needs long-term strategic choices where priorities and investment matter: do we envisage smaller class sizes, extensive new technologies or better-trained teachers, for example? How do we make these decisions sustainable? How do we balance responsibility for them in the tiers and structures of the system? Some suggest the sustainability of a representative national education executive (perhaps, as a Standing Advisory Council) creating longer-term policy, providing guidance and advice to which the secretary of state reports and considers evidence from an independent inspectorate and research programmes. Above all, the education strategy should enable primary educators to find meaning and motivation, to interpret creatively, harnessing their energy, alongside their learners and their communities: public service creating public value.

Where power is devolved and distributed through the middle-tier the emphasis needs to turn to supporting a healthy diversity in the system which promotes collaboration and addresses issues of equity and inclusion; that acts as a champion for vulnerable children and assesses the extent that public value is created, providing checks and balances on institutional self-interest. It should address the challenges of geographic isolation, socio-economic deprivation and cultural isolation so that these can become priorities (e.g. Ovenden-Hope and Passy, 2016), particularly where inter-generational patterns are embedded and where differential investment is needed (remembering that short-term injections of funding are unlikely to have a long-term effect).

Arguing in favour of a self-improving education system is one thing but in doing so, it moves well beyond calls for professional autonomy and raises many questions. For example, how does the system of primary education manage its professionals, their ethics and practice? How does such a system collectively conceptualise pedagogy and how does it examine, research and study its effectiveness? How will it decide on the best forms of education and use evidence to identify its issues and inform the development of structures, processes and pedagogy effectively? If the self-improving system is dominated by larger, corporate-style MATs, what will this mean for local areas and how will they address growing calls for equity, parental engagement and community voice? For primary education to progress, there are key strategic questions (Table 7.4).

Table 7.4: Questions for education as a collaborative system

- How primary education is framed, judged and valued
- How the professional knowledge of primary education is codified, distributed and accessed and on whose terms
- How the needs of localities are understood and the commitment to responding sensitively and powerfully to them to address equity and social justice
- How any tensions between supporting the needs of the most vulnerable children and institutional self-interest are resolved
- How primary education achieves and demonstrates its public value

A self-improving system needs the security of structures (to keep children safe and ensure probity, for example), but flexibility and creativity too: an environment conducive to system leadership in a range of forms. When the system is envisaged as a collaborative venture and when thinking focuses on the needs of children and their communities rather than the institutions that serve them, when it is motivated by ensuring a high-quality primary education for every child and that the system is fair and equitable and respects contexts and the realities of everyone, then investment in the collaborative endeavour and the capacities to enable it would be worthwhile.

There is much to be done to ensure that the future system has public legitimacy, listens to the voices of its stakeholders and that genuine recourse for individuals is not lost in corporate bureaucracy. As the Association of School and College Leaders noted, more imagination and courage is needed to bring the power of endogenous development to bear (Cruddas, 2015). To illustrate, we need even more stories of successful change from a range of perspectives, especially our children and their families.

Vitor and Boynton describe co-configuration (see Chapter 3); namely, building a sustained and integrated system that can 'sense, respond, and adapt' (1988, p. 195). There is no finished product, rather a living and growing network; it requires the dispositions to recognise and engage with the expertise distributed across a rapidly changing environment, always with an eye to capacity-building (Elmore, 2004).

Collaboration has to impact on lived realities. It is a very challenging perspective, in part because we each experience change differently, exciting because it relates essentially to the complexity of human relationships and the myriad and compelling possibilities for improving primary education: the intention is collective impact and this can only be done together.

Delving deeper

David Hargreaves produced a series of reports for the National College for School Leadership (Hargreaves, 2010, 2011). They remain important to the journey of the self-improving education system he explores and proposes. His maturity models demonstrate that it is still 'a work in progress'.

Next: This chapter has focused on collaboration, a self-improving system and 'systemness', bringing this section to a close. In the conclusions that follow, I return to Bronfenbrenner's model and propose eight emergent and expansive opportunities for primary education.

Conclusions

These conclusions bring Part 2 to an end. They summarise some of the key areas identified in its four chapters. It asks whether science and the human spirit are coming together as complementary driving forces for primary education.

It summarises: *childhood • active learning • powerful pedagogy • expansive leadership • the collaborative system*

A socio-cultural approach to primary education

This exploration of primary education through the lenses of childhood, learning, pedagogy, leadership, collaboration and, eventually, the wider system reveals the remarkable scope and complexity of the enterprise (Figure 3). A socio-cultural perspective proposes a system of primary education where: children have a strong sense of agency; there are powerful and diverse pedagogies; leadership is expansive within a collegial culture and community connections; and there is collaboration for collective impact. It connects

Figure 3: Connecting: from childhood to system

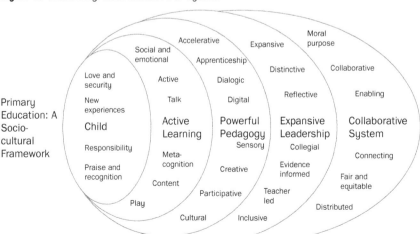

through the five features of a socio-cultural approach drawn from Wells and Claxton's (2002) analysis: fostering a mind to learn; enculturation and transformation; a communicative core; cultural relativism; and pedagogic communities of practice.

If access and entitlement have been resolved in the English education system, that is not the end of the story – new issues constantly emerge. If every child matters, if equity and social justice are key features of our education system, then the signals for the leadership and governance of our school system are set: they are systemic and collective challenges. Finding ways of creating cultures not just within but across schools and with other partners, which deepen pedagogies; building a system architecture to structure connection and collaboration, increasingly reflecting the science of teaching: these matters are open to debate but not inaction. It requires the energies of the *human spirit*.

Table P2 sets out nine expansive opportunities for the development of primary education. They emerge from two viewpoints. First, there is a strong human emphasis on the learning of children, their identity ('a mind to learn') and, alongside this, the role and empowerment of their teachers. The second theme is the increasingly evidence-informed system rooted in research and increasingly *scientific approaches* coupled with the emergent potential of new technologies.

Table P2: Expansive opportunities for the development of primary education

- Recognise that identity (the development of self, connections and understanding of the world) is in continuous formation and should be a prime purpose of education
- New technologies may be disruptive (to notions of curriculum expertise and the construction of knowledge) and need to be pro-actively harnessed by primary educators
- Pedagogy should have requisite variety and be fit for purpose to develop knowledge, skills and understanding
- Leadership is a key component that must be expansive, connecting, ambitious and adaptive
- A new era of collegial teacher leadership will be a vital and emergent component of a self-improving system
- Collaboration based in trust can be used to develop systemic capacity and resilience
- The political, policy and media environments should be enabling for institutions, allowing them autonomy and creativity
- Social justice is a moral responsibility of education but will need to cross boundaries and reach beyond education to impact fully
- Accountability needs to be contextually situated and evolve into a formative approach

Those who come to primary education now and in the future, as parents, carers, teachers, leaders and governors will find that dilemmas, tensions and controversies still abound and there is always so much to be done: the message for them and through them needs to be one of hope and aspiration; through partnerships creating the conditions where children learn well and live together successfully. Now as we search for educational wisdom the two significant features that come together in a more holistic primary education are 'science' and the 'human spirit'.

Next: If science and the human spirit are coming together, the next section considers whether it is time for a new 'holistic' version of primary education and what will be necessary to make this a reality.

Part 3

Towards Holistic Primary Education

This section begins to explore what next and why for primary education. It considers the sustainability and robustness of the system (noting the impact of Covid-19) and suggests that what is needed is something more holistic. It explores the idea of 'pioneering' in primary education before proposing 'productive trails' that might emerge in an 'evolutionary' period of primary education.

It explores: *the impact of Covid-19 • holistic approaches • aims and values • pioneering • a pedagogical index • productive possibilities • primary education as a whole*

Covid-19 had a profound effect on our lives as a whole and impacted hugely on primary education; it shifted our life conditions profoundly. The response of the system as a whole was remarkable. It served to galvanise educators into recognising that beyond the pandemic something different was both necessary and possible. This section explores this possibility by suggesting a new evolutionary and holistic period, connecting science and the human spirit, might be ahead of us.

Looking back on the pandemic there were many significant events but 4 January 2021 was among the most notable for primary education. In the aftermath of a torrid year and the strangest of Christmas periods, many shuddered at the enormity of it all: a rapidly spreading Covid-19 variant, partial school closures (in London and where section 44 was called), calls for further widespread closure and enmity between trade unions (which roared again) and the Department for Education about the best course of action. There were competing priorities, of course: health, well-being, education and the economy. Opening primary schools seemed to be characterised by political ideology, indecision and, some argued, derogation of responsibility for the committed but concerned body of teachers and school leaders (why no priority for vaccinations?). And then, one day after children's return, a remarkable U-turn, arguably much needed, after the event and inexplicably late in the day. Neoliberal narratives of 'autonomy' and 'choice', now, actually mattered little; when it came down to it, centralised decision-making in England revealed itself in a form that was far from fit for purpose and too often divisive as a public service ethic reasserted its value.

Intense energy was revealed in the collective responses of communities: the bond between school and home was, despite many families being tested to the limits in so many realms of their lives, more tangible than ever and came to be seen as the basis on which to build an education system. If our education system is to thrive in the future there was a basis in the dedicated professionalism, cohesion and the pedagogical innovation shown throughout the pandemic.

These changes in human life and society produced changes in consciousness and behaviour: from those pressures, from the reaction of communities, from accumulating action, new meaning emerged.

Reflection point

What was the impact of Covid-19 on primary education? What can we learn from it and how do we translate this into a version of primary education that is fit for purpose in the twenty-first century?

Next: What follows is in two parts. An exploration of our potentially changing 'life conditions' and their implications for primary education, followed by an agenda for change that suggests some fruitful areas for innovation and development.

8 | Wholeness

This chapter is about recognising what might be possible in primary education following on from the effects of the pandemic. It is suggestive of a holistic approach set within expansive educational aims and values. The concept of a 'pedagogical index' is proposed to capture the breadth and depth of thinking that should accompany primary education.

It explores: *the impact of Covid-19 • next stages in the spiral of development • holistic approaches • revisiting aims and values • a pedagogical index • evolutionary organisations*

The impact of Covid-19

For development to take place, it is we humans who must grow: for that is what we have control over. By altering our attitudes of mind we alter our lives.

The 'unprecedented' impact of Covid-19 on our world, arguably, put our aims and values to their sternest test since the Second World War. Carpenter (2020) identified five losses for children: of routine, structure, friendship, opportunity and freedom and their deep psychological effects. Processes of socio-cultural dynamics intensified, society felt huge strain: nonetheless, amid unprecedented pressures there emerged a renewed commitment to getting things 'right'.

Confidence in the teaching profession increased as primary educators 'made the weather': urged to complain to Ofsted if not satisfied with their school's provision, the large majority of the correspondence was positive praise (see Ofsted, 2021). While much was made of the lauded Oak Academy in providing online resources, it was the relationships and the creativity of teachers, the enthusiasm of children and the rapid appropriation of digital technologies that was remarkable. Perhaps it was the fostering of even stronger relationships, between children and teachers, between home and school that offered most. If confidence in the profession is rising, it needs to be matched with trust from politicians in the form of a new settlement.

Children's experiences of 'lockdown' had been extraordinarily varied, revealing the extent of inequalities and exacerbating them (EEF, 2021). Inevitably after children's absence from school there was concern about educational gaps increasing (Ofsted, 2020b; Worth and Faulkner-Ellis, 2021), about children's mental health (Carpenter, 2020; Education Support, 2020; Young Minds, 2021) and there was much talk of 'catching up', 'lost learning', 'recovery' and 'building back better' and, more importantly, happy and excited children returning to school (Save the Children, 2021). Access to education was much more than attending school: the availability of tools and technologies for remote learning moved into focus along with access to the expertise to support children's learning (e.g. Mundy and Hares, 2020).

The appointment of an education recovery commissioner created a more optimistic narrative and he was quick to recognise the social and emotional needs of children (though his subsequent resignation raised more concerns about lack of funding). There were powerful, deeper changes to life conditions at play too, stretching beyond Covid-19. They concerned, among other things: democracy in the United States, concern for the environment and the Black Lives Matters movement. It was timely that the Foundation for Education Development (FED, 2021) engaged a debate about the long-term vision for English education, and the on-going work of campaigning organisations such as the Fair Education Alliance, BAMEd and the Life-Based Learning Forum sat alongside a variety of reports, including that on the right drivers for whole-system success (Fullan, 2021): the result being a series of movements, shifting dynamics, with some differences but many similarities. As primary educators emerged from what Hargreaves (2020) called the 'long, dark tunnel', their perspectives evolved, now demanding greater connection, synergy, togetherness and fulfilment – a greater sense of wholeness.

Movement forward will require determination and will (Shirley, 2020a), together with vision and values. There will be push-backs and the pandemic revealed primary education's conservative forces: was 'catch up', especially through investment, predominantly in tutoring, a euphemism for 'back to basics'? Moreover, any revival of fear and blame (the discourse of derision) will stifle attempts to re-imagine primary education, especially if it undermines the profession. Nor can we simply produce a plan, organise the next cycle and implement the programme – our existential educational challenges are changing, requiring adaptive leadership. Primary education doesn't need a 'revolution'; rather, an open, evolutionary and expansive developmental period where the spaces for innovation and improvement are released and firmly grasped. Wegerif's (2013) description of three educational processes – 'opening', 'widening' and 'deepening' – is apt; the intention now must be to emphasise quality in the system of primary education.

There is now a curious juxtaposition of science and the human spirit meeting in new configurations: as science advances, so do our understandings of what it means to be human along with our consciousness of the world. New understandings are emerging from biogenetics and the neurosciences telling us that well-being is central to human flourishing and that it is under threat from the strain and drain from being caught in continuous cycles of striving to meet narrow, externally imposed improvement measures that eventually prove dispiriting for children and teachers. Connections to communities are increasingly front and centre; there are concerns for equity and pluralism and, through the development of 'inner work', the growth of identity. Technological advances may not be an educational panacea but they provide potential bridges for pedagogy and their pervasiveness cannot be ignored.

We are entering a new 'holistic' period: one that recognises the interdependencies of education that include but transcend narrow 'standards' dimensions so that intellectual, personal, social, emotional and spiritual flourishing are integrated and connected – even though they will each, at times, need their own focus. This period also reveals the power of collaboration: future challenges will be distinct because they may not be resolved by individuals no matter how much they learn; they will require collective responses – as we saw with Covid-19, some of these will be complex adaptive challenges on a level we cannot yet understand or comprehend.

Primary education now needs sustainable and holistic pedagogies, for as Ralph Waldo Emerson said, 'we do not inherit the earth from our ancestors; we borrow it from our children'. Can primary education make a vital transformation where science and the human spirit in combination provide the basis for further progress?

The next stage in the spiral of development: holistic and evolutionary

Beck and Cowan (1996), in their flow of spiral dynamics, recognise the potential for mankind to enter a new era or 'tier' of existence. Their referent is the term Flex-Flow (1996, pp. 274–285): the move to a multi-modal, intuitive and integrating approach with flows, networks and holism. This would mean a continued deepening and extension of the rich combinatory pedagogies, creative leadership and disciplined collaboration serving children's learning and development. Beck and Cowan also recognise how mankind's activity has put 'everything in jeopardy' (seen in the world's fragilities) while at the same time developments in science and technology are opening up 'unprecedented opportunities' where new priorities (1996, p. 277) and possibilities emerge. It signifies a move from mankind's 'subsistence' levels into a new human phase of 'Being' to address our changing 'life conditions'. Laloux, in his book *Reinventing Organizations* (2016), also recognises that a 'new stage of consciousness is coming to the fore'. He uses the term 'evolutionary' and observes that it 'is a profoundly new worldview that opens radical possibilities' (2016, p. 38).

Laloux's metaphor is 'living systems'. He argues: 'Change in nature happens everywhere, all the time' without central control and this opens new horizons. Imagine, he continues, if we treated organisations and systems in this way 'fuelled by the evolutionary power of life itself' (2016, p. 54). There is no one correct approach; rather, a combining together through disciplined enquiry. A new understanding of the human spirit allowing us to contemplate 'who' as well as 'what' primary education is for, as we recognise collective imperatives and even greater mutual interdependencies (Beck and Cowan, 1996). Azorin asked whether a new education was possible: it does seem that primary education has the potential to develop what she describes as a 'fairer and more supportive educational system that really can change lives' (2020, p. 388).

What might this mean for primary education? This new innovative period emerges, in part, from 'frustration', for example, with the negative effects of performance type cultures, especially high-stakes testing and inspection but also from 'dissatisfaction' with some forms of consensus where over-elaborated processes fail to ignite sufficient change. On entering this new 'evolutionary' phase, there is still significant value to be found in what has come before: it is not an outright rejection of 'stability, standards and subjects', rather a transformation towards *wholeness* that builds on strengths. Rich, high-quality learning experiences, deepening well-being for children, ambitious aims, high expectations, and achievement and reflective self-evaluation do not lose their value; rather, ideology diminishes to be replaced with a commitment to evidence, equity and inclusion and a concern for what is 'necessary, natural and next' (Beck and Cowan, 1996). This will move beyond espoused theory to theories-in-action (Argyris and Schön, 1977): tacit and unexamined beliefs will be subject to reflective, professional scrutiny and studied developmental processes.

What is 'holistic' education?

Holistic primary education takes the concept of an integrated whole that has both integrity and identity: it sees the child as themselves and their education in spacious, inclusive terms yet also part of a wider system. The 'holistic' concept in education has a long history. There are references, for example, in ancient Greek and Aboriginal culture; mention can be found in Comenius, Froebel, Thoreau and Montessori, and more recently in Noddings' (2003, 2006) 'care for the world', where education helps children develop their 'best selves'. Eisler's 'partnership model of education' (see Eisler and Fry, 2019) also serves to place vital values at the heart of education. Arguably in England, it was the 'Every Child Matters' (DfES, 2004) strategy that has come closest to such an approach. The suggestion here is that well-being, learning and achievement come together in a symbiotic relationship. This is not about clearing away all the obstacles in children's paths but as Shirley argues, building capacities of fortitude and resilience in the pursuit of worthy goals; wholeness supporting 'the dynamic unfolding of the individual over time' (2020b, p. 553).

Holistic primary education connects with the central motivations of children, influencing their aims and aspirations, shaping their goals, and helping give them their sense of direction as they create meaning from and through the world. It sits comfortably with the socio-cultural approaches of Chapter 5. It recognises identity and what sets a child apart, but there is connection, much is accomplished together through the community of learning and beyond. As Shirley argues: 'the young should be brought together across the world in pursuit of the common good as never before' (2020b, p. 546). Darling-Hammond et al. (2019) carefully assemble the science of learning and development that could support a holistic approach: in their terms, academic, cognitive, ethical, physical, psychological and social-emotional.

The educational journey can be reconstructed in pursuit of holism, as it becomes more acutely sensitive to context, more definitively capable, it senses where it is drawn to go (Beck and Cowan, 1996). This is a paradigm where we might seek:

- pedagogies that are combinatory of mind, body and spirit;
- highly skilled teachers who capitalise on the multitude of available resources creating powerful modes of instruction, personalising learning to children's interests and creating powerful social contexts for children to find their voice and agency;
- advances in enquiry-based models where the potential of collaborative learning emerges in new forms;
- increases in information and connection so that learning has many bridges across communities and the world as children access expertise in a variety of fields;
- cognitive diagnostics and learning enabled by using the analytic algorithms of information technologies to tailor learning experiences to children's needs;
- stretching of the school day as children access learning in an increasingly agile way and the power of their communications to bridge gaps between home and school.

Broadly, expect an increasingly kaleidoscopic repertoire of pedagogies implemented with precision and children continuing to exceed our expectations of them. (*Note*: This creates important professional challenge and responsibilities for the teaching profession.)

A holistic system of primary education will have many qualities and be describable through many lenses, but the combination of science and the human spirit is a powerful beginning in understanding the movement. This evolutionary phase will take primary education into new and dynamic forms, beyond the warm recognition of primary education's many achievements, with the knowledge that even this can be transformed into something more, something that recognises and values the past but transcends it. Yet it, too, will face enormous challenges: humankind is likely to face developments that improve its own capacities as new intelligences more powerful than our own emerge. What will this mean for primary age children? This new understanding of the human spirit will mean we must contemplate 'who we are' as we are faced with collective imperatives and even greater mutual interdependencies.

This worldview suggests a promising course for humanity, and offers an insight for all of us regarding how we can expand our perspective and move towards a deeper experience – where science and the human spirit come together. Evolutionary primary education is not the creation necessarily of new but greater recognition and deepening understanding of what already is and realising of what might be. As Beck and Cowan comment:

> Life is a kaleidoscope of natural hierarchies, systems and forms; The magnificence of existence is valued over material possessions; Flexibility, spontaneity and functionality have the highest priority; Knowledge and competency should supersede rank, power, status; Difference can be integrated into interdependent, natural flows. (Beck and Cowan, 1996, p. 47)

It will require high levels of pedagogical acuity and sensitive, intuitive responsiveness to context, adept leadership managing both certainty and ambiguity but with values that support personal freedom without harm to others and integrated and interconnected on scales only just being imagined. It's a cultural shift that lands in the hands of everybody who chooses to make the journey: ownership, enterprise and action are needed. A holistic primary education is comprehensive in equipping children with the whole range of knowledge, dispositions and understanding they need for the significant challenges of life: it opens up critical dimensions of education without being either highly specified (standardised) or ideologically determined.

Reflection point

Are we ready to move into an evolutionary phase, moving towards an increasingly holistic approach to primary education? What will we need to learn and enable to make this happen?

Three pillars of holistic primary education

> The glue that binds the effective drivers together is the underlying attitude, philosophy, and theory of action. The mindset that works for whole system reform is the one that inevitably generates individual and collective motivation and corresponding skills to transform the system. (Fullan, 2011, p. 5)

If primary education is to find ways forward, three components combine:

1 Constancy of educational purpose (our direction, what we aim to do for children) supported by the related systems of policy, resourcing and system architecture (see Chapter 7).

2 A pedagogical index (our theory and practices of primary education and approaches to how we go about achieving our purpose) that includes our system of teaching.

3 A commitment to self-evaluation processes (ways of knowing how well we are doing, co-configuration that 'senses, responds and adapts'; Viktor and Boynton, 1988) that is open to public scrutiny and analysis.

Pillar 1: Aims and purpose

At its best, primary education is full of meaning and motivation found in vibrant classrooms full of rich experience and in the expression of highly skilled teachers: but it needs direction from aims and purpose, or in Dilts' (2018) model (see Chapter 6) 'vision, values and identity'. Aims and purpose can be constructed in many ways but their intention should be to create such a powerful energy that they become well-understood arbiters of meaning, becoming among the most powerful expressions of primary education. Clearly articulated aims and purpose are means of making the journey worthwhile, as well as something to turn back to in times of difficulty. Values are equally indispensable: if aims relate to purpose, then values relate to the principles and beliefs held to be important; Barnes (2021) argues that together they hold cultures and subcultures together. When primary educators build values into the curriculum – tolerance, for example, in the study of a history unit, studying the use of power in religious education or the ethical issues surrounding energy in science – they come to life (see Barnes, 2021). There is surely an opportunity to create an inclusive framework to guide everyone concerned with primary education; the consultation in itself could be a powerfully engaging process. And, of course, they should relate back to the principles we espouse as a democratic nation, set too in a world of much fragility.

Aims focus on what we want: in 1904 the Morant Code for Public Elementary Schools attempted to establish aims for the primary phase (Gordon, 2002); White (2010) notes that they were the most comprehensive and coherent set of aims prior to 1999! The purpose of primary education, it argued, was strengthening character and developing the intelligence of children with practical preparation for work and life, including a united effort between home and school. In the twenty-first century, we might consider how those aims have evolved (Hannon and Peterson, 2021): children's well-being is symbolic of our times, as are sustainability and stewardship and a concern for our environment, our cultural diversity too, alongside, of course, learning and achievement.

Talk of aims raises also questions of 'who by' and for 'what ends' (Noddings, 2006; Thomson et al., 2012). Elliott's (2000) argument was for a stronger emphasis on socio-cultural interrelationships, personal aspiration and organisational context as a way forwards – a point that resonates with many commentators (Duguid and Brown, 2002; Alexander, 2008; Leach and Moon, 2008; Hopkins, 2013), one that alludes to and includes the vitality of pedagogy and children's voices in primary education. Rethinking aims and purpose requires a necessary shift: they must be adaptive and open, they should be genuinely evolutionary for present and future generations to thrive – economically, socially and morally – through nurturing human potential. It includes a deeper recognition of being healthy and happy based in the strongest of relationships. Knowledge is vital, but as it proliferates and is stored increasingly in complex networks, it creates epistemic questions and we may need to redefine our relationship with it.

There is always a political dimension to education systems demanding dialogue: without it aims remain unexplored for they are meaningless without debate, critique and generative understanding. Change, development and growth become core concepts too: the aims and purpose of education cannot always fix problems but they can galvanize action and in doing so would have seven qualities:

- *Holistic*: a recognition that education is multidimensional, interconnected and explicable by reference to the whole rather than component parts.
- *Inclusive*: includes everybody and actively removes barriers to participation.
- *Public*: available and understood by all while reflecting both the civic rights and responsibilities of education.
- *Relatable*: in an accessible form, easily understood and adaptable to context.
- *Ambitious*: sets a compelling but challenging agenda for the system.
- *Fairness*: engages with the diversity of the education system and seeks to promote fairness throughout.
- *Focused*: targeted on the right things including purpose, well-being and achievement.

How might this translate into a working framework? Who decides the ambition and agenda? The Cambridge Primary Review is exemplary (Alexander, 2010b): born from extensive consultation, its aims were interwoven with a curricular framework and set a standard while Scotland's' 'Curriculum for Excellence' recognises the need for children to know themselves and build relations with others; gain the knowledge, skills and attributes to thrive in a rapidly changing world; and be democratic citizens and active shapers of the world. Importantly, they are expressed in meaningful terms for children. This search for coherence between aims, values, pedagogy and curriculum is a powerful quest also taken up by the OECD in their Learning Compass 2030 (OECD, 2019). Leach and Moon (2008) suggest that we build learning by identifying 'the big ideas' and then find pedagogical strategies that lead to understanding. In Ontario, an education strategy was devised to develop themes that contribute across a range of domains (see Glaze et al., 2006).

Fullan and Langworthy's (2013) six 'C's inform the New Pedagogies for Deep Learning project. They are radically different from what is measured through current standardised tests or detailed in some modern curriculum models: they offer a powerful panoptic vision of what could constitute wholeness in education.

- *Character education* – honesty, self-regulation and responsibility, perseverance, empathy for contributing to the safety and benefit of others, self-confidence, personal health and well-being, career and life skills.
- *Citizenship* – global knowledge, sensitivity to and respect for other cultures, active involvement in addressing issues of human and environmental sustainability.
- *Communication* – communicate effectively orally, in writing and with a variety of digital tools; listening skills.
- *Critical thinking and problem solving* – think critically to design and manage projects, solve problems, make effective decisions using a variety of digital tools and resources.
- *Collaboration* – work in teams, learn from and contribute to the learning of others, social networking skills, empathy in working with diverse others.
- *Creativity and imagination* – economic and social entrepreneurialism, considering and pursuing novel ideas, and leadership for action. (Fullan and Langworthy, 2013, p. 3)

Within this type of framework, any movement towards exploring 'indicators' of educational success will need far more subtlety in engagement than is currently the case: how, for example, do we assess citizenship?

Aims should offer, in the search for a complete and harmonious 'whole', a challenging agenda, deeply imbued with humanity. In setting aims and purpose, their descriptions should:

- represent the whole child, integrating development across a range of domains: academic, personal, social, emotional and intellectual skills, qualities and knowledge;
- include a framework of challenging expectations for children and their schools and retain a strong emphasis on the communicative core;
- enable a curriculum that builds on children's curiosity and uses rich experiences and real-world contexts as vehicles for the development of knowledge, skills and understanding and a love of learning;
- encourage relationships which enable values to thrive (respect and tolerance, for example) and include a deep reverence for life and our world;
- enable agency, particularly from children, and recognise that it is through empowerment that change is realised;
- have a commitment to an education system that is fundamentally inclusive and enables all to succeed.

> **Reflection point**
>
> Which aims and values are most important moving forwards? Can we justify primary education as important in its own right without reference to other phases or ambitions (e.g. economic success)?

Pillar 2: A pedagogical index

While cultural relativism is a feature of a socio-cultural approach, this does not imply any lack of rigour; aims and purpose need a system, in Dilts' (2018) terms the 'capacities, practices and environment' of primary education. The term 'index' is useful here: defined as a framework that collects the theories and practices that can be seen in individual or collective configuration. While primary education in its various layers and manifestations is always an intricate fusion, this doesn't mean it cannot or should not be captured: primary education should be underpinned by theory and evidence. Increasingly, there are wide-ranging, evidence-based frameworks to inform us. Joyce, Weil and Calhoun's (2015) 'Models of Teaching' provide extensive summaries of a range of pedagogical approaches forming a clear, expansive and meticulously researched framework. The Education Endowment Foundation, Hattie (2009) and Coe et al. (2014) offer others. Elsewhere, there are Hopkins and Craig's (2014) four whole-school and six teacher 'theories of action' that form the 'elements' of a system. The five pedagogical domains I proposed in Chapter 5 also reflect an ambitious combinatory framework (deep learning as an accelerative apprenticeship; learning through a guided participatory and dialogic process; learning as a rich multi-sensory, experiential and creative process; learning as organised, skilful and critical inquiry; and learning supporting the formation of identity through a sense of well-being and belonging). From an even wider perspective, Darling-Hammond et al. offer a set of supportive environments (promoting strong attachments, relationships, a sense of safety and belonging, and relational trust), productive instructional strategies (that connect to children, support conceptual understanding and meta-cognitive abilities), a system of support (to enable healthy development, meet student needs and address learning barriers), and social and emotional development (to promote skills, habits and mindsets that enable self-regulation, interpersonal skills, perseverance and resilience) (2019, p. 3). In this vein, Deming (1982) describes a 'theory of profound knowledge' comprising: appreciation of a system, knowledge of variation, a theory of knowledge and an understanding of psychology; he understood, too, that people are the source of value in a system.

A pedagogical index is a system of knowledge that should offer meaning applied to practice – a basis for decision-making, self-evaluation and for further evolution. Without such an index there is nothing to reference. Reflecting through such an index allows its users to see how strong or common a practice might be and allow it to be explored in depth and developed.

In primary education there is a complex 'index' at play, including both tacit and explicit knowledge that operate to guide our choices and behaviours. For primary education I propose six domains. First, a *theory of learning* must be at its heart, one that moves beyond experience and is tested in practice every day and is visible through the observation of associated *pedagogical systems*, which include assessment processes. In a socio-cultural approach, voice and its expression reveal achievement through the eyes of others, so the third domain is the *voice of the community*. Fourth, a *theory of change* to reflect an evolutionary approach, while a *theory of organisational psychology* embraces the leadership dimensions in creating expansive and evolutionary processes as well as the meaning and motivation that are vital to well-being and to the release of energy. The final and sixth dimension relates to *systems of governance*, which reflect the need for ethics, probity, strategy and structure as part of effective systems of primary education.

A pedagogical index would draw on wide-ranging sources that reveal the extent of primary education: from theory, research, evidence and practice; and in this context from socio-cultural dynamics, from signature pedagogies and theories of action and collaboration, from concerns for equity and inclusion.

- *A theory of learning*: informed by aims, this will include understandings from neuroscience and cognitive psychology and be the basis of development and include particular expertise for supporting children who have special educational needs or who need particular attention to their inclusion in school. It includes support for socio-emotional needs and developing mindset. Curriculum design processes and models will reflect these understandings. (**Domain 1**)
- *Pedagogical systems*: informed by theory and research, understandably complex and adaptive, fit for purpose, built on the basis of a thorough understanding of child development, epistemological knowledge and instructional skill. They include curriculum design, building learning communities including systems for evaluating learning and children's progress and a system of support for children. Teachers, in particular, must understand curriculum and pedagogy in holistic terms. Pedagogical systems have consistency and capacity to implement them. (**Domain 2**)
- *Voice of the community*: an in-depth approach to engaging learners, their families, the community and other stakeholders so that they connect and feel a strong sense of partnership with the school. An understanding of social transformation. A commitment to making the boundaries between school and community permeable. (**Domain 3**)
- *A theory of change*: leadership as direction finding, an understanding of how organisations can continually develop their activity in ways that reflect the changing environment in which they operate. (**Domain 4**)
- *A theory of organisational psychology*: how to orient participants around an object that is jointly constructed and which is enabling of all to contribute as

child / teacher / community leaders: the heart that generates motivation and meaning. (**Domain 5**)

- *Systems of governance*: ensuring probity and that institutions are safe, nurturing and of high quality. A repository for protocols about pedagogy and assessment, a means of setting strategy and holding the school to account. (**Domain 6**)

Reflection point

What would be the theories and features of your own pedagogical index? How holistic would it be? What evidence and research would you use to justify this?

Pillar 3: Self-evaluation

A powerful pedagogical index needs three active attributes: (1) a reference back to aims, theory and evidence so that it is principled, evidenced and justifiable; (2) engagement with a repertoire of approaches with requisite variety that are fit for purpose; and (3) development through studied collaborative enquiry. Self-evaluation is its bedrock enabling adoption, adaptation and continual improvement. It provides a lens and enables the making of a map of the landscape as the success of the index is tested.

> Smart schools are those which have, and know how to use, simple, economical and routine evaluation tools – shadowing, photographs and videos, spot checks, focus groups, diaries, interviews, feedback boxes, surveys or questionnaires. These are the media through which the intelligence of an organisation ... expands and enriches. (MacBeath, 1999, p. 7)

Self-evaluation (MacBeath, 1999) sits at the heart of an evolutionary approach: all organisations exchange information with their environment, with those with whom they work directly and indirectly, formally and informally. Sophisticated organisations generate development from feedback: for example, from external evaluation, data about staff turnover, a negative reaction from a parent or through assessment processes. Kaptelinin and Nardi (2006) offer an explanation of this: they reference sensory, perceptual and intelligent (evolutionary) responsiveness. Organisations which make *sensory* responses to their surrounding environment recognise simple phenomena and respond to causal stimuli – a new policy directive or instruction, for example – and engage with only limited representations of their context, possibly detecting problems and taking corrective action, possibly missing or avoiding more subtle, potentially critical aspects. *Perceptual* responses are on a higher plane and are more broadly attuned; the information is processed within existing organisational constructs that are not subject to change, which means that at a perceptual level a problem-solving mode is applied. Organisations that are perceptual in response are able to adapt their object and reorganise activity in these terms. *Evolutionary* responses in organisations are characterised by the development of sophisticated mental representations of situations. By their very nature organisations whose responsiveness is evolutionary are able to both develop and where necessary transform their object and recast their 'pedagogical index' accordingly. Moreover, they often serve to turn stressors into positives by connecting them to object. Learning is fast and knowledge transfers across the organisation.

An accountability model figures as an important feature in debates (see Chapter 7) but not mass inspection concerned to judge one against another or to pronounce failure too late in the day (though an immediate inspectorial function, arguably, should be available when, for example, misconduct or behaviour of serious concern is suspected); rather, it is evaluation focused on the self-generated standards constructed locally. It is vital that there is a system of external advice, that the system is not self-reliant and that it remains open to challenge and responsive; if not, it will run the risk of accountability through politics and the media rather than skilled and constructive evaluation.

Summary

Pedagogies here are a deliberate form of production that attempt to affect changes which alter the relationships within the system. There are numerous examples of 'catalytic' activity aiming to re-programme or 'reconfigure' an inert system. For genuine innovation (Greany, 2018), for holistic approaches to thrive, the layers and elements in the system must connect together with concerted and dynamic energy. Famously, albeit in particular conditions, the radical educator, Paulo Freire, working in South America showed, in *Pedagogy of the Oppressed* (1972), how pedagogy could be enabling and emancipatory. To be successful, in Freire's conceptualisation, teachers need to be passionate about their work, authoritative (knowledgeable) and expert but also to see pedagogy with a 'curiosity that is critical, bold and adventurous' (Freire, 1998). His vision, crucially, was socially constructed in the dialogue which culturally contextualised it: for him literacy was not just of the 'word' but of the 'world'.

Now primary education is embracing science and the human spirit: there are increasingly carefully designed, systematically organised, evidence-informed yet kaleidoscopic approaches to pedagogy to which the profession is increasingly contributing through expansive approaches to development. This combines with the human spirit – including our emotions, creativity, insight, and courage – symbolising and realising what we want for our children. We can, to conclude this chapter, see this through the lens of our six questions about primary education from Part 1 and suggest descriptors that anchor them within a holistic approach (Table 8.1).

Table 8.1: Guiding language for a holistic pedagogy of primary education

Foundation	Descriptor
Purpose – why	Holistic, sustainable, deep
Content – what	Combinatory, challenging, communicative
Quality – how	Active, curious, creative, cultural
Partnership – where	Bridging, collaborating, belonging
Voices – who	Teacher leadership, children's agency
Time – when	Open, integrated

Reflection point

Reflecting on this chapter, what does a holistic approach mean for you in your context? What pedagogies would emerge further in such an approach? How can primary education move towards them?

Next: In the next chapter, I explore some possibilities for the development of evolutionary approaches and holistic pedagogies.

9 Evolutionary purpose

> **This chapter** is about the need for pioneers and architects in primary education. It explores some trails associated with an evolutionary approach under the banners of development, pedagogies, community and innovation.
>
> **It explores:** *pioneers and architects • thematic trails: development, pedagogies, community, innovation • creating the conditions*

Pioneers and architects

The teacher creating a new environment in their nursery classroom designed to spark imaginative play; the precise design of content in Key Stage 2 to support children's conceptions of the earth in space; a teacher-educator demonstrating the links between speaking and writing using rich literary texts; a chief executive building the culture and systems of a Multi-Academy Trust through creating 'instructional rounds' where teachers study pedagogy across different schools and year groups – these are the pioneers of primary education, those who, even on a very small scale, accomplish something new, sometimes pushing through accepted orthodoxies or critique into new territory. Before them, as inspiration, are notable historical figures – Robert Owen, Susan Isaacs and Charlotte Mason – and, more recently, Robin Alexander and the Cambridge Primary Review team, the pioneers of evidence-based practice, and the many, often unsung, practitioners changing pedagogy day by day. Pioneers and architects enter new territories, using new techniques, discovering and developing approaches that push the boundaries. Pioneering is an ethic for primary educators: bringing knowledge, personality, evidence and experience together they project forwards, envisaging and enacting innovation, in David Hopkins' (2020) words, 'unleashing greatness'. Architecture matters because young children's education depends upon it: it must be designed, often through emergent processes, rather than stumbled upon or hurriedly assembled.

The September 2018 issue of *Impact*, the journal of the Chartered College of Teaching, exemplified curriculum pioneers who were building their own architecture: a 'knowledge rich curriculum' (Dennis and Kilsby, 2018); 'a curriculum to nurture compassionate citizens' (Biddulph, 2018); 'a curriculum to develop a love of learning' (Perona-Wright and Fletcher, 2018); 'a global curriculum' (Hooper and Cornes, 2018); and 'an ethically vibrant curriculum in a church school' (Humphreys and Feil, 2018). 'Pre-figurative practice' (Fielding and Moss, 2011) is gaining ground as a concept: we can take this to mean the creation and living of the forms of social relations which we would anticipate to be representations of types of decision-making, practices and approaches we have ambitions to realise – it is hoped by creating the new in the context of the old. Pre-figurative practice is about building the 'exemplary'. Note the ironic reversal in Wood and colleagues' (2018) commentary on how Sir Alec Clegg's visionary and 'pioneering' work in 1960s and 1970s West Yorkshire provided leadership of communities and supportive school partnerships that would be timely now.

Pre-figurative practices are evolutionary, realising change through practices that are exemplary, serving as desirable models for others (e.g. Fielding and Moss, 2011). In deeply challenging times, it is the energy of pioneers who drive the spiral to shift once again from collective approaches towards the individuals who take on the personal responsibilities of the global context (Beck and Cowan, 1996). Selfless rather than selfish, underpinned by the philosophy of 'I am as you are', a core understanding based in a genuine curiosity and openness to learning new things where new integrated ways of thinking emerge (Beck and Cowan, 1996). Following Beck and Cowan's insights, we should expect to see leaders (at every level) who begin to recognise and address

Table 9.1: Characteristics of pioneering leadership

- Capacity for systematic and disciplined activity creating integrative and open systems and practices (necessary because they will have responsibility for adroitly negotiating a finely balanced system of interlocking forces and demands).
- A professional element that will be highly competent: scientific and technological, curious and creative across a range disciplines yet able to balance their autonomy with a distinctive concern for the greater good, particularly empowering children and a deep respect for value and difference.
- A deep rigour which questions the efficacy of existing pedagogy and discovers new forms: there will be both spontaneity and simplicity; a concern for a range of interests, not just one, and a disciplined application of technology aiming for minimal consumption.
- Recognition that power is diffuse, reflective in expertise rather than hierarchy; this is the new age of teacher leadership and initiative combining with the power of children's voices and agency.
- They will need a sense of what Myatt (2021) calls 'essentialism': an ability to define and refine what is important; what needs to be done and, of equal import, what does not.

From Beck and Cowan (1996).

powerful productive forces by turning and tuning into change forces: transformational new technologies, changes in children's values and identities, the impact of environmental and ecological crises, the demands of huge population masses and the economic patterns which sweep across the planet. These pioneers recognise a responsibility to develop children who are creative, reflective, productive, compassionate and contributing.

The 'New Pioneers' of this 'evolutionary' period in education will be well-informed, cerebral and understanding practitioners capable of exploiting the affordances of their environment and technology, in particular, allowing the blending and harmonising of the collective energies of individuals within integrated systems (Beck and Cowan, 1996). Responses may well be radical: perhaps anticipating minimalist living and a strongly ecological element to educational philosophy. Primary education will generate a deep understanding of the mind/body relationship and the feeling dimensions will be brought together with the cognitive. Education in the holistic meme will need to develop a new version of spirituality: one of wonder, awe and reverence that coincide with the demise of ego – the vitality of all life where 'my' needs are less important (see Beck and Cowan, 1996). It focuses on co-existence – anything less than success for all is not enough.

There is a need for criticality too – to assess affordances and constraints within the system and, above all, harness agency, in a process of evolution that includes recognition that wherever possible:

1 Loyalties and identities to specific, often myth-based approaches should be exposed to constructive, evidence-based challenge.
2 Absolutist, ethnocentric values and 'truths' are placed in perspective with pluralistic conceptions.
3 Central control is rebalanced with increasing ownership by communities and localities.
4 The headlong drive for higher standards is recognised for causing high levels of stress in teachers and children.
5 Achievement for some is not enough; everyone must have that opportunity.

For those pioneers responsible at the highest levels of the education system, the challenge for their leadership is to create motivational frameworks building on strong theory and evidence and to resist the constant risk of being driven back to limited authoritarian memes which lack the sophistication, openness and integrity which 'holistic' primary education promises. We need to research not just characteristics but increasingly trajectories (Hallinger and Heck, 2011) and the stepping-off points. As Beck and Cowan (1996) acknowledge, this is systematic and interdependent but also rigorous and demanding: it must be open if it is to remain healthy and compassionate, for the warning is of what might appear in a form of ruthless leadership falling back to previous, more self-centred approaches.

Reflection point

What does pioneering mean for you? What approaches and qualities are needed for this new evolutionary period? What are the new educational 'frontiers'?

Towards wholeness

> Education ... needs to be radically rethought — partly to stop the boredom, but mostly to blow the lid off learning, whereby students and teachers as partners become captivated by education day in and day out. (Fullan and Langworthy, 2013, p. 1)

We are not starting again with primary education: this is a paradigm shift, an expansion and evolution rather than revolution. Principles, values, evidence and research act as guides as unfounded ideologies fade away. The evolution of primary education needs a creative space that encourages innovation. Engeström (2009) argues that a key metaphor for development is that of a 'zone', or a terrain of activity to be dwelled in and explored. Entering the zone is the first stage and he argues that in the network society we see 'patterns of pulsation, swarming, and multidirectional criss-crossing'. This, usually collaborative, activity is important because it allows those involved in innovation to begin to create trails. By constructing trails of new practices, in pedagogical terms, then challenge is made to what is already there, further exploration and development fortify practice to the point at which they break through. Innovation is thus grounded, evidenced and robust.

Table 9.2: Building developmental trails

Entering	Exploring	Socialising	Systemising
Gather information, reflect (book scrutiny and lesson study), learn from others, seek external viewpoints, experiment, explore research, debate ideas	Trial ideas, shape practices and knowledge together, build models, refine, test, learn in 'communities', generate 'theories of action', inform with evidence	Create ground rules, distil knowledge, confirm in documentation, review, revisit, share the narrative, build case studies, share practices, reflect, induct, maintain, modify	Share, publish, debate, engage others, externally validate

Leithwood and colleagues' (2006) argument is to normalise experimentation, an approach which would need the skills of evaluating and informing next steps (see Porritt et al., 2017). Building agency and collective action will then allow the trails to be further tested, stabilised and made durable.

I now turn to four aspects that help to generate a potential *agenda for primary education*, which we might see as evolutionary and productive, trails which are developed through activity and which eventually we can move beyond creating new pathways (Table 9.3).

The first trail explores *development* (through governance; evidence, expertise and research; collaboration; and collegial professionalism). The second trail is that of *pedagogies* (exploring dialogue and voice; knowledge and enquiry; digital technologies; neuroscience and meta-cognition; and assessment tools). The third is *community and agency* (looking beyond the school day; equity and inclusion; social pedagogies; and agency and identity). The last trail is *innovation* (a collective-expansive approach; pedagogic development work; and pre-figurative practices).

Table 9.3: Four development trails

Development (holistic, sustainable, global/local, altruistic):
• Governance
• Evidence, expertise and research
• Collaboration
• Collegial professionalism

Pedagogies (flexible, deep, ambitious, connected, combinatory):
• Dialogue and voice
• Knowledge and enquiry
• Digital technologies
• Neuroscience and meta-cognition
• Assessment tools

Community (agency, open, integrated, fair, bridging):
• Beyond the school day
• Equity and inclusion
• Social pedagogies
• Agency and Identity

Innovation (enabling, supporting, open):
• Collective-expansive
• Pedagogic development work
• Pre-figurative practice

Trail 1: Development

This trail is about building stronger forms of professional development, creating an evidence-informed profession, extending professional repertoires and demonstrating the impact of primary education.

Table 9.4: Development

Application	What is at issue	Into practice
Application 1: Make the space that allows innovation and creates professional dialogue, dynamism and trust	• Demand to develop teaching is ever present • Teachers can continually improve when offered the right opportunities (Reeve and Su, 2013) • Sometimes teachers can become hemmed in by 'habits' and the loss of the feedback signal (Allen, 2019)	• Governance supports the creation of 'conducive contexts' (Wiliam, 2016) for development (protected time, for example) • Differentiate between early careers teachers' needs (Kraft and Papay, 2014) and longitudinal processes such as coaching (Bambrick-Santoyo, 2012; Wiliam, 2016; Kraft et al., 2018)
Application 2: Gradually build evidence-informed practice by integrating it within the professional learning that occurs on a day-by-day basis	• Bridging the gap between theory and practice • Creating evidence-informed primary education • Increasing knowledge and awareness, practice-based evaluations • Schools justifying their decision-making	• Build understanding of evidence-informed resources, e.g. Teaching and Learning Toolkit (Higgins et al., 2015) • Help teachers to 'read' the research, exploring its status and its reliability and validity alongside its relevance and relatability (Cordingley, 2019) • Recognise that the link between research evidence and its translation into practice is an on-going journey
Application 3: Create the conditions of extended professionalism, searching out collaborative opportunities that involve learning so deeply that teachers know how and in what context to use the full pedagogic repertoire	• Helping teachers command the professional knowledge they need for their role (Alexander, 2016) • Creating the capacity for pedagogy to be 'intelligent, adaptive action' (Shulman and Shulman, 2004) • Supporting teachers in developing 'internal' psychological tools for action (Bedny and Harris, 2005)	• Collaborate: use teacher wisdom to help practice travel from site to site, classroom to classroom (Berliner, 2019) • Strengthen collaborative professional development (Elmore, 1996), including lesson study, coaching, mentoring, instructional rounds

(Continued)

Application	What is at issue	Into practice
Application 4: Publicly demonstrate primary education's professionalism and its impact	• Making the professional practice of teaching public (Goepel, 2012) • Demonstrating the efficacy of schools • Promoting the respectability of the profession; improvement of service quality; professional standards	• Public display of ethics, collegiality, rigorous self-regulation, serious policy activism and a commitment to building professional knowledge (see Demirkasimoglu, 2010; Goepel, 2012)

Trail 2: Pedagogies

This trail is about building stronger pedagogies that have both requisite variety and are fit for purpose. They recognise the emergent power of dialogue, audience and purpose, together with well-being and digital technologies. They are a reminder to consider whose knowledge we are teaching and its power, as well as continuing to focus on high-quality assessment.

Table 9.5: Pedagogies

Application	What is at issue	Into practice
Application 5: Develop dialogic teaching, building into the pedagogic repertoire structured opportunities for voice and argument in curriculum contexts (Alexander, 2020)	• Building a holistic 'communicative core' with talk at its heart (e.g. Voice21.org) • Engaging children's voice and participation (Cruddas, 2007; Maybin, 2013) to know how they feel about school • Building a repertoire of pedagogy: transactional, expository, interrogatory, exploratory, deliberative, imaginative, expressive and evaluative (Alexander, 2020)	• Plan opportunities for children 'to talk, discuss, marshal evidence and argue their case' (Alexander, 2020, p. 197) • Reciprocal reading, debate, school councils and family groups, Philosophy for Children (Lipman, 1980), structured controversies, 'Mantle of the Expert', Thinking at the Edge (Claxton, 2006)

(Continued)

Table 9.5: (Continued)

Application	What is at issue	Into practice
Application 6: Develop pedagogic repertoires that keep knowledge alive through meta-cognitive approaches, and expand opportunities for audience and purpose of children's learning	• There is a balance between core knowledge, skills and dispositions to participate in solving the problems that children are likely to encounter (Wells, 1999, p. 199) • A curriculum with a unifying narrative that connects together (Myatt, 2018)	• Prioritise audience and purpose to create meaning and motivation: publishing writing, hosting art exhibitions, concerts in the community, performances of dance and drama • Where possible 'turn the demanding work over to the learners, not to do all of the relating, negotiating, and reconciling for them.' (Scardamalia, 2000, p. 6) • Teach meta-cognitive skills (Quigley et al., 2018)
Application 7: Develop children's well-being and identity, helping them to understand the power of self	• Children develop positive self-image and feel a sense of agency which reflects in their learning and development	• Teach for well-being, including breathing techniques, mindfulness practices, regular exercise, reading for pleasure or relaxing with music (for example, www.mindfulnessinschools.org; www.themindfulnessinitiative.org) • Enable children to create rich, personal 'imprints' and 'archives' reflecting their learning (life-logging) • Encourage children to work with 'living knowledge' (photography, for example), to publish and exchange their work with others
Application 8: Engage digital technologies in ways that positively transform pedagogy	• Technology is purposefully adopted which bringing benefits to learning rather than simply being consumed • Children know and understand the impact of digital technologies and develop control over their use	• Invest in professional development for teachers in understanding educational technologies • Identify the benefits for pedagogy in adopting technology, rather than simply use the capacities of the technologies • Teach children to use the affordances of the technology in purposeful ways

(Continued)

Application	What is at issue	Into practice
Application 9: Re-imagine accountability to place formative assessment and learning diagnostics at the heart of primary education	• Build assessments and systems for monitoring children's progress around a holistic picture of the child • That formative assessment is recognised as a vital tool in pedagogy (Black and Wiliam, 1998)	• Challenge fixed conceptions of ability – above average, less able (Hart et al., 2004) • Ensure all teachers are skilled in formative assessment • Where possible use learning diagnostics to improve provision
Application 10: Recognise the power relations inherent in pedagogy, knowledge and curriculum choices	• That school knowledge reflects positively our diverse communities and the backgrounds of our children • Equity is promoted through access for all children to rich pedagogies and action taken when more support or experience is needed • Children feel empowered to succeed in our education system	• Build a curriculum that empowers a sense of belonging and identity in children • Enable children to develop the knowledge and skills to engage in debate about 'the best that has been thought and said' (Robinson, 2018)

Trail 3: Community

This is about engaging children, families and communities, amplifying their power and voice through better understanding, building bridges and engaging with civic responsibilities.

Table 9.6: Community and agency

Application	What is at issue	Into practice
Application 11: Build increasingly sophisticated understandings of childhood and development	• Our understanding of modern childhood and ability to meet children's 'real' needs	• Recognise the active strategies of a learning culture and positive psychology (Seligman, 2011); responding to setbacks, where 'grit', for example, is needed (Tough, 2012; Duckworth and Yeager, 2015) • Build 'growth mindset' (Dweck, 2006)

(Continued)

Table 9.6: (Continued)

Application	What is at issue	Into practice
Application 12: Build bridges between home, school and community	• That children's education is seen as an equal partner-ship between home and school • Children value education and feel a sense of belonging and achievement • That the patterns of schooling are re-thought for the twenty-first century	• Consider the 'Flipped School' concept (Groves and West-Burnham, 2020) • Develop a local model and frame-work for social justice – encourage children to be involved in community projects • Use community and technological resources to extend the concept of school (clubs, sports groups, environmental campaigns)
Application 13: Elaborate the concepts of civic responsibility, 'common' schools and collective impact	• The sense that schools 'serve' communities – Fielding and Moss's (2011) 'common' school • Enable a long-term vision, sustaina-bility and community leadership	• Embrace the 'collective impact' ethos by addressing local issues, such as those raised by Marcus Rashford, for example: food poverty, housing issues, cultural behaviours • Where possible use social pedago-gies to engage children beyond the school

Trail 4: Innovation

Patterns often repeat in practice, continuing to do so until we learn how to change our path. This trail is about the management of change: Engeström (2015) articulates the individual-explosive (tending towards the singular impact of individuals), invisible-gradual (which is largely focused on maintenance and stability) and collective-expansive. The latter constantly builds for the future, is optimistic, energetic and involving, and avoids the pitfalls of determinism and self-preservation (Berliner, 1994).

Table 9.7: Innovation

Application	What is at issue	Into practice
Application 14: Develop change processes that are collective-expansive	• Pedagogy is consistently and creatively renewed through active involvement in planned ways • Teaching remains in clear focus and there is consistent attention to children's learning	• Use a range of productive practices to continually focus pedagogy (pupil progress meetings, self-evaluation, assessment) • Elaborate and specify pedagogies (Hopkins and Craig, 2014) • Bring groups together to address identified issues with focus and clarity
Application 15: Use pre-figurative practices – namely, building working models that match aims and values to pedagogies	• Searching for common understandings, bringing evidence to bear and creating exemplary practice is a powerful means of building pedagogy	• Create exemplary micro-cosms of possible practices (change laboratories) • Intensify and focus approaches rather than scatter and disperse (Elmore, 1996)
Application 16: Pedagogic design work (see Gay and Hembrooke, 2004) involves a process of constructive enquiry searching for holistic pedagogies	• Pedagogy is actively constructed and developed • Children's voice is engaged as a central component of the process	• Engage children in the design process; design in context to understand classroom processes; make processes flexible, adaptive and rooted; build practice together and, wherever possible, explore other similar contexts
Application 17: Use 'boundary objects' or emerging pedagogies (Star and Griesemer, 1989) as a stimulus for development	• Accessing the best ideas, concepts, evidence and practice from other contexts and using them as a stimulus	• Use instructional rounds (Hopkins and Craig, 2014), for example, to look beyond immediate context • Engage in a wide range of networks and productive partnerships

Reflection point

Collective-expansive, pre-figurative practice and pedagogic design work offer variations to managing change. Which would fit best with your approach? What is missing from them that would be important in your context?

Cultural conditions

As might be expected with a socio-cultural approach, critical conflict does emerge when 'trails' are explored but can be overcome. It is increasingly possible, enabled through new technologies and their communication power, to turn emergent practices into practical, accessible resources. It is increasingly likely that innovations can cross organisational boundaries as the pioneers and innovators meet with other colleagues, share their achievements and move their knowledge around. In his views of effect sizes, Hattie (2009), for example, rates innovation highly, in the sense of willingness to try new methods. The increasing publication of extensively researched approaches, combined with skilfully constructed 'exemplary' practice in accessible forms for practitioners through, for example, the Education Endowment Fund and Chartered College, enables knowledge transfer. Enabling innovation will be key to allow 'boundary objects' to emerge and expand: they will need to be supported through a system that:

- makes it as easy as possible to innovate within a negotiated authorising environment, wherever possible allowing social construction;
- reduces elements of the rule system which limit innovative practices;
- provides support for innovative groups by enabling and resourcing their activity;
- makes available meaningful and accessible forms of research evidence generated through multiple methods;
- provides incentives in the areas for development by creating 'zones';
- enables new collaborative groups to gather together across organisations;
- maintains a focus on equitable access to developmental opportunities and resources.

Innovation is powerful when constructed ethically within and beyond organisations because:

1 These conditions create respect for solutions which emerge from the situation in which professionals find themselves. At their very best these are co-constructed in communities and with children.
2 These approaches reflect the contextual differences to be found in school and are likely to be successful because of this sensitivity.
3 A culture of positivity and identity can emerge because the process of self-efficacy emerges at the individual and organisational level.

This means trusted teaching professionals have positive energy, routes for their voices and diverse points of view are heard. Endeavour combined with deliberate action produces positive outcomes. As Wegerif comments: 'It has long been clear that learning anything significantly changes who we are and how we make sense of the world around us' (Wegerif, 2013, p. 89).

Deep, energising change is participative and communal; it is long-term work; it engages the commons, connects to movements but is carefully analytic of what is right – it has collegiality in a place where people are forging pedagogies with others. The journey matters because it reflects how people feel about a place: it may never be complete but the energy of that travel is vital to take participants beyond the cult of 'transformism' (Avis, 2009). The journey is a psychological challenge but with a constancy that Wrigley (2003) would see as full of 'hope' – an understanding that there will be short-term setbacks but the destination remains constant and possible.

Next: This section has proposed a holistic version of primary education and an evolutionary approach. The concluding chapter provides some final thoughts about socio-cultural dynamics and an expansive, evolutionary, exemplary and equitable system.

Part **4**

Conclusion

10 Primary education: pedagogy as a whole

> **This chapter** draws the book to its conclusion, summarising some of the key points drawn out of the socio-cultural approach that runs through the book.
>
> **It re-iterates** the potential of an *evolutionary*, *expansive*, *exemplary* and *equitable* approach to developing a holistic primary education.

In many ways, primary education retains a strong connection with its past with financial, structural, physical, professional and pedagogical continuities. When we look at primary education through a lens of socio-cultural dynamics, we see a system that is huge: it caters for 4.5+ million children in 16,000+ schools! It is a system that has been subject to powerful generative forces (international comparison; performativity and accountability; the knowledge-rich curriculum; autonomy and the new school system; the self-improving concept; debates about teachers and the teaching profession; and matters of social justice) but historical legacies (the generalist class teacher and 'stability, standards and subjects') still constantly constrain and influence how we think.

The Covid-19 pandemic interrupted primary education and we learned some key things. Four of them stand out here:

- Under pressure the capacity to adapt and to respond to demanding challenges was clearly demonstrated by the system (though, of course, with degrees of variation and lessons to be learned).
- Primary educators are driven by a very strong moral purpose; this commitment to children often overrode other considerations.
- The potential of new technologies to impact on the construction of education and learning experiences could be part of reshaping pedagogy.
- The role of primary schools as 'children's centres' became more overt: the sense of responsibility for children's needs in their widest sense was powerful.

The story of the pandemic can teach us something, too, about motivation: doing the best for children in adversity arguably unleashed a powerful intrinsic force concerned to get things right for children. So, while history does suggest a system with a tendency to conservatism, there should be a strong sense of pride alongside optimism and the courage to allow an evolutionary process of innovation that fosters what Donohoo et al. (2018) call 'collective efficacy'. The context is changing too and an over-emphasis on control and standardisation may not serve us well in the future in an increasingly networked world. Fullan (2021) warns of simply getting better at a bad game.

Table 10.1: Understanding primary education: eight socio-cultural features

Primary education is constantly evolving – there is constant construction and reconstruction of object and pedagogies as human consciousness evolves. Primary education is emergent, distributed and developmental, so it is vital to set direction.

Primary education goes hand in hand with organisation – primary schools provide a vital organising function for society by safeguarding, socialising and nurturing children. Our organisation must, however, be focused, first and foremost, on learning.

Primary education is socially, culturally and historically situated – Daniels (2012) argues that we never 'speak from nowhere': as we appropriate ideas and approaches with their affordances and constraints, they are defined by culture and history (these include the class teacher system and 'stability, standards and subjects')

Primary education is an innately social process – language underpins everything, it determines consciousness, what Wertsch calls 'the inherent dialogicality of human life' (1998, p. vii). How we talk about primary education will influence its development. Primary education has an important role to advocate for children and their families.

There is a regulative discourse that surrounds primary education – it is bound by the sense that Daniels (2012) suggests surrounds the morals, attitudes and community relations of primary schools. Taken further this implies an interrelationship between the design of learning environments and the dominant educational ideology: they influence and shape each other.

Culture has a significant influence on primary education – dominant ideologies colour our perception of what should be present and what is effective. What transpires externally has a shaping effect. (Note the antecedents for British values.)

Leadership (in its widest sense) is a major determinant – 'the culture and politics of schools have a major role in explaining why a school is or is not effective' (Hattie, 2009, p. 69).

The structural and organisational features of the system of primary education offer affordances and constraints – they denote choices and decisions and act as critical regulators (Alexander, 2000): finance and school planning are predicated on units of thirty children.

The system of primary education is replete with fascinating socio-cultural dynamics (objects, motives, cultural context, voices, histories and contradictions; see Chapter 1). They need to be understood because they constrain and define (see Table 10.1) but when unlocked release the rich potential of the system.

Primary education stands on a cusp: while issues of access, entitlement and many aspects of practice might appear settled, other pressing challenges of social equity and creating a 'holistic' approach fit for purpose for our time generate energies to take us forward. The promise of a socio-cultural perspective is that through pioneering leadership and creating the right systemic architecture, primary education can evolve and develop.

Two things must happen. First, if primary education is to exploit the transformative potential in the longer term with the same immediacy that the pandemic demanded, the object must evolve. As Edwards explains:

> Systems learn, that is, change, through the expansion of the object that is being worked on. The object is expanded when the variety of interpretations that may be available and the contradictions that arise are revealed and explored. (Edwards, 2009, p. 210)

The object must expand so that there can be a reshaping in the thinking in the system so that policy development recognises the value of primary education as a phase in its own right, is truly collaborative and generative with a strong emphasis on pedagogy and teacher leadership.

Second, all of this requires a long-term strategy (not a quick fix of short-lived policies caught in changing political priorities) and the creation of an innovation ecosystem. Hannon et al. argue that:

> .... creating the conditions for a flourishing ecosystem of innovation should be our objective if organised learning is to adapt adequately to the pressures and opportunities for change. (Hannon et al., 2011, p. 18)

There is a recognition among primary educators that the old model is ready for change, the challenge is to actively build the new. The collegiality of teachers (and therefore those who lead our schools) matters hugely in such a process: they will be the architects and pioneers. Doing so means understanding and working through the socio-cultural features of the system and, as Chapter 1 argued, remembering that pedagogy is the most vital ingredient: 'how' we teach and 'what' we teach should be in a powerful mutually constitutive dynamic with 'who' and 'why' we teach. Yet, increasingly this future is more difficult to anticipate; dynamic and adaptive processes of development are needed and Gerver captures the challenge (we could extend the descriptor school to encompass the whole 'system'):

> The school of the future recognises that the future will always be unknown but that, by learning to deal with it, live within it and be excited by it, we will provide our children with the education they will need and that they deserve. (Gerver, 2009, p. 152)

If primary education is to continue to evolve into something more holistic, it cannot shy away from our existential challenges. It may seem paradoxical that a more individualistic period where taking the personal responsibilities of leadership may be needed to ignite the changes, but this coupled with a powerful altruism is needed for our collective challenges. The collective-expansive sets the tone for primary education that pushes boundaries, it is about 'anticipating, steering and mastering' (Engeström, 1987) and driving purpose and meaning into the system: creating a new holistic paradigm that releases energy. These calls for change, for evolution, lead us back then to five areas covered in Part 2: framed into questions they ask us what do we want of 'learners', 'pedagogy', 'leadership', 'organisations' and the 'system'?

Table 10.2: Socio-cultural approaches: learners, pedagogy, leadership, organisation and system

Question	Possibilities
What kind of learners do we want?	**Balanced, knowledgeable, resilient, self-confident and capable children** – learners with character; who practise citizenship; who communicate effectively though a range of media; critical thinkers and problem-solvers; those who can collaborate and work well in teams; and learners who exercise creativity and imagination (Fullan and Langworthy, 2013)
What kind of pedagogy do we want?	**Where well-being, learning and achievement come together** – where deep learning involves an accelerative apprenticeship; through a guided participatory and dialogic process; in a rich, multi-sensory and creative form; through organised, skilful and critical inquiry and by supporting the formation of identity through a sense of well-being and belonging.
What kind of leadership do we want?	**Leadership that is expansive and collegial** – leaders who set direction; build relationships and develop people; who develop the organisation to support desired practices and improve the instructional (pedagogical) programme (from Leithwood et al., 2019).
What kind of organisations do we want?	**'Civic institutions' that are deeply caring, committed and with high levels of pedagogic capacity** – build community connections; have distinctive character; a culture of collegiality; enable teacher leadership and engage in collaboration and public value partnership.
What kind of system do we want?	**A collaborative system with clear aims and purpose; an innovation-oriented ecosystem and a deep concern for equity** – conditions of trust and reciprocity with resilience and distributed capacity creating sustainable innovation and expansive energy.

Helping all children to flourish requires a commitment to fairness not sameness. The term 'collective impact' captures the new ethic well, building social entrepreneurialism and public value partnerships. Simply: systems don't change when only one party takes action (Fullan and Langworthy, 2014). It also takes educators into partnership beyond the school gates, for while food poverty, overcrowded housing and remarkably wide pay gaps exist, it will need collective endeavour and our cultural behaviours will be key. Strong social pedagogies that bridge between home and school (see Groves and West-Burnham, 2020) mean setting up the system to support children – education being seen as an interconnecting experience. Partnership will be vital, it cannot happen through education alone. As Gorard advises: 'Education policy cannot be expected to solve issues such as child poverty alone, in the short term, or even at all' (2018, p. 205).

Constructing this new system must answer questions about equity. MacBeath et al. (2018) suggest four integrity tests are applied: (1) redistribution, (2) recognition, (3) representation and (4) parity of participation. In this model, *redistribution* asks whether health and welfare concerns figure in meeting children's needs and whether the combined programme is inclusive and directive of resources where appropriate. It asks whether minority knowledge is valued. Through *recognition* it asks whether the child's culture world is visibly valued. Whether capabilities to function in the social setting are included and if children's varied paths to learning are recognised. *Representation* means asking whether teachers, parents and children are involved in decision-making, particularly around the curriculum. And finally, *parity of participation* considers whether minority voices are sought out and heard and whether leadership is shared. Equity needs to be a focus of the collective energies of primary educators but with a recognition that it will require collaborative strategies extending beyond schools to support and engage all children and their families (Gorard, 2018; Groves and West-Burnham, 2020).

Three tensions at the heart of the system

The potential for innovation always exists in systems but what is released depends on what is valued and why. Developing primary education will not be without constantly emerging dilemmas, tensions and contradictions, three of which are currently strategically important and worthy of further comment.

The tension between public value partnership and corporate governance

Osborne (2006) describes an emergent phase of New Public Governance where the relationship is increasingly between government and the private sector (in England largely in the form of Multi-Academy Trusts) managed through contracts and agreements with providers under pressure to be increasingly 'corporate, bureaucratic and standardised' (Greany and Higham, 2018). This discourse can leave a contradiction between competitive elements of the system and the collegiality needed to protect all children's interests: in 2021, this was yet to be fully reconciled. Socio-cultural dynamics recognises the benefits of strong corporate governance but also suggests subsidiarity to release and express the energies found in localities. In Chapter 7, the potential of 'public value partnerships' was explored. How the system is structured, particularly in the middle-tier, has great importance moving forwards, otherwise 'public value partnerships' may find that the road has many obstacles if the system allows 'winners and losers' (Greany and Higham, 2018).

Our vision of the system will matter greatly here. Greany and Higham's (2018) study also observes the relationship between Multi-Academy Trust size and achievement – as MATs continue to proliferate we need to understand much more about this and rigorously learn the lessons for design purposes from those that succeed. Maintaining openness will be vital. For example, the principle of the 'common' school might reflect an alternative aspiration for equity premised not on uniformity but on diversity and plurality:

> [first] through a personalist approach but with deep respect for otherness and the absolute singularity of the individual within the relational context of a restless inclusive community; second through a desire and readiness to experiment, to explore new possibilities that emerge from democratic processes. (Fielding and Moss, 2011, p. 113)

Debates about curriculum and key epistemological questions

Questions of knowledge have been increasingly significant in primary education: the narrowness of 'standards'; what is meant by 'knowledge-rich, direct instruction' (Claxton, 2021); Ofsted's (2020c) 'intent, implementation and impact', and debates about the extended purposes of primary education (Alexander, 2010b) present many questions. Alexander argues that epistemological knowledge and its debates are important because leaders have a responsibility to understand a school's 'pool of curriculum capacity' so that it can meet 'children's entitlement to a curriculum of consistent quality as well as breadth' (2013, p. 11).

Some aspects of learning are not easily measurable by traditional forms of assessment (e.g. Gipps, 2002) or easily evaluated through research: they remain important even though they cannot be measured. It is suggested, too, that introducing new technology will further impact on the epistemic (Luckin et al., 2012; Luckin, 2018) and pedagogic balance. It is already possible to support specific cognitive skills in reading and numeracy through technological systems incorporating learning analytics – but how far should this go? These will become increasingly vital questions in the very near future. What kind of reliance might we put on such systems?

The debate may be as important as the outcomes. Robinson (2018) suggested the importance of extending children's horizons so that they can skilfully join and contribute to the Arnoldian debate about the 'best that has been thought and said'. Without continued open debate, we may remain firmly locked in inferior versions of 'standards and subjects' and restrict opportunities to engage with alternative models, new technologies and the needs of today's children along the powerful lines Fullan and Langworthy (2013) explore in 'New Pedagogies for Deep Learning'.

The future leadership of primary education

The development of the teaching profession and leadership of a self-improving system are 'under construction': there is much still to be done. Teachers must become advocates: 'not only fighting for better conditions for themselves; rather it is about advocating for education and for pedagogy' (MacBeath et al., 2018, p. 160). However, they must do this in a way that reflects the wider values, evidence and voices that surround them; if they retreat to ideological positions or close the doors, they weaken their position and potentially leave themselves open to public vilification. Development is still needed in the way practitioners are influenced and convinced of the quality of research. In the DfE's extended evaluation it became clear that for teachers making the link between research evidence and its translation into their practices will, understandably, be an on-going journey (Greany and Brown, 2017). Collins and Coleman describe this well: 'There is a clear difference between being an evidence-rich system and a system where evidence is a central part of day-to-day operations' (Collins and Coleman, 2017, p. 17).

Teachers will need to be open to theoretical and empirical discourse, so that change becomes self-reflexive (Wardekker, 2000). Brown and Rogers (2014) comment that developing practice with and through expert practitioners requires engagement with knowledge 'creation'. Perhaps Vygotsky's idea of a 'pedology', an extensive multi-disciplinary understanding of the development of the 'whole' child, will be needed: a comprehensive open system that begins to combine key areas of understanding. It would have to be a dynamic framework, bringing complexity together; however, the link between phonics and orthographic mapping, for example, might be found together with new insights into models of sensory attention, alongside evidence from randomised controlled trials in a comprehensive semantic framework.

Together these three tensions reflect power and control in the system; our approaches to learning and professional attitudes and expertise. They are stepping-off points that enable us to reflect and recognise that the system still needs significant further development on its evolutionary journey.

All three of these areas must be kept in dialogue, as Alexander commented:

> Dialogue is essential to how we respond to the cultural and existential crises that confront us, but only if we are able to defend those of its ingredients that are currently under attack: voice, argument and truth. (Alexander, 2020, p. 198)

Final thoughts

There is very successful pedagogy within the English system of primary education and plenty of it too. The lens of socio-cultural dynamics recognises the commitment, skill and energy expended every day in every lesson in every classroom. There are a series of constraints too but the will exists to further release primary education's potential while keeping the rigour, ambition and vigour that characterise its most powerful iterations. The lens of socio-cultural dynamics suggests interconnecting productive approaches that are evolutionary, expansive, exemplary and equitable.

The recognition in this account, given the fast-changing world, is that of an *evolutionary* approach: this means taking steps beyond the here and now, into the world of digital media, of research and evidence, to real-world challenges and bringing them to the heart of our pedagogies. Pedagogies will for example be enhanced by technology but it falls on education to be ahead of the technology, thinking through its application, not losing sight of the importance of children's agency. This means *expansive* leadership – to realise that leaders can co-create the system, although that means all of the layers need the space for innovation and all of the component parts of the system being designed to enable success for all. Pedagogy should be designed so, third, the challenge is to create and recreate that which is *exemplary*, rooted in powerful 'prefigurative' developments that emerge from practice and are well evidenced. This means celebrating the practices of primary education that are realised with children and building our futures from these: justified, articulated and tested. A system can flourish from exemplary practice that is not just full of content but deep and full of meaning too. Last but not least there is a commitment to *equity* and to engage in partnerships and approaches that offer agency, optimism and the knowledge, skills and understanding for every child to succeed. This cannot be done by primary education alone – it requires partnership. This is a final reminder in primary education that relationships are at its core, rediscovered once again in what it means to be human and what brings us together: wellbeing, learning and achievement and in our modern world science combining with the human spirit in a holistic pedagogy for a sustainable future.

The development of the World Wide Web provides a possible analogy for the socio-cultural dynamics of primary education. The internet of Web 1.0 was largely static, filled with information and with limited interactivity: a broad parallel, perhaps, with some similarities to models of education based in transmission or broadcast. The evolution to Web 2.0 was towards increasing social connectivity and collaboration. It finds a rejoinder in the increasing interactivity of pedagogies seen in various guises. What we are seeing now is the emergence of Web 3.0, the so-called semantic web, resulting from developments across a range of technologies ('block chain', for example), and through which users increasingly easily create, share and connect. It is highly accessible, hugely flexible and inherently more demanding. It presents users with many affordances but, arguably, as many challenges. Like Web 3.0, a holistic version of primary education is similarly demanding but potentially rewarding with a multiplicity of purposes and pedagogies. Perhaps like Web 3.0 it will not be born on a specific date but is already present, emergent and evolving from policy and practice together, rising as a 'living system'. And expect there to be what Christian (2020) calls, in the context of technological advance, alignment problems that will create challenges and need to be resolved.

Of course, the analogy has limitations, but if we think of holistic primary education as v3.0, then it reframes and expands our relationship with children, knowledge and pedagogy, increasingly emphasising dialogic approaches, well-being and diversity. There will be an increasing need to explore key concepts – what, for example, constitutes character education with 3- and 4-year-olds? How do we assess the qualities of citizenship? How can we introduce new technologies and manage adaptive systems that offer benefits, for example, around hard-to-teach content (Luckin, 2018; Christodoulou, 2020)? How can we combine understandings emergent from science, research and evidence?

A fundamental characteristic of our future lives appears that not only humans will be able to make connections, increasingly so will the web: hence the descriptor 'the semantic web' and the idea of connective intelligence, concepts, applications and people. Ultimately, we may then begin to ask more fundamental questions about why, for example, we choose to bring children together in the ways that we do; or consider shifts to the school day and the sacrosanct school year (Dale, 2008). Nevertheless, the sense of belonging and engagement so central to a socio-cultural interpretation in no way advocates the end of formal schooling for primary education but does suggest new flexible 'hybrid' forms of pedagogy that encourage dialogue and creativity and might eventually serve us better as schools move further towards their communities. Evolution helps us remember too that Web 4.0 is just around the corner (Almeida, 2017)!

To see primary education as one of our 'commons', as one of the key resources of twenty-first-century life, is to recognise a wealth that belongs to us all, something of great value yet in constant renewal. If the challenge is accepted, our ability to grasp the changing nature of primary education is at the heart of creating understandings that sustain change recognising that in our current world these can become 'runaway objects' (Engeström, 2009). Such objects are powerful, sometimes frighteningly so, for they gather intense momentum, overturning established ideas. Runaway objects are also contested and can be both controversial and dramatic – primary education will need to embrace stability and possibility. From such an environment Laloux concludes that these are extraordinary times:

> Often confusing but full of possibilities. It is up to us to invent a new path. There is an old saying ... that seems particularly relevant to me as we embark on the shift to more life-giving organisations – *We are the people we have been waiting for.* (Laloux, 2016, p. 159)

Bibliography

Adams, P. (2011) Continuity and the coalition: Primary pedagogy as craft and primary pedagogy as performance, *Educational Review*, 63 (4), 467–483.

Advisory Group for Citizenship (1998) *Education for citizenship and the teaching of democracy in schools* (The Crick Report), London: Department for Education.

Ainscow, M. (2015) *Towards Self-Improving School Systems: Lessons from a City Challenge*, London: Routledge.

Ainscow, M., Conteh, J., Dyson, A. and Gallannaugh, F. (2010) Children in primary education: Demography, culture, diversity and inclusion, in R. Alexander (ed.) *The Cambridge Primary Review Research Surveys*, London: Routledge.

Ainscow, M., Dyson, A., Goldrick, S. and West, M. (2012) *Developing Equitable Education Systems*, London: Routledge.

Aldrich, R. (ed.) (2001) *A Century of Education*, London: Routledge/Falmer.

Aldrich, R. (2003) The three duties of the historian of education, *History of Education*, 32 (2), 133–143.

Aldrich, R. (2013) Neuroscience, education and the evolution of the human brain, *History of Education*, 42 (3), 396–410.

Alexander, R. (1984) *Primary Teaching*, London: Cassell.

Alexander, R. (1989) Core subjects and autumn leaves: The National Curriculum and the languages of primary education, *Education 3–13*, 17 (1), 3–8.

Alexander, R. (1991) *Primary Education in Leeds: Twelfth and final report from the Primary Needs Independent Evaluation Project*, Leeds: University of Leeds.

Alexander, R. (1992) *Policy and Practice in Primary Education*, London: Routledge.

Alexander, R. (1995) *Versions of Primary Education*, London: Routledge.

Alexander, R. (2000) *Culture and Pedagogy: International Comparisons in Primary Education*, Oxford: Blackwell.

Alexander, R. (2004) Still no pedagogy? Principle, pragmatism and compliance in primary education, *Cambridge Journal of Education*, 34 (1), 7–34.

Alexander, R. (2008) *Essays on Pedagogy*, London: Routledge.

Alexander, R. (2010a) *Reform, retrench or recycle? A curriculum cautionary tale*, Keynote address, National Curriculum Symposium, University of Melbourne, 25–27 February.

Alexander, R. (ed.) (2010b) *Children, Their World, Their Education: Final Report and Recommendations of the Cambridge Primary Review*, London: Routledge.

Alexander, R. (ed.) (2010c) *The Cambridge Primary Review Research Surveys*, London: Routledge.

Alexander, R. (2012) *International evidence, national policy and classroom practice: Questions of judgement, vision and trust*, Closing session keynote address, Third Van Leer International Conference on Education, Jerusalem, 24 May [https://cprtrust.org.uk/wp-content/uploads/2014/06/20120524_Van_Leer_Alexander.pdf].

Alexander, R. (2013) *Curriculum freedom, capacity and leadership in the primary school: Expert perspective*, Nottingham: National College for School Leadership [https://eprints.whiterose.ac.uk/76338/1/Alexander_Nat_Coll_curric_capacity.pdf].

Alexander, R. (2016) *What works and what matters: Education in spite of policy*, Keynote address, Cambridge Primary Review Trust National Conference, London, 18

November [https://cprtrust.org.uk/wp-content/uploads/2016/11/Alexander-CPRT-keynote-final-3.pdf].

Alexander, R. (2018) Developing dialogic teaching: Genesis, process, trial, *Research Papers in Education*, 33 (5), 561–598.

Alexander, R. (2020) *A Dialogic Teaching Companion*, London: Routledge.

Allard, A. and Santoro, N. (2006) Troubling identities: Teacher education and students' construction of class and ethnicity, *Cambridge Journal of Education*, 36 (1), 115–129.

Allen, B. (2019) Improving teachers' instructional practice: Critically important, but incredibly hard to do, in C. Scutt and S. Harrison (eds.) *Teacher CPD: International trends, opportunities and challenges*, London: Chartered College of Teaching [https://my.chartered.college/wp-content/uploads/2019/11/Chartered-College-International-Teacher-CPD-report.pdf].

Almeida, F. (2017) Concepts and dimensions of Web 4.0, *International Journal of Computers and Technology*, 16 (7), 7040–7046.

Altrichter, H. and Kemethofer, D. (2015) Does accountability pressure through school inspections promote school improvement? *School Effectiveness and School Improvement*, 24 (1), 32–56.

Ancona, D., Malone, T., Orlikowski, W. and Senge P. (2008) In praise of the incomplete leader, *Harvard Business Review*, February, 111–121.

Anyon, J. (1981) Social class and school knowledge, *Curriculum Inquiry*, 11 (1), 3–42.

Anyon, J. (2005) *Radical Possibilities: Public Policy, Urban Education and a New Social Movement*, London: Routledge.

Apple, M. (1996) *Cultural Politics and Education*, Boston, MA: Teachers College Press.

Apple, M. (1998) What reform talk does: Creating inequalities in education, *Educational Administration Quarterly*, 24 (3), 257–271.

Apple, M. (2013) *Can Education Change Society?* London: Routledge.

Archer, M. (1984) *Social Origins of Educational Systems*, London: Sage.

Argyris, C. and Schön, D. (1977) *Organizational Learning: A Theory of Action Perspective*, Reading, MA: Addison-Wesley.

Arnold, M. (1869/1993) Culture and anarchy, in S. Collini (ed.) *Culture and Anarchy and Other Writings*, Cambridge: Cambridge University Press.

Asbury, K. and Plomin, R. (2014) *G is for Genes: The Impact of Genetics on Education and Achievement*, Chichester: Wiley.

Ashby, W. (1958) Requisite variety and its implications for the control of complex systems, *Cybernetica*, 1 (2), 83–99.

Atwal, K. (2019) *The Thinking School: Developing a Dynamic Learning Community*, Oxford: Blackwell.

Auerbach, S. (ed.) (2012) *School Leadership for Authentic Family and Community Partnerships: Research Perspectives for Transforming Practice*, London: Routledge

Auld, R. (1976) *The William Tyndale Junior and Infants Schools Public Inquiry: A report to the Inner London Education Authority by Robin Auld QC*, London: ILEA.

Avis, J. (2009) Transformation or transformism? Engeström's version of activity theory, *Educational Review*, 61 (2), 151–165.

Azorin, C. (2020) Beyond COVID-19 supernova: Is another education coming?, *Journal of Professional Capital and Community*, 5 (3/4), 381–390.

Baines, E., Blatchford, P. and Chowne, A. (2007) Improving the effectiveness of collaborative group-work in primary schools: Effects on science attainment, ESRC Teaching and Learning Research Programme Special Issue, *British Educational Research Journal*, 33 (5), 663–680.

Ball, S. (1994) *Education Reform*, Buckingham: Open University Press.

Ball, S. (2003) The teacher's soul and the terrors of performativity, *Journal of Education Policy*, 18 (2), 215–222.

Ball, S. (2007) *Education plc: Understanding Private Sector Participation in Public Sector Education*, London: Routledge.

Ball, S. (2008) *The Education Debate*, Bristol: Policy Press.

Bambrick-Santoyo, P. (2012) *Leverage Leadership: A Practical Guide to Building Exceptional Schools*, San Francisco, CA: Jossey-Bass.

Bangs, J. and Frost, D. (2012) *Teacher self-efficacy, voice and leadership: Towards a policy framework for Education International: A report on an international survey of the views of teachers and teacher union officials*, Cambridge: University of Cambridge, Faculty of Education and the Education International Research Institute [https://download.ei-ie.org/Docs/WebDepot/teacher_self-efficacy_voice_leadership.pdf].

Bangs, J., MacBeath, J. and Galton, M. (2011) *Reinventing Schools, Reforming Teaching: From Political Visions to Classroom Reality*, London: Routledge.

Barber, M. (1996) *The Learning Game: Arguments for an Education Revolution*, London: Gollancz.

Barber, M. and Mourshed, M. (2007) *How the World's Best Performing School Systems Come out on Top*, London: McKinsey.

Barenberg, J. and Dutke, S. (2019) Testing and metacognition: Retrieval practise effects on metacognitive monitoring in learning from text, *Memory*, 27 (3), 269–279.

Barnes, J. (2021) Intimations of Utopia: Values, sustaining environments and the flourishing of children and teachers, in V. Bower (ed.) *Debates in Primary Education*, London: Routledge.

Barron, B. and Darling-Hammond, L. (2010) Prospects and challenges for inquiry-based approaches to learning, in H. Dumont, D. Istance and F. Benavides (eds.) *The Nature of Learning: Using Research to Inspire Practice*, Paris: OECD Publishing [https://doi.org/10.1787/9789264086487-11-en].

Bates, A. (2013) Transcending systems thinking in education reform: Implications for policy-makers and school leaders, *Journal of Education Policy*, 28 (1), 38–54.

Baxter, J. (2019) Multi-Academy trusts in England: What drives them to grow? British Educational Research Assocation. 06.11.2019 https://www.bera.ac.uk/blog/multi-academy-trusts-in-england-what-drives-them-to-grow

Beck, D. and Cowan, C. (1996) *Spiral Dynamics: Mastering Values, Leadership and Change*, Oxford: Blackwell.

Beckett, L. and Wood, J. (2012) Talking honestly in a challenging primary school: England, in T. Wrigley, P. Thompson and B. Lingard (eds.) *Changing Schools: Making a World of Difference*, London: Routledge.

Bedny, G. and Harris, S. (2005) The systemic-structural theory of activity: Applications to the study of human work, *Mind, Culture and Activity*, 12 (2), 128–147.

Bedny, G. and Karkowski, W. (2004) Activity theory as a basis for the study of work, *Ergonomics*, 47 (2), 134–153.

Belfield, C., Crawford, C. and Sibieta, L. (2018) *Long-run comparisons of spending per pupil across different stages of education*, London: Institute for Fiscal Studies [https://ifs.org.uk/publications/8937].

Benn, M. (2011) *Schools Wars: The Battle for Britain's Education*, London: Verso.

Bereiter, C. (2002) *Education and Mind in the Knowledge Age*, Hillsdale, NJ: Erlbaum.

Berliner, D. (1994) Expertise: The wonder of exemplary performance, in J. Mangieri and C. Block (eds.) *Creating Powerful Thinking in Teachers and Students*, Fort Worth, TX: Holt, Rinehart & Winston.

Berliner, D. (2004) Expert teachers: Their characteristics, development and accomplishments, *Bulletin of Science, Technology and Society*, 24 (3), 200–212.

Berliner, D. (2011) Rational responses to high stakes testing: The case of curriculum narrowing and the harm that follows, *Cambridge Journal of Education*, 41 (3), 287–302.

Berliner, D. (2019) Teachers' analyses of educational research as a source of professional development, in C. Scutt and S. Harrison (eds.) *Teacher CPD: International trends, opportunities and challenges*, London: Chartered College of Teaching [https://my.chartered.college/wp-content/uploads/2019/11/Chartered-College-International-Teacher-CPD-report.pdf].

Biddulph, J. (2018) Designing a curriculum to nurture compassionate citizens, *Impact: Journal of the Chartered College of Teaching*, September [https://impact.chartered.college/article/designing-a-curriculum-to-nurture-compassionate-citizens/].

Biesta, G. (2010) Why 'what works' still won't work: From evidence-based education to value-based education, *Studies in Philosophy and Education*, 29 (5), 491–503.

Biesta, G. (2020) Risking ourselves in education: Qualification, socialisation and subjectification revisited, *Educational Theory*, 70 (1), 89–104.

Bisra, K., Liu, Q. and Nesbit, J. (2018) Inducing self-explanation: A meta-analysis, *Educational Psychology Review*, 30, 703–725.

Black, P. and Wiliam, D. (1998) Inside the black box: Raising standards through classroom assessment, *Phi Delta Kappan*, 80 (2), 139–144.

Blair, C. and Diamond, A. (2008) Biological processes in prevention and intervention: The promotion of self-regulation as a means of preventing school failure, *Development and Psychopathology*, 20 (3), 899–911.

Blanton, W., Moorman, G. and Zimmerman, S. (2000) *Ways of knowing, ways of doing, ways of transporting: Mastering social practices in the fifth dimension*, Boone, NC: Laboratory of Learning and Technology, Appalachian State University.

Blatchford, P. (2012) *Reassessing the Impact of Teaching Assistants: How Research Challenges Practice and Policy*, London: Routledge.

Blatchford, R. (2014) *The Restless School*, London: John Catt.

Blatchford, P., Hallam, S., Ireson, J. and Kutnick, P., with Creech, A. (2010) Classes, groups and transitions: Structures for teaching and learning, in R. Alexander (ed.) *The Cambridge Primary Review Research Surveys*, London: Routledge.

Blyth, A. (1967a) *English Primary Education: A Sociological Description*, vol. 1: *Schools*, London: Routledge & Kegan Paul.

Blyth, A. (1967b) *English Primary Education: A Sociological Description*, vol. 2: *Background*, London: Routledge & Kegan Paul.

Blyth, A. (1984) *Development, Experience and Curriculum in Primary Education*, London: Croom Helm.

Board of Education (1931) *Report of the Consultative Committee on the Primary School* (The Hadow Report), London: HMSO [http://www.educationengland.org.uk/documents/hadow1931/hadow1931.html].

Bourdieu, P. (1974) The school as a conservative force: Scholastic and cultural inequalities, in J. Eggleston (ed.) *Contemporary Research in the Sociology of Education*, London: Methuen.

Bourdieu, P. (1977) *Outline of a Theory of Practice*, Cambridge: Cambridge University Press.

Bourdieu, P. and Passeron, J.-C. (1990) *Reproduction in Education, Society and Culture*, London: Sage.

Bradford, H. and Wyse, D. (2020) Two-year-old and three-year-old children's writing: The contradictions of children's and adults' conceptualisations, *Early Years* [https://doi.org/10.1080/09575146.2020.1736519].

Breuleux, A., Laferrière, T. and Lamon, M. (2002) *Capacity building within and across countries into the effective use of ICTs*, 2002 Pan-Canadian Education Research Agenda Symposium, Montreal, Quebec, 30 April–2 May.

Brighouse, T. (1997) Leading and managing primary schools: The changing world of the local education authority, in C. Cullingford (ed.) *The Politics of Primary Education*, Buckingham: Open University Press.

Brighouse, T. (2011) *Decline and fall: Are state schools and universities on the point of collapse?*, First Annual Lecture, Lady Margaret Hall, Oxford.

Brighouse, T. (2012) Paper delivered to the North of England Education Conference, Leeds, 5 January.

British Broadcasting Company (BBC) (2020) Marcus Rashford calls for government free school meals U-turn, *BBC Sport Online*, 15 June [https://www.bbc.co.uk/sport/football/53042684].

Britton, J., Farquharson, C. and Sibieta, L. (2019) *2019 Annual report on education spending in England*, London: Institute for Fiscal Studies [https://ifs.org.uk/publications/14369].

Bronfenbrenner, U. (2005) *Making Human Beings Human: Bioecological Perspectives on Human Development*, Thousand Oaks, CA: Sage.

Bronfenbrenner, U. and Morris, P. (2006) The bio-ecological model of human development, in R. Lerner and W. Damon (eds.) *Handbook of Child Psychology: Theoretical Models of Human Development*, Chichester: Wiley.

Brown, B. (2018) *Dare to Lead: Brave Work, Tough Conversations, Whole Hearts*, London: Vermilion.

Brown, C. and Rogers, S. (2014) Knowledge creation as an approach to facilitating evidence-informed practice: Examining ways to measure the success of using this method with early years practitioners in Camden (London), *Journal of Educational Change*, 15 (1), 79–99.

Brown, C., Husbands, C. and Woods, D. (2017) Leadership to transform outcomes in one deprived urban area, in P. Earley and T. Greany (eds.) *School Leadership and Education System Reform*, London: Bloomsbury.

Bruner, J. (1971) *Towards a Theory of Instruction*, Cambridge, MA: Harvard University Press.

Bruner, J. (1973) Organization of early skilled action, *Child Development*, 44 (1), 1–11.

Bruner, J. (1996) *The Culture of Education*, Cambridge, MA: Harvard University Press.

Bryk, A., Gomez, L., Grunow, A. and LeMahieu, P. (2015) *Learning to Improve: How America's Schools Can Get Better at Getting Better*, Cambridge, MA: Harvard Education Press.

Buckingham, D. (2005) *Schooling the digital generation: Popular culture, the new media and the future of education*, London: Institute of Education.

Buckingham, D. (2007) Childhood in the age of global media, *Children's Geographies*, 5 (1), 43–54.

Bukodi, E. and Goldthorpe, J. (2018) *Social Mobility and Education in Britain: Research, Politics and Policy*, Cambridge: Cambridge University Press.

Burgess, H. (2010) Primary workforce management and reform, in R. Alexander (ed.) *The Cambridge Primary Review Research Surveys*, London: Routledge.

Bush, T., Bell, L. and Middlewood, D. (2019) *Principles of Educational Leadership and Management*, London: Sage.

Cairns, J., Gardner, R. and Lawton, D. (eds.) (2000) *Education for Values: Morals, Ethics and Citizenship in Contemporary Teaching*, London: Routledge.

Callaghan, J. (1976) *A rational debate based on the facts*, Speech, Ruskin College, Oxford, 18 October [http://www.educationengland.org.uk/documents/speeches/1976ruskin.html].

Campbell, R. (1985) *Developing the Primary School Curriculum*, London: Cassell.

Campbell, R. (1993) A dream at conception: A nightmare at delivery, in R. Campbell (ed.) *Breadth and Balance in the Primary Curriculum*, London: Falmer Press.

Campbell, R. (1998) Primary teaching: Roles and relationships, in C. Richards and P. Taylor (eds.) *How Shall We School Our Children? Primary Education and Its Future*, London: Falmer Press.

Campbell, R. (2001) The colonisation of the primary curriculum, in R. Philips and J. Furlong (eds.) *Education, Reform and the State: Twenty-Five Years of Politics, Policy and Practice*, London: Routledge.

Carpenter, B. (2020) A recovery curriculum: Loss and life for our children and schools post pandemic [blog], *Specialist Schools and Academies Trust*, 1 May [https://www.ssatuk.co.uk/blog/a-recovery-curriculum-loss-and-life-for-our-children-and-schools-post-pandemic/].

Carr, N. (2010) *The Shallows: How the Internet is Changing the Way We Think, Read and Remember*, New York: W.W. Norton.

Carter, B., Stevenson, H. and Passy, R. (2010) *Industrial Relations in Education: Transforming the School Workplace*, London: Routledge.

Carter, D. (2020) *Leading Academy Trusts: Why Some Fail, but Most Don't*, London: John Catt.

Cassen, R. and Kingdon, G. (2007) *Tackling Low Educational Achievement*, York: Joseph Rowntree Foundation.

Castells, M. (1997) *The Information Age: Economy, Society and Culture*, vol. II: *The Power of Identity*, Oxford: Blackwell.

Castells, M. (1998) *The Information Age: Economy, Society and Culture*, vol. III: *End of Millennium*, Oxford: Blackwell.

Castells, M. (2000) *The Information Age: Economy, Society and Culture*, vol. I: *The Rise of the Network Society*, 2nd edition, Oxford: Blackwell..

Castells, M. (2009) *Communication Power*, Oxford: Oxford University Press.

Central Advisory Council for Education (1967) *Children and their primary schools* (The Plowden Report), London: HMSO [http://www.educationengland.org.uk/documents/plowden/plowden1967-1.html].

Chapman, C., Muijs, D. and MacAllister, J. (2011) *A study of the impact of school federation on student outcomes*, Nottingham: National College for School Leadership [https://dera.ioe.ac.uk/12140/1/download%3fid=155373&filename=the-impact-of-school-federation-on-student-outcomes.pdf].

Chapman, L. and West-Burnham, J. (2010) *Education for Social Justice: Achieving Wellbeing for All*, London: Continuum.

Chawla-Duggan, R. and Lowe, J. (2010) Aims for primary education: Changing global contexts, in R. Alexander (ed.) *The Cambridge Primary Review Research Surveys*, London: Routledge.

Cheang, C. and Goh, E. (2018) Why some children from poor families do well: An in-depth analysis of positive deviance cases in Singapore, *International Journal of Qualitative Studies on Health and Well-Being*, 13 (suppl. 1) [https://doi.org/10.1080/17482631.2018.1563431].

Children's University (2021) *The difference we make* [https://www.childrensuniversity.co.uk/about-us/the-difference-we-make/].

Chitty, C. (2007) *Eugenics, Race and Intelligence in Education*, London: Continuum.

Chitty, C. (2014) *Education Policy in Britain*, 3rd edition, London: Palgrave Macmillan.

Christian, B. (2020) *The Alignment Problem: Machine Learning and Human Values*, New York: W.W. Norton.

Christian, D. (2004) *Maps of Time: An Introduction to Big History*, London: University of California Press.

Christodoulou, D. (2020) *Teachers vs Tech: The Case for an Ed Tech Revolution*, Oxford: Oxford University Press.

Chronaki, A. (2000) Computers in classrooms: Learners and teachers in new roles, in M. Ben-Peretz, S. Brown and B. Moon (eds.) *Routledge International Companion to Education*, London: Routledge.

City, E., Elmore, R., Fiarman, S. and Teitel, L. (2009) *Instructional Rounds in Education: A Network Approach to Improving Learning and Teaching*, Cambridge, MA: Harvard Education Press.

Claxton, G. (2002) Education for the learning age: A sociocultural approach to learning to learn, in G. Wells and C. Claxton (eds.) *Learning for Life in the 21st Century: Sociocultural Perspectives on the Future of Education*, Oxford: Blackwell.

Claxton, G. (2006) Thinking at the edge: Developing soft creativity, *Cambridge Journal of Education*, 36 (3), 351–362.

Claxton, G. (2021) *The Future of Teaching and the Myths that Hold it Back*, London: Routledge.

Claxton, G., Costa, A. and Kallick, B. (2016) Hard thinking about soft skills, *Educational Leadership*, 73 (6), 60–64.

Clayton, G. (2012) The alarming democratic void at the heart of our school system, *The Guardian*, 26 April [https://www.theguardian.com/commentisfree/2012/apr/26/democratic-void-school-system].

Coe, R., Aloisi, C., Higgins, S. and Elliot Major, L. (2014) *What makes great teaching? Review of the underpinning research*, October, Sutton Trust [https://www.suttontrust.com/wp-content/uploads/2019/12/What-makes-great-teaching-FINAL-4.11.14-1.pdf].

Coe, R., Rauch, C., Kime, S. and Singleton, D. (2020) *Great teaching toolkit: Evidence review*, Evidence Based Education in partnership with Cambridge Assessment International Education [https://www.cambridgeinternational.org/Images/584543-great-teaching-toolkit-evidence-review.pdf].

Coffield, F. (2017) The research evidence for and against Ofsted [blog], *The BERA Blog*, 2 November [https://www.bera.ac.uk/blog/the-research-evidence-for-and-against-ofsted].

Cole, M. (1996) *Cultural Psychology: A Once and Future Discipline*, Cambridge, MA: Harvard University Press.

Collins, J. (2001) *Good to Great: Why Some Companies Make the Leap and Others Don't*, London: Random House.

Collins, K. and Coleman, R. (2017) Evidence-informed policy and practice, in P. Earley and T. Greany (eds.) *School Leadership and Education System Reform*, London: Bloomsbury.

Committee on Standards in Public Life (1995) *Guidance: The seven principles of public life*, London: Committee on Standards in Public Life [https://www.gov.uk/government/publications/the-7-principles-of-public-life/the-7-principles-of-public-life–2].

Conroy, J., Hulme, M. and Menter, I. (2010) Primary curriculum futures, in R. Alexander (ed.) *The Cambridge Primary Review Research Surveys*, London: Routledge.

Cooperrider, D. and Whitney, D. (2005) *Appreciative Inquiry: A Positive Revolution in Change*, San Francisco, CA: Berrett-Koehler.

Cordingley, P. (2009) Research and evidence-informed practice: Focusing on practice and practitioners, *Cambridge Journal of Education*, 38 (1), 37–52.

Cordingley, P. (2019) Collaborative engagement in and with research: A central part of the CPD landscape, in C. Scutt and S. Harrison (eds.) *Teacher CPD: International trends, opportunities and challenges*, London: Chartered College of Teaching [https://my.chartered.college/wp-content/uploads/2019/11/Chartered-College-International-al-Teacher-CPD-report.pdf].

Cordingley, P., Higgins, S., Greany, T., Buckler, N., Coles-Jordan, D., Crisp, B. et al. (2015) *Developing great teaching: Lessons from the international reviews into effective professional development*, London: Teacher Development Trust [http:// TDTrust.org/dgt].

Covey, S. (1989) *The Seven Habits of Highly Effective People*, London: Simon & Schuster.

Covey, S. (2006) *The Speed of Trust*, London: Simon & Schuster.

Cox, B. and Dyson, A. (1971) *The Black Papers on Education*, London: Davis-Poynter.

Crehan, L. (2016) *Cleverlands*, London: Unbound.

Cremin, T. (2020) Reading for pleasure: Challenges and opportunities, in J. Davison and C. Daly (eds.) *Debates in English Teaching*, 2nd edition, London: Routledge.

Crenshaw, K. (1991) Mapping the margins: Intersectionality, identity politics, and violence against women of color, *Stanford Law Review*, 43 (6), 1241–1299.

Cruddas, L. (2007) Engaged voices – dialogic interaction and the construction of shared social meanings, *Educational Action Research*, 15 (3), 479–488.

Cruddas, L. (2015) *Leading the way: Blueprint for a self-improving system*, Leicester: Association of School and College Leaders [https://www.ascl.org.uk/ASCL/ media/ASCL/Our%20view/Campaigns/ASCL-blueprint-for-a-self-improving-system.pdf].

Cummins, J. (2000) *Language, Power and Pedagogy*, Clevedon: Multilingual Matters.

Cunningham, P. (1988) *Curriculum Change and the Primary School since 1945: Dissemination of the Progressive Ideal*, Lewes: Falmer Press.

Cunningham, P. (2012a) *Politics and the Primary Teacher*, London: Routledge.

Cunningham, P. (2012b) Structures and systems and bodies and things: Historical research on primary schooling and its professional relevance, *History of Education*, 41 (1), 73–86.

Cunningham, P. and Raymont, P. (2010) Quality assurance in English primary education, in R. Alexander (ed.) *The Cambridge Primary Review Research Surveys*, London: Routledge.

Dale, R. (2008) Neoliberal capitalism, the modern state and the governance of education, *Tertium Comparationis*, 13 (2), 183–198.

Daly, J. and Finnigan, K. (2011) The ebb and flow of social network ties between district leaders under high-stakes accountability, *American Educational Research Journal*, 48 (1), 39–79.

Damasio, A. (1999) *The Feeling of What Happens: Body and Emotion in the Making of Consciousness*, London: Harcourt.

Damasio, A. (2010) *Self Comes to Mind: Constructing the Conscious Brain*, London: Pantheon.

Daniels, H. (2001) *Vygotsky and Pedagogy*, London: Routledge.

Daniels, H. (2012) Institutional culture, social interaction and learning, *Learning, Culture and Social Interaction*, 1 (1), 2–11.

Darling, J. (1986) Child-centred, gender-centred: A criticism of progressive curriculum theory from Rousseau to Plowden, *Oxford Review of Education*, 12 (1), 31–40.

Darling-Hammond, L., Flook, L., Cook-Harvey, C., Barron, B. and Osher, D. (2019) Implications for educational practice of the science of learning and development, *Applied Developmental Science*, 24 (2), 97–140.

Das, P. and Naglieri, J.A. (2001) The Das–Naglieri Cognitive Assessment System in theory and practice, in J.W. Andrews, D.H. Saklofske and H.J. Janzen (eds.) *Handbook of Psychoeducational Assessment*, New York: Academic Press.

Davidson, R. and Begley, S. (2013) *The Emotional Life of Your Brain: How Its Unique Patterns Affect the Way You Think, Feel, and Live – And How You CAN Change Them*, London: Hodder.

Dawes, L. with Warwick, P. (2012) *Talking Points: Discussion Activities in the Primary Classroom*, London: Routledge.

Day, C., Sammons, P., Hopkins, D., Harris, A., Leithwood, K., Gu, Q. et al. (2010) *10 strong claims about successful school leadership*, Nottingham: National College for School Leadership [https://assets.publishing.service.gov.uk/government/uploads/system/uploads/attachment_data/file/327938/10-strong-claims-about-successful-school-leadership.pdf].

Deakin-Crick, R., Taylor, M., Ritchie, S., Samuel, E. and Durant, K. (2005) *A systemic review of the impact of citizenship education on student learning and achievement*, London: EPPI Centre, Institute of Education [https://eppi.ioe.ac.uk/cms/Default.aspx-?tabid=129].

Dearden, R. (1968) *The Philosophy of Primary Education*, London: Routledge & Kegan Paul.

Dearden, R. (1976) *Problems in Primary Education*, London: Routledge & Kegan Paul.

Deci, E. and Ryan, R. (2008) Self-determination theory: A macrotheory of human motivation, development and health, *Canadian Psychology*, 49 (3), 182–185.

DeFlaminis, J. (2013) *The implementation and replication of the distributed leadership program: More lessons learned and beliefs confirmed*, paper presented at the Annual Meeting of the American Educational Research Association, San Francisco, CA, 27 April–1 May.

Dehaene, S. (2020) *How We Learn: Why Brains Learn Better Than Any Machine … for Now*, London: Random House.

Deming, E. (1982) *Quality, Productivity and Competitive Position*, Cambridge, MA: MIT Press.

Deming, E. (1994) *The New Economics for Industry, Government, Education*, Cambridge, MA: MIT Press.

Demirkasimoğlu, N. (2010) Defining 'teacher professionalism' from different perspectives, *Procedia Social and Behavioural Sciences*, 9, 2047–2051.

Dennis, D. and Kilsby, J. (2018) Designing a primary knowledge-rich curriculum: Where we've been, where we are, where we are going, *Impact: Journal of the Chartered College of Teachers*, September [https://impact.chartered.college/article/designing-primary-knowledge-rich-curriculum-where-been-are-going/].

Department for Education (DfE) (2017a) *Schools, pupils and their characteristics: January 2017*, SFR28/2017, London: DfE [https://www.gov.uk/government/statistics/schools-pupils-and-their-characteristics-january-2017].

Department for Education (DfE) (2017b) *School workforce in England: November, 2016*, SFR25/2017, London: DfE [https://www.gov.uk/government/statistics/school-workforce-in-england-november-2016].

Department for Education (DfE) (2021a) *Open academies, free schools, studio schools and UTCs and academy projects in development*, London: DfE [https://www.gov.uk/government/publications/open-academies-and-academy-projects-in-development].

Department for Education (DfE) (2021b) *Compare school performance service*, London: DfE [https://www.compare-school-performance.service.gov.uk/schools-by-type?-step=default&table=mats&hasperfdata=true&for=primary&hasperfdata=true].

Department for Education and Employment (DfEE) (1997) *White Paper: Excellence in schools*, London: HMSO [http://www.educationengland.org.uk/documents/wp1997/excellence-in-schools.html].

Department for Education and Skills (DfES) (2003) *Excellence and enjoyment: A strategy for primary schools*, London: HMSO.

Department for Education and Skills (DfES) (2004) *Every child matters: Change for children*, Nottingham: DfES [http://www.educationengland.org.uk/documents/pdfs/2004-ecm-change-for-children.pdf].

Department of Education and Science (DES) (1978) *Primary education in England: A survey by HM Inspectors of Schools*, London: HMSO [http://www.educationengland.org.uk/documents/hmi-primary/hmi-primary.html].

Desforges, C. and Abouchaar, A. (2003) *The impact of parental involvement, parental support and family education on pupil achievement and adjustment: A literature review*, Research Report RR433, London: DfES [https://www.nationalnumeracy.org.uk/sites/default/files/documents/impact_of_parental_involvement/the_impact_of_parental_involvement.pdf].

Dewey, J. (1900) *The School and Society*, Chicago, IL: University of Chicago Press.

Dewey, J. (1910) *How We Think*, Boston, MA: D.C. Heath.

Dewey, J. (1916) *Democracy and Education*, New York: Macmillan.

Dewey, J. (1938) *Logic: The Theory of Inquiry*, New York: Holt, Rinehart & Winston.

Dilts, R. (2018) *Changing Belief Systems with NLP*, Scotts Valley, CA: Dilts Strategy Group.

Doidge, N. (2007) *The Brain that Changes Itself: Stories of Personal Triumph from the Frontiers of Brain Science*, London: Penguin.

Donaldson, M. (1978) *Children's Minds*, London: Fontana.

Donohoo, J., Hattie, J. and Eells, R. (2018) The power of collective efficacy, *Educational Leadership*, 75 (6), 40–44.

Downes, T. (2002) Blending play, practice and performance: Children's use of the computer at home, *Journal of Educational Enquiry*, 3 (2), 21–34.

Doyle, W. (1979) Classroom tasks and students' abilities, in P. Peterson and H. Walberg (eds.) *Research on Teaching: Concepts, Findings and Implications*, Berkeley, CA: McCutchan.

Doyle, W. (1983) *Basic questions in research on teaching*, Austin, TX: Research and Development Centre for Teacher Education. University of Texas, Austin.

Doyle, W. and Ponder, G. (1977) The practicality ethic and teacher decision-making, *Interchange*, 8 (3), 1–12.

Duckworth, A. and Yeager, D. (2015) Measurement matters: Assessing personal qualities other than cognitive ability for educational purposes, *Educational Researcher*, 44 (4), 237–251.

Duguid, P. and Brown, J.S. (2002) *The Social Life of Information*, Boston, MA: Harvard Business School Press.

Dweck, C. (2000) *Self-theories: Their Role in Motivation, Personality and Development*, London: Routledge.

Dweck, C. (2002) Messages that motivate: How praise molds students' beliefs, motivation, and performance (in surprising ways), in J. Aronson (ed.) *Improving Academic Achievement*, New York: Academic Press.

Dweck, C. (2006) *Mindset: The New Psychology of Success*, New York: Random House.

Earley, P. (2013) *Exploring the School Leadership Landscape: Changing Demands, Changing Realities*, London: Bloomsbury.

Earley, P. (2017) Conceptions of leadership and leading the learning, in P. Earley and T. Greany (eds.) *School Leadership and Education System Reform*, London: Bloomsbury.

Earley, P., Higham, R., Allen R., Allen, T., Howson, J., Nelson, R. et al (2012) *Review of the school leadership landscape*, Nottingham: National College for School Leadership [http://www.lcll.org.uk/uploads/3/0/9/3/3093873/review_of_school_leadership_landscape_2012_dec.pdf].

Eaude, A. (2019) *Identity, Culture and Belonging: Educating Young Children for a Changing World*, London: Bloomsbury.

Edge, K., Galdames, S. and Horton, J. (2017) Diversity: New leaders and new leadership, in P. Earley and T. Greany (eds.) *School Leadership and Education System Reform*, London: Bloomsbury.

Education Endowment Foundation (EEF) (2021) *Impact of Covid-19 disruptions in primary schools: Attainment gaps and school responses*, London: EEF [https://educationendowmentfoundation.org.uk/projects-and-evaluation/projects/covid-19-disruptions-in-primary-schools-attainment-gaps-and-school-response/].

Education Policy Institute (EPI) (2016) *Education in England: Annual Report 2016*, London: EPI [https://epi.org.uk/publications-and-research/education-england-annual-report-2016/].

Education Support (2020) *Covid-19 and the classroom: Working in education during the coronavirus pandemic*, London: Education Support [https://www.educationsupport.org.uk/resources/research-reports/covid-19-and-classroom-working-education-during-coronavirus-pandemic].

Edwards, A. (2009) Agency and activity theory: From the systemic to the relational, in A. Sannino, H. Daniels and K. Guttierez (eds.) *Learning and Expanding with Activity Theory*, Cambridge: Cambridge University Press.

Egan, K. (1997) *The Educated Mind*, Chicago, IL: University of Chicago Press.

Eisler, R. and Fry, D. (2019) *Nurturing Our Humanity: How Domination and Partnership Shape Our Brains, Lives and Future*, Oxford: Oxford University Press.

Elliott, J. (2000) Towards a synoptic vision of educational change in advanced industrial society, in H. Altrichter and J. Elliott (eds.) *Images of Educational Change*, Buckingham: Open University Press.

Elmore, R. (1996) Getting to scale with good educational practice, *Harvard Educational Review*, 66 (1), 1–26.

Elmore, R. (2004) *School Reform from the Inside Out: Policy, Practice and Performance*, Cambridge, MA: Harvard Education Press.

Elmore, R. (2008) Leadership as the practice of improvement, in B. Pont, D. Nusche and D. Hopkins (eds.) *Improving School Leadership*, vol 2: *Case Studies on System Leadership*, Paris: OECD.

Engel, S. (2015) *The Hungry Mind: The Origins of Curiosity in Childhood*, London: Harvard University Press.

Engeström, Y. (1987) *Learning by Expanding: An Activity Theoretical Approach to Developmental Research*, Helsinki: Orienta-Konsultit.

Engeström, Y. (1999a) Activity theory and individual and social transformation, in Y. Engeström, R. Miettinen and R.-L. Punamäki (eds.) *Perspectives on Activity Theory*, Cambridge, Cambridge University Press.

Engeström, Y. (1999b) Innovative learning in work teams: Analysing cycles of knowledge creation in practice, in Y. Engeström, R. Miettinen and R.-L. Punamäki (eds.) *Perspectives on Activity Theory*, Cambridge, Cambridge University Press.

Engeström, Y. (2000) Activity theory as a framework for analysing and redesigning work, *Ergonomics*, 43 (7), 960–974.

Engeström, Y. (2001) Expansive learning at work: Toward an activity theoretical reconceptualization, *Journal of Education and Work*, 14 (1), 133–156.

Engeström, Y. (2007a) From communities of practice to mycorrhizae, in J. Hughes, N. Jewson and L. Unwin (eds.) *Communities of Practice: Critical Perspectives*, London: Routledge.

Engeström, Y. (2007b) From stabilization knowledge to possibility knowledge in organizational learning, *Management Learning*, 38 (3), 1–5.

Engeström, Y. (2009) The future of activity theory: A rough draft, in A. Sannino, H. Daniels and K. Gutierez (eds.) *Learning and Expanding with Activity Theory*, Cambridge: Cambridge University Press.

Engeström, Y. (2015) *Learning by Expanding: An Activity-Theoretical Approach to Developmental Research*, 2nd edition, Cambridge: Cambridge University Press.

Engeström, Y. and Ahonen, H. (2001) On the materiality of social capital: An activity theoretical exploration, in H. Hasan, E. Gould, P. Larkin and L. Vrazalic (eds.) *Information Systems and Activity Theory*, vol. 2: *Theory and Practice*, Wollongong, NSW: University of Wollongong Press.

Engeström, Y. and Miettinen, R. (1999) Introduction: Perspectives on activity theory, in Y. Engeström, R. Miettinen and R.-L. Punamäki (eds.) *Perspectives on Activity Theory*, Cambridge, Cambridge University Press.

Engeström, Y., Engeström, R. and Suntio, A. (2002) Can a school community learn to master its own future? An activity-theoretical study of expansive learning among middle school teachers, in G. Wells and C. Claxton (eds.) *Learning for Life in the 21st Century: Sociocultural Perspectives on the Future of Education*, Oxford: Blackwell.

Facer, K. (2011) *Learning Futures: Education, Technology and Social Change*, London: Routledge.

Facer, K. (2012) Taking the 21st century seriously: Young people, education and socio-technical futures, *Oxford Review of Education*, 38 (1), 97–113.

Fazackerley, A., Wolf, R. and Massey, A. (2010) *Blocking the best: Obstacles to new independent state schools*, London: Policy Exchange/New Schools Network [https://www.policyexchange.org.uk/wp-content/uploads/2016/09/blocking-the-best-mar-10.pdf].

Feldman Barrett, F. (2017) The theory of constructed emotion: An active inference account of interoception and categorization, *Social Cognitive and Affective Neuroscience*, 12 (1), 1–23.

Ferrari, M. (2011) What can neuroscience bring to education, *Educational Philosophy and Theory*, 43 (1), 31–36.

Fielding, M. and Moss, P. (2011) *Radical Education and the Common School: A Democratic Alternative*, London: Routledge.

Fink, D. (2010) *The Succession Challenge: Building and Sustaining Leadership Capacity through Succession Management*, London: Sage.

Finnigan, K. and Daly, A. (2012) Exploring the space between: Social networks, trust and urban school district leaders, *Journal of School Leadership*, 22 (3), 493–500.

Fitz-Gibbon, C. (1996) *Monitoring Education: Indicators, Quality and Effectiveness*, London: Continuum.

Fitz-Gibbon, C. and Tymms. P. (2002) Technical and ethical issues in indicator systems: Doing things right and doing wrong things, *Educational Policy Analysis Archives*, 10, 1–26.

Flynn, J. (2007) *What is Intelligence? Beyond the Flynn Effect*, Cambridge: Cambridge University Press.

Forrester, G. and Garratt, D. (2016) *Education Policy Unravelled*, London: Bloomsbury.

Foundation for Education Development (FED) (2021) *National education consultation report*, London: FED [https://www.youthemployment.org.uk/dev/wp-content/uploads/2021/04/FED-NECReport-2021.pdf].

Frazzetto, G. (2013) *How We Feel: What Neuroscience Can – and Can't – Tell Us About Our Emotions*, New York: Doubleday.

Freire, P. (1972) *Pedagogy of the Oppressed*, New York: Continuum.

Freire, P. (1998) *Pedagogy of Freedom: Ethics, Democracy, and Civic Courage*, Lanham, MD: Rowman & Littlefield.

Friedman, T. (2005) *The World is Flat: A Brief History of the Globalized World in the 21st Century*, London: Penguin.

Fullan, M. (1982) *The Meaning of Educational Change*, New York: Teachers College Press.

Fullan, M. (2001) *The New Meaning of Educational Change*, London: Routledge.

Fullan, M. (2010) *All Systems Go: The Change Imperative for Whole System Reform*, Thousand Oaks, CA: Corwin Press.

Fullan, M. (2011) *Choosing the wrong drivers for whole system reform*, Summary of Seminar Series Paper no. 204, May, East Melbourne, VIC: Centre for Strategic Education [http://michaelfullan.ca/wp-content/uploads/2016/06/13396088160.pdf].

Fullan, M. (2021) *The right drivers for whole system success*, East Melbourne, VIC: Centre for Strategic Education [https://michaelfullan.ca/wp-content/uploads/2021/03/Fullan-CSE-Leading-Education-Series-01-2021R2-compressed.pdf].

Fullan, M. and Langworthy, M. (2013) *Towards a new end: New pedagogies for deep learning*, June, Seattle, WA: Collaborative Impact [http://www.newpedagogies.nl/images/towards_a_new_end.pdf].

Fullan, M. and Langworthy, M. (2014) *A Rich Seam: How New Pedagogies Find Deep Learning*, London: Pearson.

Fullan, M. and Quinn, J. (2010) *Capacity building for whole system reform* [https://michaelfullan.ca/wp-content/uploads/2016/06/Untitled_Document_8.pdf].

Furlong, J. (2014) *Research and the teaching profession: Building capacity for a self-improving education system*. Final Report of the BERA-RSA Inquiry into the Role of Research in the Teaching Profession, London: BERA [https://www.thersa.org/globalassets/pdfs/bera-rsa-research-teaching-profession-full-report-for-web-2.pdf].

Gagné, R. (1985) *The Conditions of Learning*, 4th edition, New York: Holt, Rinehart & Winston.

Galton, M. (2007) *Learning and Teaching in the Primary School*, London: Sage.

Galton, M. and MacBeath, J. (2008) *Teachers Under Pressure*, London: Sage (in association with the National Union of Teachers).

Galton, M., Simon, B. and Croll, P. (1980) *Inside the Primary Classroom*, London: Routledge.

Galton, M., Hargreaves, L., Comber, C., Wall, D. and Pell, A. (1999) *Inside the Primary Classroom: 20 Years On*, London: Routledge.

Gardner, H. (1999) *The Disciplined Mind: What All Students Should Understand*, London: Prentice-Hall.

Gay, G. and Hembrooke, H. (2004) *Activity-Centered Design: An Ecological Approach to Designing Smart Tools and Usable Systems*, Cambridge, MA: MIT Press.

Gazeley, L. and Dunne, M. (2007) Researching class in the classroom: Addressing the social class attainment gap, *Journal of Education for Teaching*, 33 (4), 409–424.

Geake, J. (2009) *The Brain at School: Educational Neuroscience in the Classroom*, Maidenhead: Open University.

Gerver, R. (2009) *Creating Tomorrow's Schools Today*, London: Bloomsbury.

Gibb, R. and Kolb, B. (eds.) (2018) *The Neurobiology of Brain and Behavioural Development*, London: Academic Press.

Gibton, D. (2017) Regulation, governance of education and the oversight of autonomous schools, in P. Earley and T. Greany (eds.) *School Leadership and Education System Reform*, London: Bloomsbury.

Gilkerson, J., Richards, J., Warren, S., Kimbrough Oller, D., Russo, R. and Vohr, B. (2018) Language experience in the second year of life and language outcomes in late childhood, *Pediatrics*, 142 (4), 1–11.

Gillard, D. (2019) *Education in England: A history* [www.educationengland.org.uk/history].

Gipps, C. (2002) Sociocultural perspectives on assessment, in G. Wells and C. Claxton (eds.) *Learning for Life in the 21st Century: Sociocultural Perspectives on the Future of Education*, Oxford: Blackwell.

Giroux, H. (1997) *Pedagogy and the Politics of Hope: Theory, Culture, and Schooling. A Critical Reader*, Boulder, CO: Westview Press.

Glasersfeld, E. von (1989) Cognition, construction of knowledge and teaching, *Synthese*, 80 (1), 121–140.

Glatter, R. (2017) Schools as organisations or institutions: Defining core purposes, in P. Earley and T. Greany (eds.) *School Leadership and Education System Reform*, London: Bloomsbury.

Glaze, A., Zegarac, G. and Giroux, D. (2006) *Finding common ground: Character development in Ontario schools, K-12*, Ministry of Education, Mowat Block, Queen's Park, Toronto, ON, October.

Goepel, J. (2012) Upholding public trust: An examination of teacher professionalism and the use of Teachers' Standards in England, *Teacher Development*, 16 (4), 489–505.

Goodenow, C. (1993) Classroom belonging among early adolescent students, *Journal of Early Adolescence*, 13 (1), 21–43.

Goodman, A. and Gregg, P. (2010) *Poorer children's educational attainment: how important are attitudes and behaviour?*, York: Joseph Rowntree Foundation [https://www.jrf.org.uk/report/poorer-children's-educational-attainment-how-important-are-attitudes-and-behaviour].

Gorard, S. (2009) Serious doubts about school effectiveness, *British Educational Research Journal*, 36 (5), 745–766.

Gorard, S. (2018) *Education Policy, Equity and Effectiveness: What Can We Learn from the Evidence?*, Bristol: Bristol University Press.

Gorard, S. and See, B. (2013) *Do parental involvement interventions increase attainment? A review of the evidence*, Briefing Paper, London: Nuffield Foundation [https://www.nuffieldfoundation.org/sites/default/files/files/Do_parental_involvement_interventions_increase_attainment1.pdf].

Gorard, S., See, B. and Davies, P. (2012) *The impact of attitudes and aspirations on educational attainment and participation*, York: Joseph Rowntree Foundation [https://www.jrf.org.uk/sites/default/files/jrf/migrated/files/education-young-people-parents-full.pdf].

Gorard, S., Siddiqui, N. and See, B. (2021) Assessing the impact of Pupil Premium funding on primary school segregation and attainment, *Research Papers in Education* [https://doi.org/10.1080/02671522.2021.1907775].

Gordon, P. (2002), Curriculum, in R. Aldrich (ed.) *A Century of Education*, London: Routledge/Falmer.

Goswami, U. and Bryant, P. (2010) Children's cognitive development and learning, in R. Alexander (ed.) *The Cambridge Primary Review Research Surveys*, London: Routledge.

Graves, C. (1970) Levels of existence: An open system theory of values, *Journal of Humanistic Psychology*, 10 (2), 131–155.

Greany T. (2014) *Are We Nearly There Yet? Progress, Issues and Possible Next Steps for a Self-improving School System*, London: IOE Press.

Greany, T. (2015) *The self-improving system in England: A review of evidence and thinking*, Leicester: Association of School and College Leaders [https://www.ascl.org.uk/ASCL/media/ASCL/Our%20view/Campaigns/The-Self-Improving-System-in-England-a-Review-of-Evidence-and-Thinking.pdf].

Greany, T. (2017) Collaboration, partnerships and system leadership across schools, in P. Earley and T. Greany (eds.) *School Leadership and Education System Reform*, London: Bloomsbury.

Greany, T. (2018) Innovation is possible, it's just not easy: Improvement, innovation and legitimacy in England's autonomous, accountable school system, *Educational Management Administration and Leadership*, 46 (1), 65–85.

Greany, T. and Brown, C. (2017) The evidence informed school system in England: Where should school leaders be focusing their efforts?, *International Journal of Education Policy and Leadership*, 12 (3) [https://files.eric.ed.gov/fulltext/EJ1154174.pdf].

Greany, T. and Higham, R. (2018) *Hierarchy, markets and networks: Analysing the 'self-improving school-led system' agenda in England and the implications for schools*, London: IOE Press [http://www.lcll.org.uk/uploads/2/1/4/7/21470046/hierarchy-markets-and-networks.pdf].

Greany, T., Gu, Q., Handscomb, G. and Varley, M. (2014) *School-university partnerships: Fulfilling the potential*, Summary Report, London: Research Councils UK and National Co-ordinating Centre for Public Engagement [https://www.publicengagement.ac.uk/sites/default/files/publication/supi_project_report_final.pdf].

Green, A. (1990) *Education and State Formation: The Rise of Education Systems in England, France and the USA*, London: Macmillan.

Greenfield, S. (2014) *Mind Change: How Digital Technologies are Leaving Their Mark on Our Brains*, London: Rider.

Greenfield, S. (2016) *A Day in the Life of the Brain: The Neuroscience of Consciousness, from Dawn till Dusk*, London: Penguin.

Gronn, P. (2002) Designer leadership: The emerging global adoption of preparation standards, *Journal of School Leadership*, 12 (5), 552–578.

Groves, M. and West-Burnham, J. (2020) *Flipping Schools: Why it's Time to Turn Your School and Community Inside Out*, London: John Catt.

Gu, Q., Rea, S., Hill, R., Smethem, L. and Dunford, J. (2014) *Teaching schools evaluation: Emerging issues from the early development of case study teaching school alliances*, Research Report, London: National College for Teaching and Leadership [https://assets.publishing.service.gov.uk/government/uploads/system/uploads/attachment_data/file/505517/RR332_-_Teaching_schools_Evaluation.pdf].

Guerriero, S. (ed.) (2017) *Pedagogical Knowledge and the Changing Nature of the Teaching Profession: Educational Research and Innovation*, Paris: OECD Publishing.

Gunter, H. (2001) *Leaders and Leadership in Education*, London: Sage.

Gunter, H. (2007) Remodelling the school workforce in England: a study in tyranny, *Journal for Critical Education Policy Studies*, 5 (1), 1–11.

Gunter, H. (2012) *Leadership and the Reform of Education*, Bristol: Policy Press.

Hall, V. and Southworth, G. (1997) *Headship, School Leadership and Management*, London: Falmer Press.

Hallinger, P. (2003) Leading educational change: Reflections on the practice of instructional and transformational leadership, *Cambridge Journal of Education*, 33 (3), 329–351.

Hallinger, P. and Heck, R. (2003) Understanding the contribution of leadership to school improvement, in M. Wallace and L. Poulson (eds.) *Learning to Read Critically in Educational Leadership and Management*, London: Sage.

Hallinger, P. and Heck, R. (2011) Exploring the journey of school improvement: Classifying and analyzing patterns of change in school improvement processes and learning outcomes, *School Effectiveness and School Improvement*, 22 (1), 1–27.

Hallinger, P., Gumus, S. and Belllibas, M. (2020) Are principals instructional leaders yet? A science map of the knowledge base on instructional leadership, 1940–2018, *Scientometrics*, 122 (3), 1629–1650.

Halsey, A., Floud, J. and Anderson, C. (eds.) (1961) *Education, Economy and Society*, New York: Free Press.

Handford, V. and Leithwood, K. (2013) Why teachers trust school leaders, *Journal of Educational Administration*, 51 (2), 194–212.

Hannon, V. and Peterson, A. (2021) *Thrive: The Purpose of Schools in a Changing World*, Cambridge: Cambridge University Press.

Hannon, V., Patton, A. and Temperley, J. (2011) *Developing an innovation ecosystem for education*, White Paper, CISCO and Innovation Unit [https://www.cisco.com/c/dam/en_us/solutions/industries/docs/education/ecosystem_for_edu.pdf].

Hanushek, E. (2011) The economic value of higher teacher quality, *Economics of Education Review*, 30 (3), 466–479.

Hargreaves, A. (2003) *Teaching in the Knowledge Society: Education in the Age of Insecurity*, Maidenhead: Open University Press.

Hargreaves, A. (2020) What's next for schools after coronavirus? Here are 5 big issues and opportunities, *The Conversation*, 16 April [https://theconversation.com/whats-next-for-schools-after-coronavirus-here-are-5-big-issues-and-opportunities-135004].

Hargreaves, A. and Fink, D. (2006) *Sustainable Leadership*, San Francisco, CA: Jossey-Bass.

Hargreaves, A. and Fullan, M. (1998) *What's Worth Fighting For Out There*, New York: Teachers College Press.

Hargreaves, A. and Fullan, M. (2012) *Professional Capital: Transforming Teaching in Every School*, New York: Teachers College Press.

Hargreaves, A. and Shirley, D. (2009) *The Fourth Way: The Inspiring Future for Educational Change*, London: Sage.

Hargreaves, D. (2001) A capital theory of school effectiveness and improvement, *British Educational Research Journal*, 27 (4), 487–503.

Hargreaves, D. (2010) *Creating a self-improving school system*, Nottingham: National College for School Leadership [https://assets.publishing.service.gov.uk/government/uploads/system/uploads/attachment_data/file/325873/creating-a-self-improving-school-system.pdf].

Hargreaves, D. (2011) *Leading a self-improving school system*, Nottingham: National College for School Leadership [https://assets.publishing.service.gov.uk/government/uploads/system/uploads/attachment_data/file/325890/leading-a-self-improving-school-system.pdf].

Harlen, W. (2011) *Students' learning in science: Implications for pedagogy and the curriculum* [http://www.score-education.org/media/7319/wh.pdf].

Harris, A. (2003) Teacher leadership as distributed leadership: Heresy, fantasy or possibility?, *School Leadership and Management*, 23 (3), 313–324.

Harris A. (2009) *Distributed School Leadership*, Dordrecht: Springer.

Harris, A. and Spillane, J. (2008) Distributed leadership through the looking glass, *Management in Education*, 22 (1), 31–34.

Harris, A., Chapman, C., Muijs, D., Reiss, J. and Stoll, L. (2006) Improving schools in challenging circumstances: Exploring the possible, *School Effectiveness and School Improvement*, 17 (4), 409–424.

Hart, R. (1992) *Children's participation: From tokenism to citizenship*, Innocenti Essays no. 4, Florence: UN Children's Fund [https://www.unicef-irc.org/publications/100-childrens-participation-from-tokenism-to-citizenship.html].

Hart, S., Dixon, A., Drummond, M.-J. and McIntyre, D. (2004) *Learning without Limits*, Maidenhead: Open University Press.

Hartley, D. (2007) The emergence of distributed leadership in education: Why now?, *British Journal of Educational Studies*, 55 (2), 202–221.

Hartley, D. (2010) The management of education and the social theory of the firm: From distributed leadership to collaborative community, *Journal of Educational Administration and History*, 42 (4), 345–361.

Hasan, H. and Kazlauskas, A. (2014) Activity theory: Who is doing what, why and how, in H. Hasan (ed.), *Being Practical with Theory: A Window into Business Research*, Wollongong, NSW: THEORI [https://ro.uow.edu.au/buspapers/403].

Hatcher, R. (2011) Social class and schooling: Differentiation or democracy, in M. Cole (ed.) *Education, Equality and Human Rights: Issues of Gender, 'Race', Sexuality, Disability and Social Class*, 3rd edition, London: Routledge.

Hattie, J. (2009) *Visible Learning: A Synthesis of Over 800 Meta-Analyses Relating to Achievement*, London: Routledge.

Hattie, J. (2011) *Visible Learning for Teachers: Maximizing Impact on Learning*, London: Routledge.

Hayes, D., Mills, M., Christie, P. and Lingard, B. (2006) *Teachers and Schooling Making a Difference: Productive Pedagogies, Assessment and Performance*, London: Allen & Unwin.

Heifetz, R. and Linsky, M. (2002) *Leadership on the Line: Staying Alive through the Dangers of Leading*, Boston, MA: Harvard Business School Press.

Henricks, T. (2014) Play as self-realisation: Towards a general theory of play, *American Journal of Play*, 6 (2), 190–213.

Higgins, D., Katsipataki, R., Coleman, P., Henderson, L., Major, R., Coe, R. et al. (2015) *The Sutton Trust-Education Endowment Fund Teaching and Learning Toolkit*, Manual, London: Education Endowment Fund.

Higgins, S. (2009) Learning to learn, *Beyond Current Horizons*, May [https://www.academia.edu/589476/Learning_to_Learn].

Higham, R. and Earley, P. (2013) School autonomy and government control: School leaders' views on a changing policy landscape in England, *Educational Management Administration & Leadership*, 41 (6), 701–717.

Higham, R., Hopkins, D. and Matthews, P. (2009) *System Leadership in Practice*, Maidenhead: Open University Press.

Hill, R. (2016) *School improvement in multi-academy trusts*, London: Ambition Institute [https://www.ambition.org.uk/blog/school-improvement-multi-academy-trusts/].

Hill, R., Dunford, J., Parish, N., Rea, S. and Sandals, L. (2012) *The growth of academy chains: Implications for leaders and leadership*, Nottingham: National College for School Leadership [https://dera.ioe.ac.uk/14536/1/the-growth-of-academy-chains%5B1%5D.pdf].

Hirsch, D. (2006) *What will it take to end child poverty? Firing on all cylinders*, York: Joseph Rowntree Foundation [https://www.jrf.org.uk/report/what-will-it-take-end-child-poverty].

Hirsch, D. (2007) *Experiences of poverty and educational disadvantage*, York: Joseph Rowntree Foundation [https://www.jrf.org.uk/report/experiences-poverty-and-educational-disadvantage].

Hirsch, E. (1999) *The Schools We Need: And Why We Don't Have Them*, New York: Anchor.

Hirsch, E. (2006) *The Knowledge Deficit: Closing the Shocking Education Gap for American Children*, Boston MA: Houghton Mifflin.

Holman, P., Devane, T. and Cady, S. (2007) *The Change Handbook: The Definitive Resource on Today's Best Methods for Engaging Whole Systems*, San Francisco, CA: Berrett-Koehler.

Hooper, A. and Cornes, A. (2018) A brave global curriculum, *Impact: Journal of the Chartered College of Teaching*, September [https://impact.chartered.college/article/a-brave-global-curriculum/].

Hopkins, D. (2007) *Every School a Great School: Realizing the Potential of System Leadership*, Maidenhead: Open University Press.

Hopkins, D. (2013) *Exploding the Myths of School Reform*, Maidenhead: Open University Press.

Hopkins, D. (2016) Building capacity for school improvement in multi-academy trusts: From the inside out, *Specialist Schools and Academies Trust Journal*, Autumn, 19–29.

Hopkins, D. (2020) Unleashing greatness: A strategy for school improvement, *Australian Educational Leader*, 42 (3) [http://www.acel.org.au/ACEL/ACELWEB/Publications/AEL/2020/3/View.aspx].

Hopkins, D. and Craig, W. (2014) *Curiosity and powerful learning*, Melbourne, VIC: McRel International [http://gateway.roxburghcollege.vic.edu.au/wp-content/uploads/2016/08/Curiosity-Powerful-Learning.pdf].

Howe, C. (2010) *Peer Groups and Children's Development*, Oxford: Blackwell.

Howe, C. and Mercer, N. (2010) Children's social development, peer interaction and classroom learning, in R. Alexander (ed.) *The Cambridge Primary Review Research Surveys*, London: Routledge.

Hoyle, E. (1974) Professionality, professionalism and control in teaching, *London Education Review*, 3 (2), 13–19.

Hughes, M. and Tizard, B. (1984) *Young Children Learning*, Cambridge, MA: Harvard University Press.

Humphreys, H. and Feil, T. (2018) Building an ethically vibrant curriculum: A church school perspective, *Impact: Journal of the Chartered College of Teaching*, September [https://impact.chartered.college/article/ethically-vibrant-curriculum-church-school/].

Hutchings, M., Greenwood, C., Hollingworth, S., Mansaray, A., Rose, A., Minty, S. et al. (2012) *Evaluation of the City Challenge programme*, Research Report DFE-RR215, London: Institute for Policy Studies in Education, Metropolitan University and Coffey International Development [https://dera.ioe.ac.uk/14820/1/DFE-RR215.pdf].

Hutchinson, J. (2016) *School inspection in England: Is there room to improve?*, London: Education Policy Institute [https://epi.org.uk/publications-and-research/school-inspection-england-room-improve/].

Hutchinson, J., Bonetti, S., Crenna-Jennings, W. and Akhal, A. (2019) *Education in England, Annual Report 2019*, London: Education Policy Institute [https://epi.org.uk/publications-and-research/annual-report-2019/].

Hutchinson, J., Reader, M. and Akhal, A. (2020) *Education in England, Annual Report 2020*, London: Education Policy Institute [https://epi.org.uk/publications-and-research/education-in-england-annual-report-2020/].

Ilyenkov, E. (1977) *Dialectical Logic: Essays on its History and Theory*, Moscow: Progress (original work published 1974).

Immordino-Yang, M. (2015) *Emotions, Learning and the Brain: Exploring the Educational Implications of Affective Neuroscience*, New York: W.W. Norton.

Immordino-Yang, M. (2016) Emotion, sociality, and the brain's default mode network: Insights into educational practice and policy, *Policy Insights from the Behavioural and Brain Sciences*, 3 (2), 211–219.

Immordino-Yang, M. and Damasio, A. (2007) We feel, therefore we learn: The relevance of affective and social neuroscience to education, *Mind, Brain and Education*, 1 (1), 3–8.

Jackson, B. (1964) *Streaming: An Education System in Miniature*, London: Routledge & Kegan Paul.

James, M. and Pollard, A. (2010) Learning and teaching in primary schools: Insights from TLRP, in R. Alexander (ed.) *The Cambridge Primary Review Research Surveys*, Routledge: London.

James, M., Black, P., Carmichael, P., Drummond, M.J., Fox, A., MacBeath, J. et al. (2007) *Improving Learning How to Learn: Classrooms, Schools and Networks*, London: Routledge.

Jeffrey, B. and Woods, P. (1999) *Creative Learning in the Primary School*, London: Routledge.

Jeffrey, B. and Woods, P. (2003) *The Creative School: A Framework for Success, Quality and Effectiveness*, London: Routledge.

Jenkins, C. (2000) New Education and its emancipatory interests (1920–1950), *History of Education*, 29 (2), 139–151.

Jennings, M. (2006) *The Seven Signs of Ethical Collapse: How to Spot Moral Meltdowns in Companies … Before it's Too Late*, New York: St. Martin's Press.

Jensen, B. (2012) *Catching up: Learning from the best school systems in East Asia*, Melbourne, VIC: Grattan Institute [https://grattan.edu.au/report/catching-up-learning-from-the-best-school-systems-in-east-asia/].

Jerrim, J., Perera, N. and Sellen, P. (2017) *English education: World class in primary?*, London: Education Policy Institute [https://epi.org.uk/publications-and-research/english-education-world-class-primary/].

Jones, P. (2015) Childhoods and contemporary practices, in D. Wyse, R. Davis, P. Jones and S. Rogers (eds.) *Exploring Education and Childhood: From Current Certainties to New Visions*, London: Routledge.

Joyce, B., Calhoun, E. and Hopkins, D. (2009) *Models of Learning, Tools for Teaching*, Maidenhead: Open University Press.

Joyce, B., Weil, M. and Calhoun, E. (2015) *Models of Teaching*, London: Pearson.

JRF Analysis Unit (2018) *UK Poverty 2018: A comprehensive analysis of poverty trends*, York: Joseph Rowntree Foundation [https://www.jrf.org.uk/report/uk-poverty-2018].

Jubilee Centre for Character and Virtues (2017) *A framework for character education in schools*, University of Birmingham [https://www.jubileecentre.ac.uk/userfiles/jubileecentre/pdf/character-education/Framework%20for%20Character%20Education.pdf].

Julius, J., Hillary, J. and Veruete-McKay, L. (2021) *Free schools: The formative first ten years*, Slough: NFER [https://www.nfer.ac.uk/media/4347/free_schools_the_formative_first_ten_years_an_analysis_of_the_impact_of_free_schools_since_2010.pdf].

Kabat-Zinn, J. (2013) *Full Catastrophe Living: How to Cope with Stress, Pain and Illness Using Mindfulness Meditation*, London: Piatkus.

Kahneman, D. (2011) *Thinking, Fast and Slow*, London: Penguin.

Kaptelinin, V. (2005) The object of activity: Making sense of the sense-maker, *Mind, Culture and Activity*, 12 (1), 4–18.

Kaptelinin, V. and Nardi, B. (2006) *Acting with Technology: Activity Theory and Interaction Design*, London: MIT Press.

Kara, B. (2021) Decolonisation, power and knowledge in the curriculum, *The Education Exchange*, Chartered College of Teaching [https://soundcloud.com/online-learning-382330170/decolonisation-power-and-knowledge-in-the-curriculum].

Kellmer-Pringle, M. (1980) *The Needs of Children*, London; Hutchinson.

Kelly, A. (2004) *The Curriculum: Theory and Practice*, London: Sage.

Kerr, K., Dyson, A. and Raffo, C. (2014) *Education, Disadvantage and Place: Making the Local Matter*, Bristol: Policy Press.

Kershaw, I. (2013) *Investigation report: Trojan Horse letter* (The Kershaw Report), Independent investigation for Birmingham City Council, London: Eversheds [https://www.birmingham.gov.uk/downloads/file/1579/investigation_report_trojan_horse_letter_the_kershaw_report].

Kirschner, P. (2015) The disturbing facts about digital natives, *3-Star Learning Experiences* [blog], 20 October [https://3starlearningexperiences.wordpress.com/2015/10/20/the-disturbing-facts-about-digital-natives/].

Kirschner, P., Sweller, J., Kirschner, F. and Zambrano, J. (2018) From cognitive load theory to collaborative cognitive load theory, *International Journal of Computer-Supported Collaborative Learning*, 13, 213–233.

Kraft. M. and Papay, J. (2014) Can professional environments in schools promote teacher development? Explaining heterogeneity in returns to teaching experience, *Educational Evaluation and Policy Analysis*, 36 (4), 476–500.

Kraft, M., Marinell, W. and Yee, D. (2016) School organizational contexts, teacher turnover, and student achievement: Evidence from panel data, *American Educational Research Journal*, 53 (5), 1411–1499.

Kraft, M., Blazar, D. and Hogan, D. (2018) The effect of teaching coaching on instruction and achievement: A meta-analysis of the causal evidence, *Review of Educational Research*, 88 (4), 547–588.

Kucirkova, N. and Cremin, T. (2020) *Children Reading for Pleasure in the Digital Age: Mapping Reader Engagement*, London: Sage.

Kuczynski, L. and De Mol, J. (2015) Dialectical models of socialization, in W. Overton, P. Molenaar and R. Lerner (eds.) *Handbook of Child Psychology and Developmental Science: Theory and Method*, London: Wiley.

Lacey, R. and Minnis, H. (2020) Practitioner review: Twenty years of research with adverse childhood experience scores: Advantages, disadvantages and applications to practice, *Journal of Child Psychology and Psychiatry*, 61 (2), 116–130.

Laloux, F. (2016) *Reinventing Organizations: An Illustrated Invitation to Join the Conversation on Next-Stage Organizations*, Millis, MA: Nelson Parker.

Lave, J. and Wenger, E. (1991) *Situated Learning: Legitimate Peripheral Participation*, Cambridge: Cambridge University Press.

Lawson, J. and Silver, H. (1973) *A Social History of Education in England*, London: Methuen.

Lawton, D. (1975) *Class, Culture and the Curriculum*, London: Routledge & Kegan Paul.

Lawton, D. (1980) *The Politics of the School Curriculum*, London: Routledge & Kegan Paul.

Lawton, D. (1987) Cutting the curriculum cloth, *Times Educational Supplement*, 1 May.

Lawton, D. (2000) Citizenship education in context, in D. Lawton, J. Cairns and R. Gardner (2000) *Education for Citizenship*. London: Continuum.

Leach, J. and Moon, B. (2008) *The Power of Pedagogy*, London: Sage.

Leadbeater, C. (2009) *We-Think: Mass Innovation Not Mass Production*, London: Profile Books.

LeDoux, J. (2003) *Synaptic Self: How Our Brains Become Who We Are*, London: Penguin.

Lee, J. and Croll, P. (1995) Streaming and subject specialism at Key Stage 2: A survey in two local authorities, *Educational Studies*, 21 (2), 155–165.

Lefstein, A. and Snell, J. (2014) *Better than Best Practice: Developing Teaching and Learning through Dialogue*, London: Routledge.

Leithwood, K. and Jantzi, D. (2005) A review of transformational school leadership research, 1996–2005, *Leadership and Policy in Schools*, 4 (3), 177–199.

Leithwood, K. and Jantzi, D. (2008) Linking leadership to student learning: The role of collective efficacy, *Educational Administration Quarterly*, 44 (4), 496–528.

Leithwood, K. and Louis, K, (2012) *Linking Leadership to Student Learning*, San Francisco, CA: Jossey-Bass.

Leithwood, K., Jantzi, D. and Steinbach, R. (1999) *Changing Leadership for Changing Times*, Buckingham: Open University Press.

Leithwood, K., Day, C., Sammons, P., Harris, A. and Hopkins, D. (2006) *Successful school leadership: What is it and how it influences pupil learning*, Research Report RR800, London: DfES Publications [http://www.nysed.gov/common/nysed/files/principal-project-file-55-successful-school-leadership-what-it-is-and-how-it-influences-pupil-learning.pdf].

Leithwood, K., Harris, A. and Hopkins, D. (2008) Seven strong claims about successful school leadership, *School Leadership and Management*, 28 (1), 27–42.

Leithwood, K., Harris, A. and Hopkins, D. (2019) Seven strong claims about successful school leadership revisited, *School Leadership and Management*, 40 (1), 5–22.

Lektorsky, V. (2009) Mediation as a means of collective activity, in A. Sannino, H. Daniels and K. Guttierez (eds.) *Learning and Expanding with Activity Theory*, Cambridge: Cambridge University Press.

Lemke, J. (1990) *Talking Science: Language, Learning, and Values*, Norwood, NJ: Ablex.

Lemke, J. (2002) Becoming the village: Education across lives, in G. Wells and C. Claxton (eds.) *Learning for Life in the 21st Century: Sociocultural Perspectives on the Future of Education*, Oxford: Blackwell.

Leontiev, A. (1981) *Psychology and the Language Learning Process*, Oxford: Pergamon Press.

Lewis, Z. (2021) What is effective pedagogy in the Reception year?, in V. Bower (ed.) *Debates in Primary Education*, London: Routledge.

Lickona, T. (2004) *Character Matters: How to Help Our Children Develop Good Judgment, Integrity, and Other Essential Virtues*, New York: Touchstone Simon & Schuster.

Lipman, M. (1980) *Philosophy in the Classroom*, Philadelphia, PA: Temple University Press.

Littleton, K. and Mercer, N. (2013) *Interthinking: Putting Talk to Work*, London: Routledge.

Lofthouse, R. and Whiteside, R. (2020) *Sustaining a vital profession: A research report into the impact of leadership coaching in schools*. Leeds: Leeds Beckett University [https://www.leedsbeckett.ac.uk/-/media/files/schools/school-of-education/sustaining-a-vital-profession–final-report.pdf?la=en].

Louis, K. (2015) Linking leadership to learning: State, district and local effects, *Nordic Journal of Studies in Educational Policy*, 3, 30321 [https://doi.org/10.3402/nstep.v1.30321].

Louis, K., Leithwood, K., Wahlstrom, K. and Anderson, S. (2010) *Learning from leadership: Investigating the links to improved student learning*, New York: The Wallace Foundation [https://www.wallacefoundation.org/knowledge-center/pages/investigating-the-links-to-improved-student-learning.aspx].

Lowndes, G. (1969) *The Silent Social Revolution: An Account of the Expansion of Public Education in England and Wales 1895–1965*, Oxford: Oxford University Press.

Luckin, R. (2018) *Machine Learning and Human Intelligence: The Future of Education for the 21st Century*. London: IOE Press.

Luckin, R., Bligh, B., Munches, A., Ainsworth, S., Crook, C. and Noss, R. (2012) *Decoding learning: The proof, promise and potential of digital education*, London: Nesta [https://www.nesta.org.uk/report/decoding-learning/].

Lupton, R. (2004) *Schools in disadvantaged areas: Recognising context and raising quality*. CASE Paper 76, London: Centre for Analysis of Social Exclusion, London School of Economics and Political Science [http://eprints.lse.ac.uk/6321/].

Lupton, R. (2006) Schools in disadvantaged areas: Low attainment and contextualised policy response, in H. Lauder, P. Brown, S. Dillabough and A. Halsey (eds.) *Education, Globalisation and Social Change*, Oxford: Oxford University Press.

Lyotard, J.-F. (1979) *The Postmodern Condition: A Report on Knowledge*, Paris: Minuit.

MacBeath, J. (1999) *Schools Must Speak for Themselves: The Case for School Self-Evaluation*, London: Routledge.

MacBeath, J., Gronn, P., Opfer, D., Lowden, K., Forde, C., Cowie, M. et al. (2009) *Recruitment and retention of headteachers in Scotland*, Edinburgh: Scottish Government [https://dera.ioe.ac.uk/402/2/0089341.pdf].

MacBeath, J., Dempster, N., Frost, D., Johnson, G. and Swaffield, S. (2018) *Strengthening the Connections between Leadership and Learning: Challenges to Policy, School and Classroom Practice*, London: Routledge.

Maguire, M., Wooldridge, T. and Pratt-Adams, S. (2006) *The Urban Primary School*, Maidenhead: Open University Press.

Mansell, W. (2016) *Academies: Autonomy, accountability, quality and evidence*, York: Cambridge Primary Review Trust [https://cprtrust.org.uk/wp-content/uploads/2016/05/Mansell-report-160527.pdf].

Mansell, W. (2021) Digging around in the undergrowth of schools reform in England, *Education Uncovered* [https://www.educationuncovered.co.uk].

Martin, R., Tyler, P., Storper, M., Evenhuis, E. and Glasmeier, A. (2018) Globalization at a critical conjuncture?, *Cambridge Journal of Regions, Economy and Society*, 11 (1), 3–16 [https://doi.org/10.1093/cjres/rsy002].

Matthews, P. and Hill, R. (2010) *Schools leading schools II: The growing impact of national leaders of education*, Nottingham: National College for School Leadership [https://dera.ioe.ac.uk/2101/1/download%3Fid%3D117657%26filename%3D-schools-leading-schools-ii.pdf].

Maybin, J. (2013) Towards a sociocultural understanding of children's voice, *Language and Education*, 27 (5), 383–397.

McCormick, R. and Scrimshaw, P. (2001) Information and communications technology, knowledge and pedagogy, *Education, Communications and Information*, 1 (1), 39–57.

Mccrea, P. (2017) *Memorable Teaching: Leveraging Memory to Build Deep and Durable Learning in the Classroom*, CreateSpace Independent Publishing.

McCulloch, G. (ed.) (2011) *The Struggle for the History of Education*, London: Routledge.

McFarlane, A. (1997) Where are we and how did we get here?, in A. McFarlane (ed.) *Information Technology and Authentic Learning: Realising the Potential of Computers in the Primary Classroom*, London: Routledge.

McGrane, J., Stiff, J., Baird, J.-A., Lenkeit, J. and Hopfenbeck, T. (2017) *Progress in International Reading Literacy Study (PIRLS): National Report for England*, London: Department for Education [https://assets.publishing.service.gov.uk/government/uploads/system/uploads/attachment_data/file/664562/PIRLS_2016_National_Report_for_England-_BRANDED.pdf].

McGregor, J., Fielding, M., Robinson, C. with Spender, B. (2006) *Footprints of practice: Exploring the sharing and development of practice through collaborative adult learning*, Learning Networks Research Legacy Paper no. 3, Nottingham: National College for School Leadership.

Mercer, N. and Littleton, K. (2007) *Dialogue and the Development of Children's Thinking: A Sociocultural Approach*, London: Routledge.

Mercer, N., Wegerif, R. and Major, L. (eds.) (2020) *The Routledge International Handbook of Research on Dialogic Education*, London: Routledge.

Meyer, A., Rose, D. and Gordon, D. (2013) *Universal Design for Learning: Theory and Practice*, Wakefield: CAST Professional Publishing.

Miettinen, R. (1999) Transcending traditional school learning: Teachers' work and networks of learning, in Y. Engeström, R. Miettinen and R.-L. Punamäki (eds.) *Perspectives on Activity Theory*, Cambridge, Cambridge University Press.

Minogue, O. and Moore, A. (2013) *Too young to fail: Closing the education achievement gap in Northern Ireland*, Policy Brief, October, London: Save the Children [https://resourcecentre.savethechildren.net/node/13964/pdf/too_young_to_fail_northern_ireland_briefing.pdf].

Mitchell, I., Mitchell, J. with McKinnon, R., Scheele, S. and Lumb, D. (eds.) (2016) *PEEL in practice: 1550 ideas for quality teaching*, Melbourne, VIC: Project for the Enhancement of Effective Learning, Monash University.

Moll, L. (2019) Elaborating funds of knowledge: Community-oriented practices in international contexts, *Literacy Research: Theory, Method and Practice*, 68 (1), 130–138.

Morris, E. (2010) Important questions still need to be answered about the Academies Bill, *The Guardian*, 27 October [https://www.theguardian.com/education/2010/jul/27/academies-bill-no-formal-consultation].

Mourshed, M., Chijioke, C. and Barber, M. (2010) *How the world's most improved school systems keep getting better*, New York: McKinsey [https://www.mckinsey.com/industries/public-and-social-sector/our-insights/how-the-worlds-most-improved-school-systems-keep-getting-better].

Mourshed, M., Krawitz, M. and Dorn, E. (2017) *How to improve student educational outcomes*, New York: McKinsey [https://www.mckinsey.com/industries/public-and-social-sector/our-insights/how-to-improve-student-educational-outcomes-new-insights-from-data-analytics].

Muijs, D. (2015) Improving schools through collaboration: A mixed methods study of school-school support partnerships in the primary sector, *Oxford Review of Education*, 41 (5), 563–586.

Muijs, D., West, M. and Ainscow, M. (2010) Why network? Theoretical perspectives on networking, *School Effectiveness and School Improvement*, 21 (1), 5–26.

Muijs, D., Kyriakides, L., van der Werf, G., Creemers, B., Timperley, H. and Earl, L. (2014) State of the art – teacher effectiveness and professional learning, *School Effectiveness and School Improvement*, 25 (2), 231–256.

Mundy, K. and Hares, S. (2020) *Equity-focused approaches to learning loss during COVID-19*, Washington, DC: Center for Global Development [https://www.cgdev.org/blog/equity-focused-approaches-learning-loss-during-covid-19].

Muschamp, Y., Wikeley, F., Ridge, T. and Balarin, M. (2010) Parenting, caring and educating, in R. Alexander (ed.) *The Cambridge Primary Review Research Surveys*, London: Routledge.

Myatt, M. (2018) *The Curriculum: Gallimaufry to Coherence*, Woodbridge: John Catt.

Myatt, M. (2021) Thinking about curriculum intent, *Mary Myatt* [blog], 27 February [https://www.marymyatt.com/blog/thinking-about-curriculum-intent].

Nash, J. (2008) Rethinking intersectionality, *Feminist Review*, 89 (1), 1–15.

National Foundation for Education Research (NFER) (2018) *Key insights for England from PIRLS, TIMSS and PISA*, NFER Education Briefing, Slough: NFER [https://www.nfer.ac.uk/media/2667/ilsa02.pdf].

New Visions for Education Group (2012) *Coherent structures of and governance for education: Economy, accountability and improving educational performance*, 27 July [http://newvisionsforeducation.org.uk].

Nias, J. (1989) *Primary Teachers Talking: A Study of Teaching as Work*, London: Routledge.

Nichols, S. and Berliner, D. (2007) *High-Stakes Testing and the Corruption of America's Schools*, Cambridge, MA: Harvard Education Press.

Noddings, N. (2003) *Happiness and Education*, Cambridge: Cambridge University Press.

Noddings, N. (2005) Identifying and responding to needs in education, *Cambridge Journal of Education*, 35 (2), 147–159.

Noddings, N. (2006) *Philosophy of Education*, London: Routledge.

November, A. (2001) *Empowering Students with Technology*, Glenview, IL: Skylight.

Nuthall, G. (2007) *The Hidden Lives of Learners*, Wellington: NZCER Press.

Oates, T. (2010) *Could do better: Using international comparisons to refine the National Curriculum in England*, Cambridge: Cambridge Assessment [https://www.cambridgeassessment.org.uk/Images/112281-could-do-better-using-international-comparisons-to-refine-the-national-curriculum-in-england.pdf].

Ofsted (2002) *The curriculum in successful primary schools*, London: Ofsted [https://dera.ioe.ac.uk/4564/1/Curriculum%20in%20successful%20primary%20schools%20(The)%20(PDF%20format).pdf].

Ofsted (2009) *Twenty outstanding primary schools: Excelling against the odds*, London: Ofsted [https://dera.ioe.ac.uk/11216/1/Twenty%20outstanding%20primary%20schools.pdf].

Ofsted (2019) *Education inspection framework 2019*, London: Ofsted [https://www.gov.uk/government/publications/education-inspection-framework].

Ofsted (2020a) *Making the cut: How schools respond when they are under financial pressure*, London: Ofsted [https://www.gov.uk/government/publications/making-the-cut-how-schools-respond-when-they-are-under-financial-pressure].

Ofsted (2020b) *Covid-19 series: Briefing on schools*, London: Ofsted [https://www.gov.uk/government/publications/covid-19-series-briefing-on-schools-october-2020].

Ofsted (2020c) *The Annual Report of Her Majesty's Chief Inspector of Education, Children's Services and Skills 2018/19*, London: Ofsted [https://www.gov.uk/government/publications/ofsted-annual-report-201819-education-childrens-services-and-skills].

Ofsted (2021) *Nearly 9 out of 10 parents say their child's school handled COVID-19 well*. Press Release, London: Ofsted [https://www.gov.uk/government/news/nearly-9-out-of-10-parents-say-their-childs-school-handled-covid-19-well].

Organisation for Economic Cooperation and Development (OECD) (2008) *Understanding the Brain: Towards a New Learning Science*, Paris: OECD Publishing.

Organisation for Economic Cooperation and Development (OECD) (2012) *Equity and Quality in Education: Supporting Disadvantaged Students and Schools*, Paris: OECD Publishing [https://www.oecd.org/education/school/50293148.pdf].

Organisation for Economic Cooperation and Development (OECD) (2015) *What do parents look for in their child's school?*, PISA in Focus no. 51, Paris: OECD Publishing [https://www.oecd.org/pisa/pisaproducts/pisainfocus/PIF-51(eng)-FINAL.pdf].

Organisation for Economic Cooperation and Development (OECD) (2016) *Teaching excellence through professional learning and policy reform: Lessons from around the world*, International Summit on the Teaching Profession, Paris: OECD Publishing [https://www.oecd.org/publications/teaching-excellence-through-professional-learning-and-policy-reform-9789264252059-en.htm].

Organisation for Economic Cooperation and Development (OECD) (2019) *OECD Future of Education and Skills 2030: Learning Compass 2030*, Paris: OECD Publishing [https://www.oecd.org/education/2030-project/teaching-and-learning/learning/learning-compass-2030/].

Orme, N. (2006) *Medieval Schools: From Roman Britain to Renaissance England*, New Haven, CT: Yale University Press.

Orr, D. (2002) The uses of mindfulness in anti-oppressive pedagogies: Philosophy and praxis, *Canadian Journal of Education*, 27 (4), 477–490.

Osborne, S. (2006) The new public governance, *Public Management Review*, 8 (3), 377–387.

Ovenden-Hope, T. and Passy, R. (2016) Changing student behaviour in schools located in areas of socioeconomic deprivation: Findings form the 'coastal academies' project,

Education Today, 66 (3), Autumn, 12–18 [https://pearl.plymouth.ac.uk/bitstream/handle/10026.1/6731/Changing%20student%20behaviour_for%20PEARL.pdf?sequence=1&isAllowed=y].

Pachler, N. (2001) Connecting schools and pupils: to what end?, in M. Leask (ed.) *Issues in Teaching Using ICT,* London: Routledge.

Palinscar, A.S. (2013) Reciprocal teaching, in J. Hattie and E.M. Anderman (eds.) *International Guide to Student Achievement,* London: Routledge.

Palinscar, A. and Brown, A. (1984) Reciprocal teaching of comprehension-fostering and comprehension-monitoring activities, *Cognition and Instruction,* 1 (2), 117–175.

Palmer, H. (2016) Professional primary school teacher identity development: A pursuit in line with an unexpressed image, *Teacher Development,* 20 (5), 682–700.

Palmer, S. (2006) *Toxic Childhood: How the Modern World is Damaging Our Children and What We Can Do About It,* London: Orion.

Papert, S. (1996) *The Connected Family: Bridging the Digital Generation Gap,* Atlanta, GA: Longstreet Press.

Park, J. (2013) *Detoxifying school accountability: The case for multi-perspective inspection,* London: DEMOS [https://www.demos.co.uk/files/Detoxifying_School_Accountability_-_web.pdf?1367602207].

Payne, C. (2008) *So Much Reform, So Little Change: The Persistence of Failure in Urban Schools,* Cambridge, MA: Harvard Educational Press.

Perkins, D. (1993) Person-plus: A distributed view of thinking and learning, in G. Salomon (ed.) *Distributed Cognitions: Psychological and Educational Considerations,* Cambridge: Cambridge University Press.

Perkins, D. (2014) *Future Wise: Educating Our Children for a Changing World,* San Francisco, CA: Jossey-Bass.

Perkins, D. and Salomon, G. (2012) Knowledge to go: A motivational and dispositional view of transfer, *Educational Psychologist,* 47 (3), 248–258.

Perona-Wright, K. and Fletcher, G. (2018) The D.E.E.P. curriculum: Creating a love of learning, *Impact: Journal of the Chartered College of Teaching,* September [https://impact.chartered.college/article/deep-curriculum-creating-love-learning/].

Phillipson, N. and Wegerif, R. (2017) *Dialogic Education: Mastering Core Concepts through Thinking Together,* London: Routledge.

Piaget, J. (1926) *The Language and Thought of the Child,* London: Routledge & Kegan Paul.

Piaget, J. (1928) *The Child's Conception of the World,* London: Routledge & Kegan Paul.

Plank, D. and Keesler, V. (2009) Education and the shrinking state, in B. Sykes, B. Schneider and D. Plank (eds.) *Handbook of Education Policy Research,* New York: Routledge.

Plant, R. (2010) *The Neo-liberal State,* Oxford: Oxford University Press.

Plomin, R. (2018) *Blueprint: How DNA Makes Us Who We Are,* London: Allen Lane.

Polanyi, M. (1958) *Personal Knowledge: Towards a Post-Critical Philosophy,* London: Routledge.

Polanyi, M. (1966) *The Tacit Dimension,* London: Routledge.

Pollard, A. (1985) *The Social World of the Primary School,* London: Cassell.

Pollard, A. (ed.) (2010) *Professionalism and pedagogy: A contemporary opportunity* (a commentary by TLRP and GTCE), London: Teaching and Learning Research Programme [http://reflectiveteaching.co.uk/media/profandped.pdf].

Pollard, A. (2012) Proposed primary curriculum: What about the pupils? [blog], *IOE London Blog,* 12 June [https://ioelondonblog.wordpress.com/2012/06/12/proposed-primary-curriculum-what-about-the-pupils/].

Porritt, V., Spence-Thomas, K. and Taylor, C. (2017) Leading professional learning and development, in P. Earley and T. Greany (eds.) *School Leadership and Education System Reform*, London: Bloomsbury.

Priestly, M. and Biesta, G. (2014) *Reinventing the Curriculum: New Trends in Curriculum Policy*, London: Bloomsbury.

Purkey W. (1978) *Inviting School Success: A Self-Concept Approach to Teaching and Learning*, Belmont, CA: Wadsworth.

Quigley, A., Muijs, D. and Stringer, E. (2018) *Metacognition and self-regulated learning*, Guidance Report, London: Education Endowment Fund [https://dera.ioe.ac. uk/31617/1/EEF_Metacognition_and_self-regulated_learning.pdf].

Reay, D. (2006) 'I'm not seen as one of the clever children': Consulting primary school children about the social conditions of learning, in Special Issue on Pupil Consultation, *Education Review*, 58 (2), 171–181.

Reay, D. (2012) *Think Piece: What would a socially just education system look like?*, London: Centre for Labour and Social Studies [http://classonline.org.uk/docs/2012_ Diane_Reay_-_a_socially_just_education_system.pdf].

Reay, A. (2017) *The Power of Character: Lessons from the Frontline*, Woodbridge: John Catt.

Reeve, J. and Su, Y.-L. (2013) Teacher motivation, in M. Gagné (ed.) *The Oxford Handbook of Work Engagement, Motivation and Self-Determination Theory*, Oxford: Oxford University Press.

Resnick, L. (1987) The 1987 Presidential Address: Learning in school and out, *Educational Researcher*, 16 (9), 13–20.

Resnick, L. (1991) Shared cognition: Thinking as social practice, in L. Resnick, J. Levine and S. Teasley (eds.) *Perspectives on Socially Shared Cognition*, Washington, DC: American Psychological Association.

Reynolds, D. and Farrell, S. (1996) *Worlds Apart? A Review of International Surveys of Educational Achievement Involving England*, London: HMSO.

Rice, B. (2006) *Against the odds*, London: Shelter [https://england.shelter.org.uk/professional_resources/policy_and_research/policy_library/against_the_odds].

Richards, C. (2002) *Primary education: A sensual approach*, presentation to the North-West Primary Advisers Conference, Liverpool.

Richards, C. (2006) The establishment of English primary education 1941–1946, *Education 3–13*, 34 (1), 5–10.

Richardson, M., Isaacs, T., Barnes, I., Swensson, C., Wilkinson, D. and Golding, J. (2020) *Trends in International Mathematics and Science Study (TIMSS) 2019: National report for England*, Research Report, London: Department for Education [https:// assets.publishing.service.gov.uk/government/uploads/system/uploads/attachment_ data/file/941351/TIMSS_2019_National_Report.pdf].

Riggall, A. and Sharp, C. (2010) The structure of primary education: England and other countries, in R. Alexander (ed.) *The Cambridge Primary Review Research Surveys*, London: Routledge.

Riley, R. (2017) Community collaboration and partnership in volatile times, in P. Earley and T. Greany (eds.) *School Leadership and Education System Reform*, London: Bloomsbury.

Rimfeld, K., Malanchini, M., Krapohl, E., Hannigan, L., Dale, P. and Plomin, R. (2018) The stability of educational achievement across school years is largely explained by genetic factors, *npj Science of Learning*, 3 (16) [https://doi.org/10.1038/s41539-018-0030-0].

Risvi, F. and Lingard, B. (2006) *Globalizing Educational Policy*, London: Routledge.

Robinson, D., Schofield, J. and Steers-Wentzell, K. (2005) Peer and cross-age tutoring in math: Outcomes and their design implications, *Educational Psychology Review*, 17 (4), 327–362.

Robinson, K. (2010) *The Element: How Finding Your Passion Changes Everything*, London: Penguin.

Robinson, M. (2018) Curriculum: An offer of what the best might be, *Impact: Journal of the Chartered College of Teaching*, September [https://impact.chartered.college/article/curriculum-an-offer-of-what-the-best-might-be/].

Robinson, V. (2007) *School Leadership and Student Outcomes: Identifying What Works and Why*, ACEL Monograph Series, no. 41, Winmalee, NSW: Australian. Council for Educational Leaders.

Robinson, V. (2015) *Open-to-learning conversations: Background paper* [https://www.researchgate.net/profile/Viviane-Robinson/publication/267411000_Open-to-learning_Conversations_Background_Paper_Introduction_to_Open-to-learning_Conversations/links/54d7cb6c0cf2970e4e755956/Open-to-learning-Conversations-Background-Paper-Introduction-to-Open-to-learning-Conversations.pdf].

Robinson, V., Hohepa, M. and Lloyd, C. (2009) *School leadership and student outcomes: Identifying what works and why – Best evidence synthesis iteration*, Wellington, NZ, New Zealand, Ministry of Education [https://www.educationcounts.govt.nz/publications/series/2515/60170].

Rogoff, B. (1990) *The Cultural Nature of Human Development*, Oxford: Oxford University Press.

Rogoff, B. (1995) Observing sociocultural activity on three planes: Participatory appropriation, guided participation, and apprenticeship, in J. Wertsch, P. del Río and A. Alvarez (eds.) *Sociocultural Studies of Mind*, Cambridge: Cambridge University Press.

Rogoff, B., Paradise, R., Mejia Arauz, R., Correa-Chavez, M. and Angelillo, C. (2003) Firsthand learning through intent participation, *Annual Review of Psychology*, 54, 175–203.

Rohrer, D., Dedrick, R. and Stershic, S. (2015) Interleaved practice improves mathematics learning, *Journal of Educational Psychology*, 107 (3), 900–908.

Rosenshine, B. (2012) Principles of instruction: Research based strategies that all teachers should know, *American Educator*, Spring [www.aft.org/pdfs/americaneducator/spring2012/Rosenshine.pdf].

Rutter, M., Maugham, B., Mortimore, P. and Ouston, J. (1979) *Fifteen Thousand Hours. Secondary Schools and Their Effects on Children*, London: Open Books.

Sahlberg, P. (2011) *Finnish Lessons: What Can the World Learn from Educational Change in Finland?* New York: Teachers College Press.

Sahlberg, P. and Doyle, W. (2020) *Let the Children Play: For the Learning, Well-being and Life Success of Every Child*, Oxford: Blackwell.

Salokangas, M. and Chapman, C. (2014) Exploring governance in two chains of academy schools: A comparative case study, *Educational Management Administration and Leadership*, 42 (3), 372–386.

Sammons, P., Sylva, K., Melhuish, E., Siraj-Blatchford, I., Taggart, B., Barreau, S. et al. (2008) *Influence of school teaching and quality on children's progress in primary school*, DCSF Research Report no. RR028, London: DCSF [https://dera.ioe.ac.uk/7915/1/DCSF-RR028.pdf].

Sannino, A. and Engeström, Y. (2018) Cultural-historical activity theory: Founding insights and new challenges, *Cultural-Historical Psychology*, 14 (3), 43–56.

Save the Children (2021) *Most children are happy and excited to return to school having missed an average of 95 days of education since March 2020*, London: Save the Children [https://www.savethechildren.org.uk/news/media-centre/press-releases/uk-children-happy-and-excited-to-return-to-school-having-missed-95-days-of-education-since-march].

Scardamalia, M. (2000) Can schools enter a knowledge society?, in M. Selinger and J. Wynn (eds.) *Educational Technology and the Impact on Teaching and Learning*, Abingdon: RM Education.

Scardamalia, M. and Bereiter, C. (2006) Knowledge building: Theory, pedagogy, and technology, in K. Sawyer (ed.) *Cambridge Handbook of the Learning Sciences*, New York: Cambridge University Press.

Seli, P., Wammes, J., Risko, E. and Smilek, D. (2016) On the relation between motivation and retention in educational contexts: The role of intentional and unintentional mind wandering, *Psychonomic Bulletin and Review*, 23 (4), 1280–1287.

Seligman, M. (2011) *Flourish: A Visionary New Understanding of Happiness and Well-being*, New York: Free Press.

Selleck, R. (1972) *English Primary Education and the Progressives, 1914 to 1939*, London: Routledge & Kegan Paul.

Sharp, R. (2002) Central and local government, in R. Aldrich (ed.) *A Century of Education*, London: Routledge/Falmer.

Sharp, R., Green, A. and Lewis, J. (1975) *Education and Social Control: A Case Study in Progressive Education*, London: Routledge & Kegan Paul.

Shirley, D. (2020a) *Optimism of the will*, Worlds of Education, 23 April [https://www.worldsofeducation.org/en/woe_homepage/woe_detail/16747/"optimism-of-the-will"-by-dennis-shirley].

Shirley, D. (2020b) Beyond well-being: The quest for wholeness and purpose in. education, *SCNU Review of Education*, 3 (3), 542–555.

Shulman, L. (1986) Those who understand: Knowledge growth in teaching, *Educational Researcher*, 15 (2), 4–14.

Shulman, L. (1987) Knowledge and teaching: Foundations of the new reform, *Harvard Educational Review*, 57 (1), 1–22.

Shulman, L. (2005a) Pedagogies, *Liberal Education*, 91 (2), 18–25.

Shulman, L. (2005b) Signature pedagogies in the professions, *Daedalus*, 134 (3), 52–59.

Shulman, L. and Shulman, J. (2004) How and what teachers learn: A shifting perspective, *Journal of Curriculum Studies*, 36 (2), 257–271.

Sikora, J., Evans, M. and Kelley, J. (2018) Scholarly culture: How books in adolescence enhance adult literacy, numeracy and technology skills in thirty-one societies, *Social Science Research*, 77, 1–15.

Silcock, P. (2013) Should the Cambridge Primary Review be wedded to Vygotsky?, *Education 3–13: International Journal of Primary, Elementary and Early Years Education*, 41 (3), 316–329.

Silver, H. (1983) *Education as History: Interpreting Nineteenth and Twentieth Century Education*, London: Methuen.

Silver, H. (1994) *Good Schools, Effective Schools: Judgements and Their Histories*, London: Cassell.

Simkins, T. (2005) Leadership in education: 'What works' or 'What makes sense'?, *Educational Management Administration and Leadership*, 33 (1), 9–26.

Simkins, T. (2015) School restructuring in England: New school configurations and new challenges, *Management in Education*, 29 (1), 4–8.

Simon, B. (1974) *The Two Nations and the Educational Structure 1780–1870*, London: Lawrence & Wishart.

Simon, B. (1981) Why no pedagogy in England?, in B. Simon and W. Taylor (eds.) *Education in the Eighties: The Central Issues*, London: Batsford.

Simon, J. (1966) *Education and Society in Tudor England*, Cambridge: Cambridge University Press.

Singh, J. (2002) Introduction: Information technologies and the changing scope of power and governance, in J. Rosenau and J. Singh (eds.) *The Changing Scope of Power and Governance*, Albany, NY: State University of New York Press.

Singh, J. (2013) Information technologies, meta-power and transformations in global politics, *International Studies Review*, 15 (1), 5–29.

Smithers, A. (2013) *Confusion in the ranks: How good are England's schools?*, Report for the Sutton Trust, February, Buckingham: Centre for Education and Employment Research, University of Buckingham [https://www.buckingham.ac.uk/wp-content/uploads/2013/01/Confusion-in-the-Ranks.pdf].

Social Mobility Commission (2019) *Social mobility in Great Britain – state of the nation 2018–2019*, Sixth Annual Report, London: Social Mobility Commission [https://www.gov.uk/government/publications/social-mobility-in-great-britain-state-of-the-nation-2018-to-2019].

Social Mobility Commission (2020) *Social mobility barometer: Public attitudes to social mobility in the UK, 2019–2020*, London: Social Mobility Commission [https://assets.publishing.service.gov.uk/government/uploads/system/uploads/attachment_data/file/858908/Social_Mobility_Barometer_2019-2020.pdf].

Southworth, G. (2002) Instructional leadership in schools: Reflections and empirical evidence, *School Leadership and Management*, 22 (1), 73–91.

Spielman, A. (2018) *HMCI commentary: Curriculum and the new education inspection framework*, 18 September, London: Ofsted [https://www.gov.uk/government/speeches/hmci-commentary-curriculum-and-the-new-education-inspection-framework].

Star, S. and Griesemer, J. (1989) Institutional ecology, 'translations' and boundary objects: Amateurs and professionals in Berkeley's Museum of Vertebrate Zoology, 1907–39, *Social Studies of Science*, 19 (3), 387–420.

Stenhouse, L. (1975) *An Introduction to Curriculum Research and Development*, London: Heinemann.

Stetsenko, A. and Arievitch, I. (2002) Teaching, learning and development: A post-Vygotskian perspective, in G. Wells and C. Claxton (eds.) *Learning for Life in the 21st Century: Sociocultural Perspectives on the Future of Education*, Oxford: Blackwell.

Stevenson, L. (2019) An improvement plan is not enough – you need a strategy, *Phi Delta Kappan*, 100 (6), 60–64.

Stone, L. (2009) *Beyond simple multi-tasking: Continuous partial attention* [https://lindastone.net/2009/11/30/beyond-simple-multi-tasking-continuous-partial-attention/].

Sutherland, G. (1971) *Elementary education in the nineteenth century*, Classic Pamphlet, London: The Historical Association.

Swann, M., Peacock, A., Hart, S. and Drummond, M.-J. (2012) *Creating Learning without Limits*, Maidenhead: Open University Press.

Sweller, J. (1988) Cognitive load during problem solving: Effects on learning, *Cognitive Science*, 12 (2), 257–285.

Sweller, J. (2011) Cognitive load theory, in J. Mestre and B. Ross (eds.) *The Psychology of Learning and Motivation: Cognition in Education*, London: Elsevier Academic Press.

Tapscott, D. and Williams, A. (2007) *Wikinomics: How Mass Collaboration Changes Everything*, London: Atlantic Books.

Theobald, M., Danby, S., Einarsdottir, J., Bourne, J., Jones, D., Ross, S. et al. (2015) Children's perspectives of play and learning for educational practice, *Education Sciences*, 5, 345–362.

Thompson, C. (2013) *Smarter than You Think: How Technology is Changing Our Minds for the Better*, London: Collins.

Thompson, M. and Wiliam, D. (2007) *Tight but loose: A conceptual framework for scaling up school reforms*, paper presented at the Annual Meeting of the American Educational Research Association (AERA), Chicago, IL, 9–13 April [https://www.dylanwiliam.org/Dylan_Wiliams_website/Papers.html].

Thomson, P. (2009) *School Leadership: Heads on the Block?*, London: Routledge.

Thomson. P. (2020) *School Scandals: Blowing the Whistle on the Corruption of Our Education System*, Bristol: Policy Press.

Thomson, P., Lingard, B. and Wrigley, T. (2012) Reimagining school change: The necessity and reasons for hope, in T. Wrigley, P. Thomson and B. Lingard (eds.) *Changing Schools: Alternative Ways to Make a World of Difference*, London: Routledge.

Timmins, N. (2001) *The Five Giants: A Biography of the Welfare State*, London: Harper Collins.

Toffler, A. (1980) *The Third Wave*, New York: Bantam Books.

Tolman, C. (1999) Society versus context in individual development: Does theory make a difference? in Y. Engeström, R. Miettinen and R.-L. Punamäki (eds.) *Perspectives on Activity Theory*, Cambridge, Cambridge University Press.

Tough, P. (2012) *How Children Succeed: Grit, Curiosity, and the Hidden Power of Character*, New York: Houghton Mifflin Harcourt.

Troman, G. (2008) Primary teacher identity, commitment and career in performative school cultures, *British Educational Research Journal*, 34 (5), 619–633.

Troman, G., Jeffrey, B. and Raggl, A. (2007) Creativity and performativity policies in primary school cultures, *Journal of Education Policy*, 22 (5), 549–572.

Tyack, D. and Cuban, L. (1995) *Tinkering Toward Utopia: A Century of Public School Reform*, Cambridge, MA: Harvard University Press.

Tymms, P. and Merrell, C. (2010) Standards and quality in English primary schools over time, in R. Alexander (ed.) *The Cambridge Primary Review Research Surveys*, London: Routledge.

Tyng, C., Amin, H., Saad, M. and Malik, A. (2017) The influences of emotion on learning and memory, *Frontiers in Psychology*, 8, 1454 [https://doi.org/10.3389/fpsyg.2017.01454].

Um, E., Plass, J., Hayward, E. and Homer, B. (2012) Emotional design in multimedia learning, *Journal of Educational Psychology*, 104 (2), 485–498.

UNICEF (1990) *The United Nations Convention on the Rights of the Child*, New York: United Nations [https://www.unicef.org.uk/what-we-do/un-convention-child-rights/].

Victor, B. and Boynton, A. (1998) *Invented Here: Maximizing Your Organization's Internal Growth and Profitability*, Boston, MA: Harvard Business School Press.

Virkunnen, J. (2009) Two theories of organisational knowledge creation, in A. Sannino, H. Daniels and K. Gutierrez (eds.) *Learning and Expanding with Activity Theory*, Cambridge: Cambridge University Press.

Virkunnen, J., Makinen, E. and Lintula, L. (2010) From diagnosis to clients: Constructing the object of collaborative development between physiotherapy educators and workplaces, in H. Daniels, A. Edwards, Y. Engeström, T. Gallagher and S. Ludvigsen (eds.)

Activity Theory in Practice: Promoting Learning Across Boundaries and Agencies, London: Routledge.

Vygotsky, L. (1962) *Thought and Language*, Cambridge, MA: MIT Press.

Vygotksy, L. (1978) *Mind in Society*, Cambridge, MA: Harvard University Press.

Vygotsky, L. (1997) *The Collected Works of L.S. Vygotsky*, vol. 4: *The History of the Development of Higher Mental Functions*, trans. M. Hall, New York: Plenum Press.

Walker, M. (2017) *Insights into the Role of Research and Development in Teaching Schools*, Slough, NFER.

Wardekker, W. (2000) Criteria for the quality of inquiry, *Mind, Culture and Activity*, 7 (4), 259–272.

Waslander, S., Pater, C. and Van der Weide, M. (2010) *Markets in education: An analytic review of empirical research in market mechanics in education*, OECD Education Working Papers no. 52, Paris: OECD Publishing.

Watkins, C. (2010) Learning, performance and improvement, *INSI Research Matters*, no. 34 (Summer), London: Institute of Education [https://www.academia.edu/2309010/Learning_Performance_and_Improvement].

Webb, R. and Vulliamy, G. (2007) Changing classroom practice at Key Stage 2: The impact of New Labour's national strategies, *Oxford Review of Education*, 33 (5), 561–580.

Webb, R. and Vulliamy, G. (2009) *Here because of the children: Primary teachers' work and well-being*, London: ATL.

Wegerif, R. (2013) *Dialogic Education for the Internet Age*, London: Routledge.

Weinstein, Y., Sumeracki, M. and Caviglioli, O. (2018a) *Understanding How We Learn: A Visual Guide*, London: Routledge.

Weinstein, Y., Madan, C. and Sumeracki, M. (2018b) Teaching the science of learning, *Cognitive Research*, 3, 2 [https://doi.org/10.1186/s41235-017-0087-y].

Wells, G. (1999) *Dialogic Inquiry: Towards a Sociocultural Practice and Theory of Education*, Cambridge: Cambridge University Press.

Wells, G. (2002) Inquiry as an orientation for learning, teaching and teacher education, in G. Wells and C. Claxton (eds.) *Learning for Life in the 21st Century: Sociocultural Perspectives on the Future of Education*, Oxford: Blackwell.

Wells, G. (2009) *The Meaning Makers: Learning to Talk and Talking to Learn*, 2nd edition, London: Multilingual Matters.

Wells, G. and Claxton, C. (2002) Introduction: Sociocultural perspectives on the future of education, in G. Wells and C. Claxton (eds.) *Learning for Life in the 21st Century: Sociocultural Perspectives on the Future of Education*, Oxford: Blackwell.

Weltman, D. (2008) Popular representations of the working class: Contested identities and social change, *Beyond Current Horizons*, Review Paper, December.

Wenger, E. (1998) *Communities of Practice: Learning, Meaning, and Identity*, Cambridge: Cambridge University Press.

Wenger, E. (2005) *Communities of practice and social learning theory*, presentation to the *Sociocultural Theory in Educational Research and Practice Conference*, University of Manchester, 8–9 September.

Wenger, E. (2007) *Communities of practice. A brief introduction* [https://www.ohr.wisc.edu/cop/articles/communities_practice_intro_wenger.pdf].

Wertsch, J. (1998) *Mind in Action*, Oxford: Oxford University Press.

West, M. (2010) School-to-school cooperation as a strategy for improving student outcomes in challenging contexts, *School Effectiveness and School Improvement*, 21 (1), 93–112.

West, A. and Wolfe, D. (2018) Academies, the school system in England and a vision for the future. Clare Market Papers No.23, Education Research Group, Department of Social Policy, London School of Economics and Political Science.

Wheatley, M. (1999) *Leadership and the New Science: Discovering Order in a Chaotic World*, San Francisco, CA: Berrett Koehler.

Whetton, C., Ruddock, G. and Twist, L. (2010) Standards in English primary education over time: The international evidence, in R. Alexander (ed.) *The Cambridge Primary Review Research Surveys*, London: Routledge.

White, J. (2010) The aims of primary education, in R. Alexander (ed.) *The Cambridge Primary Review Research Surveys*, London: Routledge.

Whitty, G. (1997) Creating quasi-markets in education: A review of recent research on parental choice and school autonomy in three countries, *Review of Research in Education*, 22 (1), 3–47.

Whitty, G. (2009) Evaluating Blair's educational legacy? Some comments on the special issue of *Oxford Review of Education*, *Oxford Review of Education*, 35 (2), 267–280.

Wiliam, D. (2010) Standardized testing and school accountability, *Educational Psychologist*, 45 (2), 107–122.

Wiliam, D. (2012) *Building learning communities: Leadership strategies for embedding a culture of formative assessment throughout schools*, presentation to the Teachology Conference, London, April [https://www.dylanwiliam.org/Dylan_Wiliams_website/Presentations.html].

Wiliam, D. (2016) *Leadership for Teacher Learning: Creating a Culture Where All Teachers Improve So that All Students Succeed*, West Palm Beach, FL: Learning Science International.

Wilkinson, R. and Pickett, K. (2009) *The Spirit Level: Why More Equal Societies Always Do Better*, London: Allen Lane.

Wilkinson, R. and Pickett, K. (2019) *The Inner Level: How More Equal Societies Reduce Stress, Restore Sanity and Improve Everyone's Well-being*, London: Allen Lane.

Willingham, D. (2010) *Why Don't Students Like School?*, San Francisco, CA: Jossey-Bass.

Willingham, D. (2018) *The Reading Mind: A Cognitive Approach to Understanding How the Mind Reads*, London: Jossey-Bass.

Wilmott, R. (2002) *Education Policy and Realist Social Theory: Primary Teachers, Child-Centred Philosophy and the New Managerialism*, London: Routledge.

Wood, M., Pennington, A. and Su, F. (2018) Pre-figurative practice and the educational leadership of Sir Alec Clegg in the West Riding of Yorkshire, England (1945–1974), *Journal of Educational Administration and History*, 50 (4), 299–315.

Woods, P. and Jeffrey, B. (1997) *Teachable Moments: The Art of Teaching in Primary Schools*, Buckingham: Open University Press.

Woods, P. and Jeffrey, B. (1998) Choosing positions: Living the contradictions of Ofsted, *British Journal of Sociology of Education*, 19 (4), 547–570.

Woods, P., Jeffrey, B., Troman, G. and Boyle, M. (1997) *Restructuring Schools, Reconstructing Teachers: Responding to Change in the Primary School*, Buckingham: Open University Press.

Worth, J. and Faulkner-Ellis, H. (2021) *Teacher labour market in England: Annual Report 2021*, Slough: NFER [https://www.nfer.ac.uk/media/4382/teacher_labour_market_in_england_annual_report_2021.pdf].

Wrigley, T. (2003) *Schools of Hope: A New Agenda for School Improvement*, Stoke on Trent: Trentham Books.

Wrigley, T., Thomson, P. and Lingard, B. (2012) Resources for changing schools: Ideas in and for practice, in T. Wrigley, P. Thomson and B. Lingard (eds.) *Changing Schools: Alternative Ways to Make a World of Difference*, London: Routledge.

Wyse, D., McCreery, E. and Torrance, H. (2010) The trajectory and impact of national reform: Curriculum and assessment in English primary schools, in R. Alexander (ed.) *The Cambridge Primary Review Research Surveys*, London: Routledge.

Young, M., Lambert, D., Roberts, C. and Roberts, M. (2014) *Knowledge and the Future School: Curriculum and Social Justice*, London: Bloomsbury.

Young Minds (2021) *Coronavirus: Impact on young people with mental health needs*, Survey no. 4, February, London: Young Minds [https://www.youngminds.org.uk/media/esifqn3z/youngminds-coronavirus-report-jan-2021.pdf].

Zhao, Y. (2017) What works may hurt: Side effects in education, *Journal of Educational Change*, 18, 1–19.

Zull, J. (2011) *From Brain to Mind: Using Neuroscience to Guide Change in Education*, Sterling, VA: Stylus Publishing.

Index